Don't Let's Go to the Dogs Tonight

ALEXANDRA FULLER

Don't Let's Go to the Dogs Tonight

AN AFRICAN CHILDHOOD

PICADOR

First published 2002 by Random House, Inc., New York

First published in Great Britain 2002 by Picador
an imprint of Pan Macmillan Ltd
Pan Macmillan, 20 New Wharf Road, London N1 9RR
Basingstoke and Oxford
Associated companies throughout the world
www.panmacmillan.com

ISBN 0 330 49023 0

The author would like to thank Ian Murphy
for permission to reproduce the photographs on pages 302 and 304
and would like to thank Ross Hilderbrand
for permission to reproduce the photographs on pages 51, 60 and 197.
All other photographs are from the Fuller family collection.

7 9 8 6

A CIP catalogue record for this book is available from
the British Library.

Typeset by Intype London Ltd
Printed and bound in Great Britain by
Mackays of Chatham plc, Chatham, Kent

To

Mum, Dad and Vanessa

and to the memory of

Adrian, Olivia and Richard

with love

Don't let's go to the dogs tonight,
For mother will be there.

– A. P. Herbert

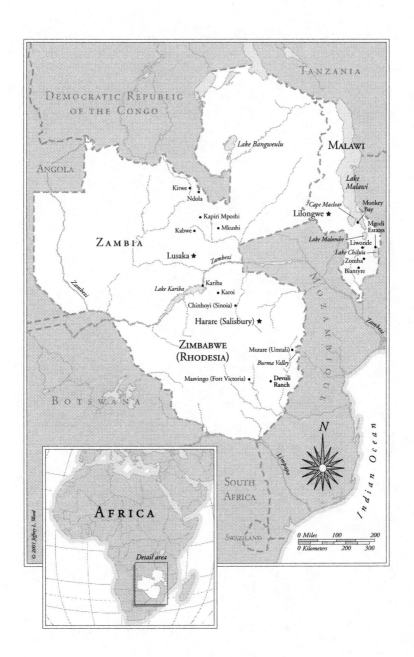

TANZANIA

DEMOCRATIC REPUBLIC
OF THE CONGO

ANGOLA

MALAWI

Lake Bangweulu

Lake Malawi

Kitwe •
Ndola •

• Kapiri Mposhi
• Mkushi

Cape Maclear
Lilongwe ★

Monkey
Bay

Mgodi
Estates

ZAMBIA

Kabwe •

Lake Malombe
Liwonde •

Lake Chilwa
Zomba •
• Blantyre

Lusaka ★ *Zambezi*

MOZAMBIQUE

Zambezi

Lake Kariba

Kariba •
• Karoi

Chinhoyi (Sinoia) •

Harare (Salisbury) ★

Zambezi

ZIMBABWE
(RHODESIA)

Mutare (Umtali) •

Burma Valley

Masvingo (Fort Victoria) •

• Devuli
Ranch

BOTSWANA

N

Limpopo

Indian Ocean

SOUTH
AFRICA

AFRICA

Detail area

SWAZILAND

0 Miles   100   200

0 Kilometers   200   300

Rhodesia, 1975

Bobo loading the FN

Mum says, 'Don't come creeping into our room at night.'

They sleep with loaded guns beside them on the bedside rugs. She says, 'Don't startle us when we're sleeping.'

'Why not?'

'We might shoot you.'

'Oh.'

'By mistake.'

'Okay.' As it is, there seems a good enough chance of getting shot on purpose. 'Okay, I won't.'

So if I wake in the night and need Mum and Dad, I call Vanessa, because she isn't armed. 'Van! Van, hey!' I hiss across the room until she wakes up. And then Van has to light a candle and escort me to the loo, where I pee sleepily into the flickering yellow light and Van keeps the candle high, looking for snakes and scorpions and baboon spiders.

Mum won't kill snakes because she says they help to keep the rats down (but she rescued a nest of baby mice from the barns and left them to grow in my cupboard, where they ate holes in the family's winter jerseys). Mum won't kill scorpions either; she catches them and lets them go free in the pool and Vanessa and I have to rake the pool before we can swim. We fling the scorps as far as we can across the brown and withering lawn, chase the ducks and geese out, and then lower ourselves gingerly into the pool, whose sides wave green and long and soft and grasping with algae. And Mum won't kill spiders because she says it will bring bad luck.

I tell her, 'I'd say we have pretty rotten luck as it is.'

'Then think how much worse it would be if we killed spiders.'

I have my feet off the floor when I pee.

'Hurry up, man.'

'Okay, okay.'

'It's like Victoria Falls.'

'I really had to go.'

I have been holding my pee for a long, long time and staring out of the window to try and guess how close it is to morning. Maybe I could hold it until morning. But then I notice that it is the deep-black-sky quiet time of night, which is the halfway time between the sun setting and the sun rising when even the night animals are quiet – as if they, like day animals, take a break in the middle of their work to rest. I can't hear Vanessa breathing; she has gone into her deep middle-of-the-night silence. Dad is not snoring nor is he shouting in his sleep. The baby is still in her crib but the smell of her is warm and animal with wet nappy. It will be a long time until morning.

*

Then Vanessa hands me the candle – 'You keep boogies for me now' – and she pees.

'See, you had to go, too.'

'Only 'cos you had to go.'

There is a hot breeze blowing through the window, the cold sinking night air shifting the heat of the day up. The breeze has trapped midday scents; the prevalent cloying of the leach field, the green soap which has spilled out from the laundry and landed on the patted-down red earth, the wood smoke from the fires that heat our water, the boiled-meat smell of dog food.

We debate the merits of flushing the loo.

'We shouldn't waste the water.' Even when there isn't a drought we can't waste water, just in case one day there is a drought. Anyway, Dad has said, 'Steady on with the loo paper, you kids. And don't flush the bloody loo all the time. The leach field can't handle it.'

'But that's *two* pees in there.'

'So? It's only pee.'

'*Agh sis*, man, but it'll be smelly by tomorrow. And you peed as much as a horse.'

'It's not my fault.'

'You can flush.'

'You're taller.'

'I'll hold the candle.'

Van holds the candle high. I lower the toilet lid, stand on it and lift up the block of hardwood that covers the cistern, and reach down for the chain. Mum has glued a girlie-magazine picture to this block of hardwood: a blond woman in few clothes, with breasts like naked cow udders, and she's all arched in a strange pouty contortion, like she's got backache. Which maybe she has, from the weight of the udders. The picture is from *Scope* magazine.

*

We aren't allowed to look at *Scope* magazine.

'Why?'

'Because we aren't those sorts of people,' says Mum.

'But we have a picture from *Scope* magazine on the loo lid.'

'That's a joke.'

'Oh.' And then, 'What sort of joke?'

'Stop twittering on.'

A pause. 'What sort of people are we, then?'

'We have breeding,' says Mum firmly.

'Oh.' Like the dairy cows and our special expensive bulls (who are named Humani, Jack, and Bulawayo).

'Which is better than having money,' she adds.

I look at her sideways, considering for a moment. 'I'd rather have money than breeding,' I say.

Mum says, '*Anyone* can have money.' As if it's something you might pick up from the public toilets in OK Bazaar Grocery Store in Umtali.

'*Ja*, but we don't.'

Mum sighs. 'I'm trying to read, Bobo.'

'Can you read to me?'

Mum sighs again. 'All right,' she says, 'just one chapter.' But it is teatime before we look up from *The Prince and the Pauper*.

*

The loo gurgles and splutters, and then a torrent of water shakes down, spilling slightly over the bowl.

'*Sis* man,' says Vanessa.

You never know what you're going to get with this loo. Sometimes it refuses to flush at all and other times it's like this, water on your feet.

I follow Vanessa back to the bedroom. The way candlelight falls, we're walking into blackness, blinded by the flame of the candle, unable to see our feet. So at the same moment we get the creeps, the neck-prickling terrorist-under-the-bed creeps, and we abandon ourselves to fear. The candle blows out. We skid into our room and leap for the beds, our feet quickly tucked under us. We're both panting, feeling foolish, trying to calm our breathing as if we weren't scared at all.

Vanessa says, 'There's a terrorist under your bed, I can see him.'

'No you can't, how can you see him? The candle's out.'

'*Struze* fact.'

And I start to cry.

'*Jeez*, I'm only joking.'

I cry harder.

'Shhh, man. You'll wake up Olivia. You'll wake up Mum and Dad.'

Which is what I'm trying to do, without being shot. I want everyone awake and noisy to chase away the terrorist-under-my-bed.

'Here,' she says, 'you can sleep with Fred if you stop crying.'

So I stop crying and Vanessa pads over the bare cement floor and brings me the cat, fast asleep in a snail-circle on her arms. She puts him on the pillow and I put an arm over the vibrating, purring body. Fred finds my earlobe and starts to suck. He's always sucked our earlobes. Our hair is sucked into thin, slimy, knotted ropes near the ears.

Mum says, 'No wonder you have worms all the time.'

I lie with my arms over the cat, awake and waiting. African dawn, noisy with animals and the servants and Dad waking up and a tractor coughing into life somewhere down at the work-shop, clutters into the room. The bantam hens start to crow and stretch, tumbling out of their roosts in the tree behind the bathroom to peck at the reflection of themselves in the window. Mum comes in smelling of Vicks VapoRub and tea and warm bed and scoops the sleeping baby up to her shoulder.

I can hear July setting tea on the veranda and I can smell the first, fresh singe of Dad's morning cigarette. I balance Fred on my shoulder and come out for tea: strong with no sugar, a splash of milk, the way Mum likes it. Fred has a saucer of milk.

'Morning, Chookies,' says Dad, not looking at me, smoking. He is looking far off into the hills, where the border between Rhodesia and Mozambique melts blue-gray, even in the pre-hazy clear of early morning.

'Morning, Dad.'

'Sleep all right?'

'Like a log,' I tell him. 'You?'

Dad grunts, stamps out his cigarette, drains his teacup, balances his bush hat on his head, and strides out into the yard to make the most of the little chill the night has left us with which to fight the gathering soupy heat of day.

Getting There: Zambia, 1987

Horses: Serioes

To begin with, before Independence, I am at school with white children only. 'A' schools, they are called: superior schools with the best teachers and facilities. The black children go to 'C' schools. In-between children who are neither black nor white (Indian or a mixture of races) go to 'B' schools.

The Indians and coloureds (who are neither completely this nor completely that) and blacks are allowed into my school the year I turn eleven, when the war is over. The blacks laugh at me when they see me stripped naked after swimming or tennis, when my shoulders and arms are angry sunburnt red.

'Argh! I smell roasting pork!' they shriek.

'Who fried the bacon?'

'Burning piggy!'

My God, I am the *wrong* colour. The way I am burned by the sun, scorched by flinging sand, prickled by heat. The way my skin erupts in miniature volcanoes of protest in the presence of tsetse flies, mosquitoes, ticks. The way I stand out against the khaki bush like a large marshmallow to a gook with a gun. White. African. White-African.

'But what are you?' I am asked over and over again.

'Where are you from *originally*?'

*

I began then, embarking from a hot, dry boat.

Blinking bewildered from the sausage-gut of a train.

Arriving in Rhodesia, Africa. From Derbyshire, England. I was two years old, startled and speaking toddler English. Lungs shocked by thick, hot, humid air. Senses crushed under the weight of so many stimuli.

I say, 'I'm African.' But not black.

And I say, 'I was born in England,' by mistake.

But, 'I have lived in Rhodesia (which is now Zimbabwe) and in Malawi (which used to be Nyasaland) and in Zambia (which used to be Northern Rhodesia).'

And I add, 'Now I live in America,' through marriage.

And (full disclosure), 'But my parents were born of Scottish and English parents.'

What does that make me?

Mum doesn't know who she is, either.

She stayed up all night once listening to Scottish music and crying.

'This music' – her nose twitches – 'is so beautiful. It makes me so homesick.'

Mum has lived in Africa all but three years of her life.

'But this *is* your home.'

'But my heart,' Mum attempts to thump her chest, 'is Scottish.'

Bo and Kenneth

Oh, *fergodsake*. 'You hated England,' I point out.

Mum nods, her head swinging, like a chicken with a broken neck. 'You're right,' she says. 'But I love Scotland.'

'What,' I ask, challenging, 'do you love about Scotland?'

'Oh the . . . the . . .' Mum frowns at me, checks to see if I'm tricking her. 'The music,' she says at last, and starts to weep again. Mum hates Scotland. She hates drunk-driving laws and the cold. The cold makes her cry, and then she comes down with malaria.

*

Her eyes are half-mast. That's what my sister and I call it when Mum is drunk and her eyelids droop. Half-mast eyes. Like the flag at the post office whenever someone important dies, which in Zambia, with one thing and another, is every other week. Mum stares out at the home paddocks where the cattle are coming in for their evening water to the trough near the stables. The sun is full and heavy over the hills that describe the Zambia–Zaire border. 'Have a drink with me, Bobo,' she offers. She tries to pat the chair next to hers, misses, and feebly slaps the air, her arm like a broken wing.

I shake my head. Ordinarily I don't mind getting softly drunk next to the slowly collapsing heap that is Mum, but I have to go back to boarding school the next day, nine hours by pickup across the border to Zimbabwe. 'I need to pack, Mum.'

That afternoon Mum had spent hours wrapping thirty feet of electric wire around the trees in the garden so that she could pick up the World Service of the BBC. The signature tune crackled over the syrup-yellow four o'clock light just as the sun was starting to hang above the top of the msasa trees. 'Lillibulero,' Mum said. 'That's Irish.'

'You're not Irish,' I pointed out.

She said, 'Never said I was.' And then, follow-on thought, 'Where's the whisky?'

We must have heard 'Lillibulero' thousands of times. Maybe millions. Before and after every news broadcast. At the top of every hour. Spluttering with static over the garden at home; incongruous from the branches of acacia trees in campsites we have set up in the bush across the countryside; singing from the bathroom in the evening.

But you never know what will set Mum off. Maybe it was 'Lillibulero' coinciding with the end of the afternoon, which is a rich, sweet, cooling, melancholy time of day.

'Your Dad was English originally,' I tell her, not liking the way this is going.

She said, 'It doesn't count. Scottish blood cancels English blood.'

*

By the time she has drunk a quarter of a bottle of whisky, we have lost reception from Bush House in London and the radio hisses to itself from under its fringe of bougainvillea. Mum has pulled out her old Scottish records. There are three of them. Three records of men in kilts playing bagpipes. The photographs show them marching blindly (how do they see under those dead-bear hats?) down misty Scottish cobbled streets, their faces completely blocked by their massive instruments. Mum turns the music up as loud as it will go, takes the whisky out to the veranda, and sits cross-legged on a picnic chair, humming and staring out at the night-blanketed farm.

This cross-leggedness is a hangover from the brief period in Mum's life when she took up yoga from a book. Which was better than the brief period in her life in which she explored the possibility of converting to the Jehovah's Witnesses. And better than the time she bought a book on belly-dancing at a rummage sale and tried out her techniques on every bar north of the Limpopo River and south of the equator.

The horses shuffle restlessly in their stables. The night apes scream from the tops of the shimmering-leafed msasa trees. The dogs set up a chorus of barking and will not stop until we put them inside, all except Mum's faithful spaniel, who will not leave her side even when she's throwing what Dad calls a wobbly. Which is what this is: a wobbly. The radio hisses and occasionally, drunkenly, bursts into snatches of song (Spanish or Portuguese) or chatters in German, in Afrikaans, or in an exaggerated American accent. 'This is the Voice of America.' And then it swoops, 'Beee-ooooeee!'

Dad and I go to bed with half the dogs. The other half of the pack set themselves up on the chairs in the sitting room. Dad's deaf, from when he blew his eardrums out in the war eight years ago in what was then Rhodesia. Now Zimbabwe. I put a pillow over my head. I can hear Mum's voice, high and inexact, trembling on the high notes: 'Speed, bonny boat, Like a bird on the wing, Over the sea to Skye,' and then she runs out of words and starts to sing, loudly to make up for the loss of words, 'La, la la laaaa!' In the other room, at the end of the hall, Dad is snoring.

In the morning, Mum is still on the veranda. The records are silent. The housegirl sweeps the floor around her. The radio is in the tree and has sobered up, with a film of shining dew over its silver face, and is telling us the news in clipped English tones. 'This is London,' it says with a straight face, as the milking cows are brought in to the dairy and the night apes curl up overhead to sleep and the Cape turtle doves begin to call, 'Work-hard-er, work-hard-er.' An all-day call, which I nevertheless associate with morning and which makes me long for a cup of tea. The bells of Big Ben sound from distant, steely-grey-dawn London, where commuters will soon be spilling sensibly out of underground stations or red double-decker buses. It is five o'clock Greenwich Mean Time.

*

When I was younger I used to believe it was called 'Mean' time because it was English time. I used to believe that African time was 'Kind' time.

*

The dogs are lying in exhausted heaps on the furniture in the sitting room, with their paws over their ears. They look up at Dad and me as we come through for our early morning cup of tea, which we usually take on the veranda but which the cook has set in the sitting room on account of the fact that Mum is lying with her forehead on the picnic table where he would usually put the tray. Still cross-legged. Still singing. I bet hardly anyone in yoga can do *that*.

We wedge Mum into the back of the pickup along with my suitcase and satchel and books and the spare tyres, next to the half-built generator we are taking into Lusaka to be fixed. She is humming 'Flower of Scotland'. And then Dad and I climb into the front of the pickup and set off down the farm road. I am going to start crying. There go the horses, two white faces and one black peering over the stable doors, waiting for Banda to bring them their breakfasts. And here come the dogs, running, ear-flapping hopeful after the pickup, willing us to stop and let them ride along in the back. And there goes the old cook, hunched and massive, his bony shoulders poking out of the top of his threadworn khaki uniform. He is almost seventy and has just sired another baby; he looks exhausted. He's sitting in the kitchen doorway with a joint the size of a sausage hanging from his bottom lip, a fragrant pillow of blue marijuana smoke hangs above his head. Marijuana grows well behind the stables, where it thrives on horseshit, cow dung, pilfered fertilizer intended for Dad's soyabean crop. Adamson raises one old hand in salute. The gardener stands to attention on his bush-broom, with which he is sweeping leaves from the dusty driveway. 'Miss Bobo,' he mouths, and raises his fist in a black power salute.

Mum leans over the rim of the pickup briefly, precariously, to blow the dogs a kiss. She waves at the staff for a moment, royally, and then collapses back into the folds of the tarpaulin.

Dad offers me a cigarette. 'Better have one while you still can,' he says.

'Thanks.' We smoke together for a while.

Dad says, 'It's tough when you can't smoke.'

I nod.

'Don't smoke at school.'

'I won't.'

'They won't like it.'

'They don't.'

It's past seven in the morning by the time we leave the farm. I have to be at school by five thirty that evening to make it in time for sign-in and supper. That leaves us half an hour for business and lunch in Lusaka and an hour to get through the border between Zimbabwe and Zambia.

I say, 'Better be polite to the blokes at the border today. We don't have time for silly buggers.'

'Bloody baboons,' mutters Dad.

*

13

When we get to Lusaka, Dad and I drop off the generator at the Indian's workshop on Ben Bella Road.

'Hello, Mr Fuller,' says the Indian, head bobbling like a bobbin of thread on a sewing machine. 'Come in, come in, for tea? Coffee? I have something for you to look at.'

'Not today,' says Dad, waving the man away, 'big hurry with my daughter, you see.' He talks between clenched teeth.

He gets in the pickup. Lights a cigarette. 'Bloody Indians,' he mutters as he reverses out of the yard, 'always up to something.'

We buy boiled eggs and slabs of white cornbread from a kiosk on the side of Cha Cha Cha Road, near the roundabout that leads to Kafue, the Gymkhana Club, or home, depending on where you get off. We wave some food at Mum, but she isn't moving. She has some oil on her face from the generator, which has been leaking thick, black engine blood. Otherwise she is very white, bordering on pale green.

We stop before Chirundu, the small hot nothing town on the Zambezi River which marks the border crossing into Zimbabwe, to make sure she is still alive. Dad says, 'We'll get into trouble if we try and take a dead body over the border.'

Mum has undone the tarpaulin which was meant to keep the dust out of my school clothes, and has wrapped herself up in it. She is asleep with a small smile on her lips.

Dad puts his forefinger under her nose to feel for breath. 'Still alive,' Dad announces, 'although she looks nothing like her passport photo now.'

From the back, as we ease into the melting hot, tarmac-shining car park in front of the customs building (broken windows like thin ice in the white sun) we can hear Mum shuffling back into life. She eases herself into a sitting position, the vast tarpaulin over her shoulders like a voluminous plastic operatic cloak in spite of the oven-breath heat. She is singing 'Olé, I Am a Bandit.'

'Christ,' mutters Dad.

Mum has sung 'Olé, I Am a Bandit' at every bar under the southern African sun into which she has ever stepped.

'Shut your mother up, will you?' says Dad, climbing out of the pickup with a fistful of passports and papers. 'Eh?'

I go around the back. 'Shhhh! Mum! Hey, Mum, we're at the border now. Shhh!'

She emerges blearily from the folds of the tarpaulin. 'I'm the quickest on the trigger,' she sings loudly.

'Oh, great.' I ease back into the front of the pickup and light a cigarette. I've been shot at before because of Mum and her singing. She made me drive her to our neighbours' once at two in the morning to sing them 'Olé, I Am a Bandit,' and he pulled a rifle on us and fired. He's Yugoslav.

The customs official comes out to inspect our vehicle. I grin rabidly at him.

He circles the car, stiff-legged like a dog wondering which tyre to pee on. He swings his AK 47 around like a tennis racquet.

'Get out,' he tells me.

I get out.

Dad gets uneasy. He says, 'Steady on with the stick, hey?'

'What?'

Dad shrugs, lights a cigarette. 'Can't you keep your bloody gun still?'

The official lets his barrel fall into line with Dad's heart.

Mum appears from under the drapes of the tarpaulin again. Her half-mast eyes light up.

'*Muli bwanje?*' she says elaborately: How are you?

The customs official blinks at her in surprise. He lets his gun relax against his hip. A smile plays around his lips. 'Your wife?' he asks Dad.

Dad nods, smokes. I crush out my cigarette. We're both hoping Mum doesn't say anything to get us shot.

But her mouth splits into an exaggerated smile, rows of teeth. She nods toward Dad and me: '*Kodi ndipite ndi taxi?*' she asks. Should I take a taxi?

15

The customs official leans against his gun for support (hand over the top of the barrel) and laughs, throwing back his head.

Mum laughs too. Like a small hyena, 'Hee-hee,' wheezing a bit from all the dust she has inhaled that day. She has a dust moustache, dust rings around her eyes, dust where forehead joins hairline.

'Look,' says Dad to the customs official, 'can we get going? I have to get my daughter to school today.'

The custom official turns suddenly businesslike. 'Ah,' he says, his voice threatening hours of delay, if he likes, 'where is my gift?' He turns to me. 'Little sister? What have you brought for me today?'

Mum says, 'You can have her, if you like,' and disappears under her tarpaulin. 'Hee, hee.'

'Cigarettes?' I offer.

Dad mutters, 'Bloody . . .' and swallows the rest of his words. He climbs into the pickup and lights a cigarette, staring fixedly ahead.

The customs official eventually opens the gate when he is in possession of one box of Peter Stuyvesant cigarettes (mine, intended for school), a bar of Palmolive soap (also intended for school), three hundred kwacha, and a bottle of Coke.

As we bump onto the bridge that spans the Zambezi River, Dad and I hang out of our windows, scanning the water for hippo.

Mum has reemerged from the tarpaulin to sing, 'Happy, happy Africa.'

If I weren't going back to school, I would be in heaven.

Chimurenga: Zambia, 1999

Kelvin

'Look,' Mum says, leaning across the table and pointing. Her finger is worn, blunt with work: years of digging in a garden, horses, cows, cattle, woodwork, tobacco. 'Look, we fought to keep *one* country in Africa white-run' – she stops pointing her finger at our surprised guest to take another swallow of wine – 'just one country.' Now she slumps back in defeat: 'We lost twice.'

The guest is polite, a nice Englishman. He has come to Zambia to show Africans how to run state-owned businesses to make them attractive to foreign investment, now that we aren't Social Humanists anymore. Now that we're a democracy. Ha ha. Kind of.

Mum says, 'If we could have kept one country white-ruled it would be an oasis, a refuge. I mean, look, what a cock-up. Everywhere you look it's a bloody cock-up.'

The guest says nothing, but his smile is bemused. I can tell he's thinking, *Oh my God, they'll never believe this when I tell them back home.* He's saving this conversation for later. He's a two-year wonder. People like this never last beyond two malaria seasons, at most. Then he'll go back to England and say, 'When I was in Zambia . . .' for the rest of his life.

'Good dinner, Tub,' says Dad.

Mum did not cook the dinner. Kelvin cooked the dinner. But Mum *organized* Kelvin.

Dad lights an after-dinner pipe and smokes quietly. He is leaning back in his chair so that there is room on his lap for his dog between his slim belly and the table. He stares out at the garden. The sun has set in a red ball, sinking behind the quiet, stretching black limbs of the msasa trees on Oribi Ridge, which is where my parents moved after I was married. The dining room has only three walls: it lies open to the bush, to the cries of the night insects, the shrieks of the small, hunted animals, the bats which flit in and out of the dining room, swooping above our heads to eat mosquitoes. Clinging to the rough white-washed cement walls are assorted moths, lizards and geckos, which occasionally let go with a high, sharp laugh: 'He-he-he.'

Mum pours herself more wine, finishing the bottle, and then she says fiercely to our guest, 'Thirteen thousand Kenyans and a hundred white settlers died in the struggle for Kenya's independence.'

I can tell the visitor doesn't know if he should look impressed or distressed. He settles for a look of vague surprise. 'I had no idea.'

'Of course you bloody people had no idea,' says Mum. 'A hundred . . . of us.'

'Cool it, Tub,' says Dad, stroking the dog and smoking.

'Nineteen forty-seven to nineteen sixty-three,' says Mum.

18

'Nearly twenty bloody years we tried to hold on.' She makes her fist into a tight grip. The sinews on her neck stand taut and she bares her teeth. 'All for what? And what a cock-up they've made of it now. Hey? Bloody, bloody cock-up.'

*

After independence, Kenya was run by Mzee, the Grand Old Man, Jomo Kenyatta. He had been born in 1894, the year before Britain declared Kenya one of its protectorates. He had come to power in 1963, an old man who had finally fulfilled the destiny of his life's work: self-government for Africans in Africa.

*

Dad says, mildly, 'Shall I ask Kelvin to clear the table?'

Mum says, 'And Rhodesia. One thousand government troops dead.' She pauses. 'Fourteen thousand terrorists. We should have won, if you look at it like that, except there were more of them.' Mum drinks, licks her top lip. 'Of course, we couldn't stay on in Kenya after Mau Mau.' She shakes her head.

Kelvin comes to clear the table. He is trying to save enough money, through the wages he earns as Mum and Dad's house-keeper, to open his own electrical shop.

Mum says, 'Thank you, Kelvin.'

*

Kelvin almost died today. Irritated to distraction by the flies in the kitchen, he had closed the two doors and the one little window in the room, into which he had then emptied an entire can of insect-killing Doom. Mum had found him convulsing on the kitchen floor just before afternoon tea.

'Bloody idiot.' She had dragged him onto the lawn, where he lay jerking and twitching for some minutes until Mum sloshed a bucket of cold water onto his face. 'Idiot!' she shrieked. 'You could have killed yourself.'

19

Now Kelvin looks as self-possessed and serene as ever. Jesus, he has told me, is his Saviour. He has an infant son named Elvis, after the other king.

Dad says, 'Bring more beers, Kelvin.'

'Yes, Bwana.'

We move to the picnic chairs around the wood fire on the veranda. Kelvin brings us more beers and clears the rest of the plates away. I light a cigarette and prop my feet up on the cold end of a burning log.

'I thought you quit,' says Dad.

'I did.' I throw my head back and watch the light-grey smoke I exhale against black sky, the bright cherry at the tip of my cigarette against deep for ever. The stars are silver tubes of light going back endlessly, years and light-years into themselves. The wind shifts restlessly. Maybe it will rain in a week or so. Wood smoke curls itself around my shoulders, lingers long enough to scent my hair and skin, and then veers towards Dad. The two of us are silent, listening to Mum and her stuck record, *Tragedies of Our Lives*. What the patient, nice Englishman does not know, which Dad and I both know, is that Mum is only on Chapter One.

Chapter One	The War
Chapter Two	Dead Children
Chapter Three	Insanity
Chapter Four	Being Nicola Fuller of Central Africa

Chapter Four is really a subchapter of the other chapters. Chapter Four is when Mum sits quietly, having drunk so much that every pore in her body is soaked. She is yoga-crosslegged, and she stares, with a look of stupefied wonder, at the garden and at the dawn breaking through wood-smoke haze and the thin grey-brown band of dust and pollution that hangs above the city of Lusaka. And she's thinking, *So this is what it's like being Me.*

Kelvin comes. 'Good night.'

Mum is already sitting yoga-crosslegged, cradling a drink on her lap. 'Good night, Kelvin,' she says with great emphasis, almost with respect (a sad, dignified respect). As if he were dead and she were throwing the first clump of soil onto his coffin.

Dad and I excuse ourselves, gather a collection of dogs, and make for our separate bedrooms, leaving Mum, the Englishman, and two swooping bats in the company of the sinking fire. The Englishman, who spent much of supper warily eyeing the bats and ducking every time one flitted over the table, has now got beyond worrying about bats.

Guests trapped by Mum have chapters of their own.

Chapter One	Delight
Chapter Two	Mild Intoxication Coupled with Growing Disbelief
Chapter Three	Extreme Intoxication Coupled with Growing Panic
Chapter Four	Lack of Consciousness

I am here visiting from America. Smoking cigarettes when I shouldn't be. Drinking carelessly under a huge African sky. So happy to be home I feel as if I'm swimming in syrup. My bed is closest to the window. The orange light from the dying fire glows against my bedroom wall. The bedding is sweet-bitter with wood smoke. The dogs wrestle for position on the bed. The old, toothless spaniel on the pillow, one Jack Russell at each foot.

'Rhodesia was run by a white man, Ian Douglas Smith, remember him?'

'Of course,' says the unfortunate captive guest, now too drunk to negotiate the steep, dusty driveway through the thick,

Mum, Dad and Van: Kenya

black-barked trees to the long, red-powdered road that leads back to the city of Lusaka, where he has a nice, European-style house with an ex-embassy servant and a watchman (complete with trained German shepherd). Now, instead of going back to his guarded African-city suburbia, he will sit up until dawn, drinking with Mum.

'He came to power in 1964. On the eleventh of November, 1965, he made a Unilateral Declaration of Independence from Britain. He made it clear that there would never be majority rule in Rhodesia.' Even when Mum is so drunk that she is practising her yoga moves, she can remember the key dates relating to Our Tragedies.

'So we moved there in 1966. Our daughter – Vanessa, our eldest – was only one year old. We were prepared' – Mum's voice grows suitably dramatic – 'to take our baby into a war to live in a country where white men still ruled.'

Bumi, the spaniel, tucks her chin onto the pillow next to my head, where she grunts with content before she begins to snore. She has dead-rabbit breath. I turn over, my face away from hers, and go to sleep.

The last thing I hear is Mum say, 'We were prepared to die, you see, to keep one country white-run.'

*

In the morning Mum is Chapter Four, smiling idiotically to herself, a warm, flat beer propped between her thighs, her head cockeyed. She is staring damply into the pink-yellow dawn. The guest is Chapter Four too, lying greyly on the lawn. He isn't convulsing, but in almost every other respect, he looks astonishingly like Kelvin did yesterday afternoon.

Kelvin has brought the tea and is laying the table for breakfast As If Everything Were Normal.

Which it is. For us.

Chimurenga: The Beginning

Village

In April 1966, the year my parents moved to Rhodesia with their baby daughter, the Zimbabwe African National Liberation Army (ZANLA) launched an attack against government forces in Sinoia to protest against Smith's Unilateral Declaration of Independence from Britain and to fight for majority rule.

Sinoia, corruption of 'Chinhoyi', was the name of the local chief in 1902.

The Second Chimurenga, it was called by the black Africans in Rhodesia, this war of which the 1966 skirmish in Sinoia was just the start.

Chimurenga. A poetic Shona way of saying 'war of liberation'.

Zimbabwe, they called the country. From *dzimba dza mabwe*, 'houses of stone'.

The whites didn't call it Chimurenga. They called it 'the troubles', 'this bloody nonsense'. And sometimes 'the war'. A war instigated by 'uppity blacks', 'cheeky kaffirs', 'bolshy muntus', 'restless natives', 'the houts'.

Black Rhodesians are also known by white Rhodesians as 'gondies', 'boogs', 'toeys', 'zots', 'nig-nogs', 'wogs', 'affies'.

We call the black women 'nannies' and the black men 'boys'.

The First Chimurenga was a long time ago, a few years after the settlers got here. The welcome mat had only been out for a relative moment or two when the Africans realized a welcome mat was not what they needed for their European guests. When they saw that the Europeans were the kind of guests who slept with your wife, enslaved your children, and stole your cattle, they saw that they needed sharp spears and young men who knew how to use them. The war drums were brought out from dark corners and dusted off and the old men who knew how to beat the war drums, who knew which rhythms would pump the fighting blood of the young men, were told to start beating the drums.

Between 1889 and 1893, British settlers moving up from South Africa, under the steely, acquiring eye of Cecil John Rhodes, had been . . . What word can I use? I suppose it depends on who you are. I could say: Taking? Stealing? Settling? Homesteading? Appropriating? Whatever the word is, they had been doing it to a swathe of country they now called Rhodesia. Before that, the land had been moveable, shifting under the feet of whatever victorious tribe now danced on its soil, taking on new names and freshly stolen cattle, absorbing the blood and bodies of whoever was living, breathing, birthing, dying upon it. The land itself, of course, was careless of its name. It still is. You can call it what you like, fight all the wars you want in its name. Change its name altogether if you like. The land is still unblinking under the African sky. It will absorb white man's blood and the blood of African men, it will absorb blood from slaughtered cattle and the blood from a woman's birthing with equal thirst. It doesn't care.

Here were the African names within that piece of land for which we would all fight: Bulawayo: the Place of Killing. Inyati: the Place of the Buffaloes. Nyabira: the Place Where There Is a Ford.

The white men came. They said, 'What name do you give this place?'

'*Kadoma*,' they said. Which in Ndebele means, 'Does Not Thunder or Make Noise'.

The white men call that place Gatooma.

'And what name do you give this place?'

'*Ikwelo*,' they said. Which in Ndebele means, 'Steep Sides of the Riverbank'.

The white men called the place Gwelo.

'What is this place?'

'*Kwe Kwe*,' said the Africans, which is the sound the frogs make in the nearby river.

The white men called the place Que Que.

'We will live in this place.'

'But this is the chiefdom of Neharawa,' said the Africans.

'And we will call it Salisbury.'

The white men named places after themselves, and after the women they were with or the women whom they had left behind, after the men they wanted to placate or impress: Salisbury, Muriel, Beatrice, Alice Mine, Juliasdale, West Nicholson.

And they gave some places hopeful names: Copper Queen, Eldorado, Golden Valley.

And obvious names: Figtree, Guinea Fowl, Lion's Den, Redcliff, Hippo Valley.

And unlikely, stolen names: Alaska, Venice, Bannockburn, Turk Mine.

In 1896 the Ndebele people had rebelled against this European-ness. They killed about one hundred and fifty European

In camp

men, women, and children in a matter of a few weeks. But within three months the settlers, with the help of military reinforcements from South Africa, had defeated the Ndebeles, and Cecil John Rhodes had negotiated a ceasefire with the Ndebele leaders at Matopo Hills.

Matopo Hills, where Cecil John Rhodes is buried, staring out over Ndebeleland in perpetuity. Matopo Hills, a corruption of 'Amatobos', meaning 'the Bald-Headed Ones'.

In the same month, June 1896, that Rhodes was settling with the Ndebeles in the south of the country, the Shonas in the central and east of the country rose up in a separate and more serious rebellion against the whites. When farmers, such as the Mashona, go to war, they are not like the Ndebele warriors, who come into the open savannah flashing their bare chests under the clear sky and waving their plumed headdresses and flaunting the skins of slaughtered lions and hunted leopards on their thighs and brows. Farmers fight a more deadly, secret kind of war. They are fighting for land in which they have put their seed, their sweat, their hopes. They are secretive, sly, desperate. They do not come with loud war drums and the bones of powerful animals around their neck. They come with one intent, sliding on their bellies, secret in the night. They don't come to be victorious in battle. They come to reclaim their land.

The Shonas killed four hundred and fifty settlers.

Reinforcements to help the settlers arrived from South Africa and England. The Africans developed a system of hiding in caves to escape from the white man's army. The settlers used dynamite to force the Africans out of the caves, killing whole villages at a time when the caves collapsed – Mashona men, women and children died by the hundreds, buried together. Survivors of the collapsed caves were executed as soon they crawled out of the ready made tombs. It took almost two years for the first Chimurenga to be quelled.

The Africans did not forget their heroes from this first struggle for independence. Kaguvi, Mkwati, and Nehanda.

Kaguvi. Also called Murenga, or Resister. From which the word Chimurenga comes.

Mkwati, famous for his use of locust medicine.

Nehanda, the woman, supra-clan mhondoro spirits. She went to her execution (with Kaguvi) on 27 April 1897, singing and dancing. 'We shall overcome. My blood is not shed in vain.'

Now how can we, who shed our ancestry the way a snake sheds skin in winter, hope to win against this history? We *mazungus*. We white Africans of shrugged-off English, Scottish, Dutch origin.

Seven ZANLA troops died on 28 April 1966, the first battle of the Second Chimurenga. A memorial stands in their name in the modern city of Chinhoyi, 'The Gallant Chinhoyi Seven'.

Adrian: Rhodesia, 1968

Mum, Adrian and Van

Mum says, 'The happiest day of my life was the day I held that little baby in my arms.' She means Rhodesia, 1968. She means the day her son, Adrian, was born.

Mum is Chapter Two, weeping into her beer. It's a sad story. It's especially sad if you haven't heard it a hundred times. I've heard one version or other of the story more than a hundred times. It's a Family Theme and it always ends badly. To begin with Mum is happy. She is freshly married, they are white (a ruling colour in Rhodesia), and she has two babies, a girl and a boy. Her children are the picture-perfect match of each other: beautiful, blond, and blue-eyed.

*

Mum

Vanessa, signature tackie lips (lips that are rosebud full), a mass of fairy-white hair, toddling cheerfully, with that overbalancing, tripping step of the small child. And tottering after her, the little boy who could be her twin. In the background, a black nanny called Tabatha, in white apron and white cap, strong, shining arms outstretched laughing, waiting to scoop them up; she is half-shyly looking into the camera. Mum is looking on from the veranda. Dad is taking the photograph.

*

Then Adrian dies before he is old enough to talk. Mum is not yet twenty-four and her picture-perfect life is shattered.

She says, 'The nurse at the hospital in Salisbury told us we could either go and get something to eat or watch our baby die.'

Mum and Dad take Vanessa to get some lunch and when they come back to the hospital their baby son, who was very sick with meningitis an hour earlier, is now dead. Cold, blond ash.

The story changes depending on what Mum is drinking. If she is very drunk on wine, then the story is a bit different than if she is very drunk on gin. The worst is if she is very drunk on

Adrian

everything she can find in the house. But the end is always the same. Adrian is dead. That's an awful ending no matter what she's been drinking.

I am eight, maybe younger, the first time Mum sits down in front of me, squiffy in her chair, leaning and keening and needing to talk. The Leaning Tower of Pissed, I say to Vanessa when I am older and Mum is drunk again. *Ha ha.*

Mum tells me about Adrian. I understand, through the power of her emotion, her tears, the way she is dissolving like soap left too long in the bath, that this has been the greatest tragedy of our lives. It is my tragedy, too, even though I was not born when it happened.

Usually, on nights when Mum is sober, and we are kissing her good night, she turns her face away from us and puckers her lips sideways, offering us a cheek stretched like dead-chicken skin. Now that she is drunk and telling me about Adrian she is wet all over me. Arms clasped over my shoulders, she is hanging around my neck, and I can feel her face crying into the damp patch on my shoulder. She says, 'You were the baby we made when Adrian died.'

I know all about making babies, being the daughter of a farmer. I have already put my hand up a cow's bum, scraped out the sloppy, warm, green-grass pile of shit and felt beyond that, for the thick lining of her womb. If the womb is swollen with a foetus I can touch the shape of it, pressing against the womb wall. A curved back, usually, or the hump of a rear, the bony fineness of a tiny head. I know about conception. Cows that don't conceive have their tails cut to differentiate them from the fertile cows, whose tails are left long. The short-tailed cows are pulled from the herd and put on a lorry and sent into Umtali where they become ground meat, sausages, glue. They become Colcom's Steak Pie.

The next morning Mum, who usually eats nothing for break-fast, has two fried eggs, fried bananas, tomatoes. A slice of toast with marmalade and butter. She swallows a pot of tea and then has a cup of coffee. She usually does not drink coffee. The coffee tastes bad because there are *sanctionson*, which means no one will sell Rhodesia anything and Rhodesia can't sell anything to anyone else, so our coffee is made from chicory and burnt maize and tastes like charcoal.

All morning, Mum is more bad-tempered than usual in spite of her enormous breakfast. She yells at the cook and the maid and the dogs. She tells me to 'stop twittering on'. I shut up. That afternoon, she sleeps for three hours while I sit quietly at the end of her bed with the dogs. We're afraid to wake her, although the dogs are ready for their walk and I am ready for a cup of tea. I am watching her sleep. Her face has fallen away into peace. The dogs sit prick-eared and watchful for a long time and then they lie with their heads in their paws and worried eyes. They are depressed.

*

Adrian is buried in the cemetery in Salisbury.

Mum and Dad leave Rhodesia. They leave the small anonymous hump of their son-child in the huge cemetery opposite the tobacco-auction floors in town. They go to England, via Victoria Falls, conceiving me in the sixties hotel next to the grand, historic, turn-of-the-century Victoria Falls Hotel.

I am conceived in the hotel (with the casino in it) next to the thundering roar of the place where the Zambezi River plunges a hundred metres into a black-sided gorge. The following March, I am born into the tame, drizzling English town of Glossop.

The plunging roar of the Zambezi in my ears at conception. Incongruous, contradictory in Derbyshire at birth.

Coming-Back Babies

Bobo: Boarfold

Some Africans believe that if your baby dies you must bury it far away from your house, with proper magic and incantations and gifts for the gods, so that the baby does not come back, time after time, and plant itself inside your womb only to die a short time after birth.

This is a story for people who need to find an acceptable way to lose a multitude of babies. Like us. Five born, three dead.

I came after a dead brother, whose body had not been properly buried in the soul-trapping roots of a tree and for whose soul there had been no proper offerings to the gods.

But I am alive.

I was not the soul of my dead brother. He had a soft soul, I think. Like my sister Vanessa has. He was blond and blue-eyed and sweet like her, too. People wanted to clutch his cheeks.

But I plucked a new, different, worldly soul for myself – maybe a soul I found in the spray thrown up by the surge of that distant African river as it plummets onto black rocks and sends up into the sun a permanent arc of a rainbow. Maybe I found a soul hovering over the sea as my parents made the passage back to England from Africa. Or, it was a soul I found floating about in working-class, damp-to-the-bone Derbyshire.

I came to earth with a shock of black hair and dark green eyes. I had a look on my face as if somebody had *already* pinched my cheeks (so that they did not need repinching). I have a pair of the signature tackie lips. Fuller lips. On me, they look over-large and sulky.

My soul has no home. I am neither African nor English nor am I of the sea. Meanwhile, Adrian's restless African soul still roamed. Waiting. Waiting to come back and take another baby under the earth.

Adrian is a Coming-Back Baby, if you can believe what some Africans say.

I should have been a Coming-Back Baby, but I didn't believe what some Africans say.

That Coming-Back soul searched for me. Undoubtedly, there was a struggle for my soul on the train coming up from Cape Town. That was the closest I came to being a Coming-Back Baby.

England, 1969

Boarfold

To begin with they lived in a semi-detached house in Stalybridge, Cheshire. But it was unthinkable to either of my parents to continue living in such ordinarily lower-middle-class circumstances. So, in spite of their lack of funds, but with their usual brazen disregard for such details, they bought a farm in bordering Derbyshire with borrowed money. There was no house on the farm, just a barn, still rank with the smell of cow shit, ancient horse pee, old dusty chicken droppings. Dad was selling agricultural chemicals to suspicious, low-browed farmers, Mum was sleeves-rolled-up running after two small children, a goat, several chickens, and a hutch of rabbits whom she couldn't bear to slaughter when the time came to turn them into rabbit pie,

Girls at Boarfold

so she let them free where they overpopulated the Derbyshire countryside.

When the rain came in the winter and as far as the eye could see a grey shroud hung over the hills, the adventure of England wore off. My parents were more broke than ever, but they were not going to rot to death under a dripping English sky. Dad quit his job. They rolled up the entire farm and sold it as turf to a gardening company, which would unroll it as lawn in suburban Manchester. They rented out the barn (now equipped with flush loos and running water, and the cow shit scraped out to reveal scrubbed old stone floors) to gullible city folk as 'rural cottages' and fled.

Dad went ahead to Rhodesia by plane. Mum followed by ship with two dogs and two children.

The ship trundled steadily down the African coast with the slow, warm winds pushing her south, past the equator, where the air felt thicker and the sun burned brighter, all the way past the welcoming, waving beaches of the tropics and to the southern tip of the continent.

When the ship veered into the Cape of Good Hope, Mum

caught the spicy, woody scent of Africa on the changing wind. She smelled the people: raw onions and salt, the smell of people who are not afraid to eat meat, and who smoke fish over open fires on the beach and who pound maize into meal and who work out-of-doors. She held me up to face the earthy air, so that the fingers of warmth pushed back my black curls of hair, and her pale green eyes went clear-glassy.

'Smell that,' she whispered, 'that's home.'

Vanessa was running up and down the deck, unaccountably wild for a child usually so placid. Intoxicated already.

I took in a face full of African air and fell instantly into a fever.

By the time we were on the train from Cape Town to Rhodesia I was so racked with illness that I was almost unconscious: trembling and shaking and with a cold-burning sweat.

Some Africans would say, 'The child is possessed, of course.' On account of the Coming-Back Baby. 'And there are various magics you can perform with the help of a witch doctor if you wish to keep her.'

Some Africans would say, 'What a load of rubbish. There's no such thing as returning babies. Wrap the child in vinegar paper.'

Some Africans would say, 'Good, let her die. Who needs another white baby, to grow into a bossy, hands-on-hips, white madam?'

But I was made of my own soul already. I was here to stay.

Mum made them stop the train. I was raced to the nearest hospital. No one could say what was wrong with me. They took my temperature and fed me aspirin which I puked up in bitter streams through my nose. They bathed my arms and legs with a damp washcloth until I sat up and demanded food.

'Say "Please,"' said Mum.

Although I had been conceived in Africa, I had been started in urban England (like a delicate vegetable started indoors, where

it is safe – at a vulnerable age – from pests and too much sun).
I had the constitution of a missionary.

Within a day I was well enough to continue the journey to
Rhodesia.

Up through South Africa, the train laboured in the heat,
pulling herself up hills, *chaka-chaka* (an Ndebele war sound)
through burning flat savannah that looked as though it might
ignite at the sight of our metallic speed, slicing on hot wheels,
ever north. This was where Cecil John Rhodes had intended for
we British to go. From Cape to Cairo had been his dream.
One long stain of British territory up the spine of Africa. He
himself, the great white bald-headed one, made it only as far as
Rhodesia.

Our train left South Africa, travelling up over the Great
Grey-Green, Greasy Limpopo (all set about, said Rudyard
Kipling, with fever-trees). Up to the long flat place where the
dust blew all day and night and the air was raw with so much
blowing. To Karoi, Rhodesia.

Karoi

The house at Karoi

A coloured topographical map of Rhodesia shows the west and the north-west of the country as pale yellow fading to green, which means that it is low and hot, barely undulating as it humps towards the Zambezi River valley. It means that when the wind blows it picks up fists of stinging sand and flings it against your skin.

Dete is there, in the flat part, in the west. Dete meaning Narrow Passage. Shithole.

When we first came back to Rhodesia, we lived in the north-west, in the flat, pale-yellow area, melted into orange in places, which meant that, unlike Dete, the land had some lift off the sunburned lowveldt. But not enough so you'd notice the difference.

You could not look to the relief of mountains or banks of green trees on a hot day when the heatwaves danced like spear-toting warriors off the grassland and when the long wide airstrip above our house and the pale yellow maize fields below our house shimmered behind dry season dust.

Grass, earth, air, buildings, skin, clothes all took on the same dust-blown glare of too much heat trapped in too little air.

We lived on a farm near Karoi.

'Karoi' meaning Little Witch. In the olden days, which aren't so olden as all that (within living memory), witches had been thrown into the nearby Angwa River, (barely deep enough to drown a small goblin). Only black witches were drowned, of course. No one would have allowed a white woman, however witchly, to be sent plunging to her death in this way.

Vanessa went to the little, flat school in town every morning. Her school looked like a bomb bunker. The playground smelled like sweat on metal from the chipped-paint swings and slides. The playground's grass was scrubbed down to bald, pale earth.

I had to stay at home with Violet, the nanny, and Snake, the cook.

Mum was don't-interrupt-me-I'm-busy all day. She rode on the farm with the dogs in the morning and then went down to the workshop, where she made wooden bookshelves and spice racks and pepper pots for the fancy ladies' shops in Salisbury.

Dad was gone at dawn, coming back when the light was dusky-grey and the night animals were starting to call, after Violet had given us our supper and bathed us. He was just in time to kiss us with tobacco-sour breath and tuck us in to bed.

In the morning, one of our horses would be brought down to the house and I was led around the garden until Mum came out to take the dogs out for their morning ride. Then I was sent outside to play. 'But not in the bamboo.'

'Why not?'

Snake and Violet settled down for plastic mugs of sweet milky tea and thick slabs of buttery bread as soon as Mum was out of sight. 'There are things in there that might bite you.'

'Like snakes?'

'Yes, like snakes.' Violet took a bite of bread and a mouthful of tea and mixed the two together in her mouth. We called this cement mixing, and we were not allowed to do it.

'Why?'

'Because it's something only *muntus* do. Like picking your nose.'

'But I've seen Euros picking their noses.'

'Rubbish.'

'I have.'

'Don't exaggerate.'

So I went into the bamboo behind the kitchen and played in the crisp fallen leaves and lay on my back and looked up at the tall, strong, grass-coloured stems, so shiny it looked as if they had been painted with thin green and thick golden stripes and then varnished. And nothing happened to me, even though Violet shook her head at me and said, 'I should beat you.'

'Then I'll fire you, hey.'

'Tch, tch.'

Then one morning, as I was playing as usual in the bamboo, I felt an intense burning bite on what my mother called *downthere*. Screaming in pain, I ran into the house and yelled for Violet or Snake to help me.

They put down their tea and put their bread over the top of the cup so that flies would not drown in their tea and they frowned at me. But they would not look *downthere*.

'Owie, owie.'

But 'Not there,' said Snake, 'I can't look there.' He picked up his bread, wafted the flies off his peels of butter, and began to drink his tea again. But the spell had been broken for him. The moment of peace in the morning was ruined by me and my bitten, burning *downthere*.

Violet hid her mouth behind her hand and giggled.

I would have to wait for my mother to get home from her ride.

'It was a spider,' said Snake.

Bobo and Van

'Or a scorpion,' said Violet, taking a bite of bread and a mouthful of tea.

'A scorpion?' I screamed louder.

'Maybe a little snake.' The cook shut his eyes.

I tugged at Violet. 'A snake? A snake!'

Violet shook me off and quickly swallowed her tea and bread without enjoyment. Glaring at me angrily as if I were giving her a stomachache.

'Help me! Owie, man!' I wondered if I was going to die.

I said, 'Look in my brookies! Please help me!' But Violet looked disgusted and Snake looked away.

I lay on the floor in the kitchen and screamed, holding my shorts, writhing and waiting to die from the poison of whatever had bitten me.

When Mum came back from her ride I ran to her before she could even slip off the horse, stripping down my shorts and crying, 'I've been bitten! I'm going to die!'

'What nonsense,' said Mum. She dismounted and handed the reins to the groom.

'On my *downthere*.'

'Bobo!'

'A scorp or a snake, I swear, I swear.'

Mum pressed her lips together. 'Oh, for god's sake.' She pulled at my wrist. 'Pull up your shorts,' she hissed.

'But it's owie, man.'

'Not in front of the servants,' she said. She dragged me into the sitting room and shut the door. 'Never, ever pull down your shorts in front of an African again.'

'Owie!'

'Do you hear me?'

'*Ja, ja*! Oh it hurts!'

She bent down and tugged at the soft, bitten skin.

'There,' she said, presenting me with a tiny tick pressed between her forefingers, 'all that fuss for a little tick.'

'What?'

'See?' The tick waved its legs at me in salute. It still had a mouthful of pink skin, *my* pink skin, in its jaws. 'Nothing to get your knickers in a twist about.'

I shook my head and wiped my nose on my arm.

'Now go and find Violet and tell her to wash your face,' said Mum. She pressed the tick between her nails until it popped, my blood bursting out of the tick and staining the tips of Mum's fingers.

*

That's how I remember Karoi. And the dust-stinging wind blowing through the mealies on a hot, dry September night. And a fold-up and rip-away lawn prickled with paper thorns. And the beginning of the army guys: men in camouflage, breaking like a ribbon out of the back of an army lorry and uncurling onto the road, heads shaved, faces fresh and blank. Men cradling guns. And the beginning of men not in camouflage anymore, looking blank-faced, limbs lost.

The Burma Valley

Bobo and Van

The central vein of Rhodesia rises up into a plateau called the Great Dyke. It is where most of the country's population have chosen to stay. The edges of the country tend toward extreme heat, flat heartless scrub, droughts, malaria. The central vein is fertile. Rhododendrons will grow here. Horses will gleam with fat, shiny coats. Children look long-limbed, high-browed, intelligent. Vitamin sufficient.

And then, in the east, beyond Salisbury, there is a thin, strangled hump, a knotted fist of highlands. And there if you look carefully, nestled into the sweet purple-coloured swellings, where it is almost always cool, and the air is sharp and wholesome with eucalyptus and pine and where there are no mosquitoes, is a deep, sudden valley. (The map plunges from purple to pink then orange and yellow to indicate one's descent into heat and flatness and malaria.) That valley, in the far east of the country, is the Burma Valley. Here, horses hang thin in the thick, wet heat, their skin stretched over hips like slings. Children are elbow-knee wormy and hollow-orange with too much heat, skin-pinching dehydration, and smoking-drinking parents. Dogs have scabs from putzi flies which lay eggs on damp patches of earth or unironed clothes, burrow under the skin, the eggs becoming maggots, bursting into living, squirming boils, emerging as full-blown, winged flies.

'Don't wear clothes that haven't been ironed.'

'Why?'

'Or you'll get putzis.' Which babies get on their bottoms from damp, cloth nappies.

Mum told us that Vanessa got them once from an unironed nappy.

'Vanessa had putzis on her bott-om. Vanessa had putzis on her bott-om.'

'*Ja*? Well at least I've never had a tick on my *downthere*.'

Mum and Dad left Karoi and bought the farm in the Burma Valley because they loved the view. When they had stood where the new veranda would one day be built on the front of the old farmhouse and when they had looked out at the view of the hills, stretching blue-green into a haze of distant forest fires, and when they had seen the innocent-looking hump of the farm stretched out at their feet toward Mozambique, it seemed to them like this farm could hold their dreams in its secret valleys and gushing rivers and rocky hills.

The plumbing was temperamental and obvious (a leach field bleeding green slime at the back of the house) and there was no electricity.

They said, 'We'll take it.'

Unsurprisingly, the valley had reminded one of its first European settlers of Burma. It was humid and thick with jungle and creepers, and cut through with rivers whose banks spilled prolific ferns and mossy rocks and lichen-dripping trees teetering on the edge of falling in, and it was fertile-foul smelling (as if on the verge of rotting) and held a green-leafy lie of prosperity in its jewelled fist.

The valley represented the insanity of the tropics so precarious for the fragile European psyche. The valley could send you into a spiral of madness overnight if you were white and highly strung. Which we were.

It was easy to leave Karoi. Karoi had always felt like a train station platform, a flat place from which we hoped to leave at any moment for somewhere more interesting and picturesque.

We loaded up two cats called Fred and Basil and three dogs called Tina, Shea and Jacko, and we drove, our worldly possessions balanced precariously on the roof of our car, clear across Rhodesia from flat west to convoluted east. We stopped to fill up the petrol tank, drink Cokes and buy bags of Willards chips ('Make music in your mouth'). Everyone, dogs included, was let out for a pee on the side of the road, behind the bougainvillea bushes.

'Go now or for ever hold your pee.'

Dad doesn't like to stop. Even if your legs are crossed and you can't see straight you have to pee so much, he doesn't like to stop. He says, 'You should have gone back there when you had a chance.'

'Ja, but I didn't need to go back there.'

Dad lights a cigarette and ignores us.

'*Agh*, please, Dad.'

'I have to pee, man.'

'She's going to widdle in her knickers,' warns Vanessa.

'Oh *fergodsake*. Tim, pull over, won't you?'

The dogs panted hotly down our necks and we itched with their irritably scratched-off hair, the cats cried angrily from their boxes, strong gusts of wind threatened to flip the mattresses off our roof. Dad smoked and we ducked his ash in the back seat.

Mum read, occasionally nodding off into broken-chicken-neck sleep. Vanessa and I fought and whined and dodged the consequent flailing hands aimed toward our bottoms.

Rebel, the horse, was on a lorry with the sofa and the dining-room table and Mum's woodwork machines. He was padded by our sheets and towels and two suitcases in which Mum had packed all our clothes. Our whole lives, everything we were and everything we owned, were in a Peugeot station wagon and a lorry. If we had been vanished away, sucked up into the atmosphere, just as we were, there would have been no trace of our little family ever having been on the planet. Not even Adrian's grave, which was never marked, would tell of our short, unimportant passage on this earth.

*

As we drove over Christmas Pass, through the Mutarandanda Hills, the small city of Umtali suddenly winked up at us in the bright eastern highland sun, which seemed more glittering and intense out here than it did in the dust-yellow western part of the country.

Umtali (corruption of the word *mutare*, meaning piece of metal), is the last city in Rhodesia before the somewhat mysterious, faintly exotic border of Portuguese-held Mozambique draws a red line across the map.

Against a cliff overlooking the road, a hedge had been planted to read WELCOME TO UMTALI. During the war, the terrorists chopped out the 'L' in WELCOME, so that the subsequent greeting read a chilling WE COME TO UMTALI. As quickly as the women from the Umtali Gardening Club directed the 'garden boys' to replant the all-important missing 'L', it was ripped out again, until the war was won (or lost, depending on whose side you were on) and the hedge was replanted to read, WELCOME TO MUTARE.

We stopped in Umtali, at the Cecil Hotel (renamed the Manica Hotel after the war). Vanessa and I were given a Coke, not out of the bottle and warm but in a glass, floating with little wondrous cubes of ice. A shiny African waiter with impeccable hands and careful, clean nails brought us little white plates of ham sandwiches with the crusts cut off and green shreds of lettuce and paper-thin tomatoes sprinkled all over them.

Mum and Dad were in the bar for a beer or two.

Vanessa and I picked the salad off the sandwiches and finished our meal quickly, eyeing each other and trying to stuff at least as much as the other into our mouths. Then we ran around on the blue patterned carpet, dizzy with luxury and Coke ('Adds life'); wall-to-wall carpeting; the unfamiliar bitter-smelling chill of air-conditioning; hushed lights; vigorously flushing loos; soft-footed waiters whose gleaming uniforms were made of thick, shiny cream nylon, crisply piped in gold, sharp-shouldered with blue epaulettes. The chairs were swallowingly soft, the colours were bubble-gold and shades of greeny-blue. A white lady with hair like a purple-rinsed haystack and long red nails frowned at us from behind the reception desk. I had never been anywhere so comfortable. I would have been happy to sleep on the floor, under one of the round, glass-topped coffee tables, for the rest of my life. I would never need to sting with sweat again, being for ever nicely, lightly chilled. No ticks or flies or scorps or snakes on this prickling, clean carpet. Cold Coke and ham sandwiches for breakfast, lunch and supper for ever and ever. Our-men.

*

On the way out of Umtali, heading always east, farther and farther toward Mozambique, we stopped at the little rural post office, Paulington, which serviced the Vumba highlands and the Burma Valley, to collect our new post-box key. And then we snaked across the rim of the mountains leading out of Umtali, barrelled across the dusty Tribal Trust Lands, and swung down off the mountains onto the floor of the valley.

It was breathtaking, that first drive into the valley, dropping off the sandy plateau of the denuded Zamunya TTL, where African cattle swung heavy horns and collected in thorny corrals for the evening and where the land was ribbed with erosion, and then banking steeply into the valley, the road now shouldered by thick, old, vine-covered trees with a dense light-sucking canopy and impenetrable undergrowth. We had gone from desert to jungle in one steep turn in the road.

Then we drove almost as far across the valley as we could go in the direction of the Mozambican hills until we arrived, dusty and stinging with sweat, coated with dog hair, at the large, ugly squat house that was to be our home for the next six years. We were going to be here until the end of the thirteen-year-long civil war.

'Home,' Mum announced cheerfully.

We scrambled out of the car, sea-sick after the choppy passage across the unfolding hills (Coke and ham sandwiches churning uncomfortably). We stared suspiciously, unimpressed at the house. It looked like an army barracks, low to the ground and solid with closed-in windows and a blank stare. The yard, littered with flamboyant pods, was big and bald and red.

Chimurenga, 1974

Dad

That was 1974, the year I turned five.

That year, in neighbouring Mozambique, a ten-year civil war between Frelimo rebels and colonial Portugal was just drawing to a close and a new civil war between Renamo rebel forces and the new Frelimo government was just beginning.

We could see the Mozambican hills from our house. Our farm ended where the Mozambican hills started.

In 1974, the civil war in Rhodesia was eight years old. In a matter of months, terrorist forces based in Mozambique under the new and guerilla-friendly Frelimo government would be flooding over the border to Rhodesia to conduct nightly raids, plant land mines, and, *they said*, chop off the ears and lips and eyelids of little white children.

*

'Do you think it hurts?'

'What?'

'To get your lips chopped off.'

'Why would you get your lips chopped off?'

I shrug.

'By whom? Who told you that?'

'Everyone knows terrs chop off your lips if they catch you.'

My sister and I both have big lips. Tackie lips, is what the other children call them. Africans have tackie lips, too. I try and remember to suck in my lips, especially for photographs in case anyone thinks I'm part *muntu*. I wouldn't mind getting my lips chopped off, or at least pared down a size or two, and then I wouldn't be teased by the other children.

'You've got tackie lips. Like a *muntu*.'

'I do not.' I suck them in.

'You're sucking in your lips.'

'Am not!'

Mum says, 'They're not tackie lips, they're full lips.' She says, 'Brigitte Bardot has full lips.'

'Is she a *muntu*?'

'No, she most certainly is not. She's very glamorous. She's French.'

But I don't care how French or glamorous Brigitte Bardot is; she is not the one getting teased about my lips.

Vanessa says, 'Getting your lips chopped off would hurt like *sterik*. Of course it hurts, man.'

Of course. It hurts.

'I wouldn't cry.'

'Yes you would.'

'Would not.'

Vanessa takes my wrist in both her hands and gently twists

the skin in opposite directions, a Chinese bangle. I have long hairs on my arms, pulled back with smears of snot from where I've wiped my nose. The snot makes a green, long pattern through the blonde, sunburnt hair.

'Yurrah man!'

'Does that hurt?'

'*Ja, ja*! Oh it hurts!' I start to cry.

'See?'

'*Ja*.'

'Now don't cry.'

'Okay.' I wipe my nose on my arm.

'Don't wipe your nose on your arm, man, yuck.'

I cry harder.

'It hurts worser than that to get your lips cut off.'

'Okay.'

'So would you cry?'

'*Ja, ja*. I'd cry, hey.'

*

Robandi, the farm, had been named by the original owner's two sons, Rob and Andy. Robandi. Almost an African word. Like the Lozi word *banani*: they have. Or the Tonga word *ndili*: I am. Or Nyanja *pitani*: to the . . .

We have moved, mother and father with two children, a couple of cats, three dogs and one horse, right into the middle, the very birth place and epicentre, of the civil war in Rhodesia and a freshly stoked civil war in Mozambique. There is no way out of the valley for us now. We have borrowed money to buy the farm. Money we might never be able to repay. And who is going to buy the farm off us now? Who is going to buy our farm and take our place in the middle of a civil war? We are stuck.

We erect a massive fence with slanting-backwards barbed wire at the top around the house. Mum plants Mauritius thorn around the inside of the fence for good measure; it bushes out with its forward-backward hooking thorns. We stop at the SPCA in Umtali and collect a host of huge dogs, and then we collect dogs abandoned by civil-war fleeing farmers. These dogs are found tied up to trees or staring hopefully down flat driveways, waiting for their nonreturning owners. Their owners have gone in the middle of the night to South Africa, Australia, Canada, England. We call it the chicken run. Or we say they gapped it. But they gapped it without their pets.

One day Dad says to Mum, 'Either I go, or some of these bloody dogs have to go.'

'But they don't have anywhere *to* go.'

Dad is in a rage. He aims a kick at a cluster of dogs, who cheerfully return his gesture with jump-up licking let's-playfulness.

Mum says, 'See? How sweet.'

'I mean it, Nicola.'

So the dogs stay with us until untimely death does them part.

The life expectancy of a dog on our farm is not great. The dogs are killed by baboons, wild pigs, snakes, wire snares and each other. A few eat the poison blocks left out in the barns for rats. Or they eat cow shit on which dip for killing ticks has splattered and they dissolve in frothy-mouthed fits. They get tick fever and their hearts fail from the heat. More dogs come to take the place of those whose graves are wept-upon humps in the field below the house.

We buy a 1967 mineproofed Land Rover, complete with siren, and call her Lucy. Lucy, for Luck.

'Why do we have the bee-ba?'

'To scare terrorists.'

But Mum and Dad don't use the siren except to announce their arrival at parties.

*

There are two roads out of the valley. We can drive up to the Vumba Highlands to the north or through Zamunya Tribal Trust Land to the east. Neither road is paved, and therefore both are easily planted with land mines. We are supposed to travel in convoy when we go to town.

A convoy is a Pookie, the mine-detecting vehicle that can drive over a matchbox without squishing it. There is something in the Pookie that beeps if it detects metal. And land mines are cased in metal. Then, two or three long crocodile-looking lorries, which are spiky with Rhodesian soldiers, their FN rifles poking out of the sides of the vehicle like so many bristles, ready to retaliate if we are ambushed. And finally, us. Farmers and their kids in ordinary vehicles, or mineproofed Land Rovers, our own guns poking from windows, on the way to town in our best clothes. If we are killed in an ambush or blown up on a mine, we will be wearing clean brookies, our best dresses, red and black necklaces made out of the very poisonous seeds from lucky-bean trees. We'll be presentable to go and sit on the left hand of *Godthefather*.

The third way out of the valley is too dangerous for casual travel now. It was possible, before the war, to climb up over the mountains, on footpaths unguarded by customs officials, to Mozambique. But these secret paths have been blocked by the mine field that has been laid along the border. Almost daily, and often at night, a mine erupts underneath the unsuspecting legs of a baboon, or a person – a fisherman coming back from the fish-rich dams in Mozambique, or a soldier in a troop of terrorists. We cheer when we hear the faint, stomach-echoing thump of a mine detonating. Either an African or a baboon has been wounded or killed.

*

'One hundred little baboons playing on the mine field. One hundred little baboons playing on the mine field. And if one little baboon

should accidentally explode, there'll be ninety-nine little baboons playing on the mine field.'

*

We had a policeman come to our school to talk to us about mines. Vanessa said he had come because I sucked my thumbs and the policeman was here to chop off my thumbs. I tucked my thumbs into my fists, but the policeman stood on the stage in the assembly hall and rocked back and forth in tight-squeaky shoes and stared over the top of our heads and didn't look towards my thumbs once.

'Mines are hidden in cake tins and biscuit tins.' He showed us. The tins were bright and promising, with pictures of roses painted on their sides, or small children with rosy cheeks in old-fashioned winter clothes running behind snow-covered trees, or butter-soft shortbread with cherry-heart centres. 'Would any of you open this tin?'

A few of us raised our hands eagerly.

'Children like you open the tins and get blown to pieces.'

We greedy, stupid few quickly sat on our hands again.

The policeman showed us pictures of holes in the ground where a mine had been.

A kid asked, pointing to the picture, 'Was a kid blown up by that mine?'

The policeman hesitated, caught between wanting to scare the hell out of us, and wanting to preserve our childish innocence. He said, 'Not this particular mine. But you can never be too careful, hey?'

We shook our heads solemnly.

'Mines can also be buried, and you will never know where they are.'

A little voice from the assembly hall asked, 'In your driveway even?'

'Oh, *ja*. Oh, *ja*.'

There was a rustle of titillated fear among the audience. The teachers look bored, cross-armed, cross-legged, watchful. Waiting for one of us to misbehave so that they could send us to detention.

I only know a few people who have gone over mines.

A girl who attended the high school in Umtali went over a mine and had her legs blown off but she lived. She was brave and beautiful and when she got married in South Africa a few years after the accident, *Fair Lady* magazine wrote a big article about her and showed photographs of her walking down the aisle of a church all frothy in a white dress and a long white veil and with the help of bridesmaids and crutches.

Fanie Vorster, who is a farmer in the Burma Valley, went over a mine, too, but he did not get his legs blown off. If he had, it might have given children a chance to run away from him when he tried to trap them in his spare bedroom and pin them to the single bed with his fat grey-hair-sprouting belly while mums and dads drank coffee in the kitchen with his stick-insect purple-mottled-bruised-and-battered wife. Fanie Vorster didn't even get a headache when he went over the mine because he was in a mineproofed Land Rover, so the back end of it blew off and left the cab intact with Fanje inside, not at all hurt. He sat on the side of the road and smoked a cigarette until help came along.

Which just goes to show, all prayers aren't answered.

*

Once Vanessa and I were driving back from a Christmas party with Mum and we were behind an African bus that had gone over a mine. It left a hole the size of the bus in the middle of the road and the bus lay blindly on its side like an eyeless, legs-in-the-air dead insect. Mum said, 'Put your heads down!' Mum said, 'Don't look.' So I put my head down and squeezed my eyes shut and Vanessa looked out the window as we drove past the bus. She said bits and pieces of Africans were hanging from the trees and bushes like black and red Christmas decorations. Some of the passengers weren't dead, Vanessa told me, but sitting on the side of the road with blood on them and their legs straight out in front of them, like people who have just had a big surprise.

She said, 'Did you look?'

I said, 'No ways, hey.'

Once at the police station I saw the army guys unload bodies in black plastic body bags from the back of a pickup and I heard the damp-dead sound of the heavy flesh hitting the ground.

I told Mum I had seen dead terrorists.

She said, 'Don't exaggerate.'

'I did. They were in bags.'

'Then you saw *body bags*,' she told me, 'not bodies.'

That's how I think of dead bodies, as things in long black bags, the ends neatly tied off. And I think of dead bodies as strips of meat hanging land-mine-blown from trees like strips of drying, salted biltong, even though I have only Vanessa's word for it.

*

We drive through the Tribal Trust Lands to get to town, past Africans whose hatred reflects like sun in a mirror into our faces, impossible to ignore. Young African men slouch aggressively against the walls of the taverns. Their eyes follow us as we hurry past, and we stare at them until they are swallowed in the cloud of dust kicked up behind the armed convoy and the mine-detecting Pookie and the snake of farmers coming into town to sell green peppers and mealies, tobacco and milk. Outside one of the African stores (which advertise Cafenol for headaches and Enos Liver Salts for indigestion and Coke for added life on bullet-pocked billboards) there is a gong hanging from a tree. When our convoy thunders through, an old woman squatting under the shade of the tree gets painfully to her feet and beats the gong with surprising vigour.

The sound of that gong echoes through the flat, dry TTL

and bounces against the hills that border them. Anyone camped in those hiding, thick hills or crouched behind boulders by the side of the road can hear the warning. We know now that we are being watched. A blink of binocular glass against the rocks up in the hills. An unnatural sway of thigh-deep grass on a still day. The shaking foliage of a tree as branches are parted, then allowed to spring back. Mum sits back in her seat and slides the Uzi forward out the window.

She says, 'Be ready to put your heads down, girls.'

War: 1976

Dad on call-up

Mum and Dad both join the police reservists, which means Dad
has to go out into the bush on patrol for ten days at a time and
find terrorists and fight them.

I watch him strip his gun and clean it; it lies on the sitting-
room floor in pieces and the house and our clothes and the dogs
reek of gun oil afterward. Dad lets me press the magazine full
of bullets.

'Faster than that. You'd have to do it a lot faster than that.'

In the back of my cupboard, stacked under my one hanging
dress (which is too hot to wear and was sent to me from England
by Granny and which smells of mothballs) are the rat packs.
Small government-issue cardboard boxes in which there are pink,

sugar-covered peanuts, small gooey packets of coffee which leak on everything else, two squares of Cowboy chewing gum, a box of matches, teabags, a tin of bully beef, a packet of powdered milk, sugar, Pronutro. Dad packs five rat packs and a flask of contraband brandy into his camouflage rucksack along with ten boxes of cigarettes.

He puts on his camouflage uniform and he has a camouflage band that Mum made to put over his watch so that it doesn't blink in the sunlight and alert the terrorists. He paints black, thick paint on his face and arms and when I ask, 'Why?' he says, 'So the terrs won't see me.' But he doesn't blend in. He stands out. He is a white human figure, hunched with the weight of a pack and his gun. He walks with his head down and his legs striding and bandy like a cowboy, without his horse, in a movie. I can see him all the way to the bottom of the driveway when he climbs into the Land Rover that has come to take him away and he doesn't turn around and wave although I am waving both arms in the air and shouting, ''Bye Dad! 'Bye Dad!'

I want to warn him that I can see him the whole way down the driveway, that he doesn't blend in at all. The terrs will easily see him and shoot him. He shouldn't walk down driveways. I shout, one last thin hysterical message into the hot air, 'Don't let the bugs bite, Dad!'

Mum says, 'Shh now. That's enough.' Dad has heaved his rucksack onto his lap and turned to take a light from a friend for his cigarette. The Land Rover pulls away. As Dad disappears from sight, as the Land Rover jolts over the bump where the snake lives in the culvert at the bottom of the driveway, he raises his hand and I think he's waving. But he's just taking a pull off his cigarette.

There's a lump in my throat that hurts when I swallow and I can't talk or I'll start to cry. Mum puts down her hand. She hardly ever lets me hold her hand. I slip my hand into hers and we begin to walk back to the house. It quickly feels strange to hold Mum's hand and too quickly there is an uncomfortable film of sweat between us. I slip out of Mum's grip, wipe my hand on my trousers, and run ahead to the house, banging into the warm, meat-smelling, fat-greasy-walled kitchen where July is making bread and the kitchen is becoming rich with the smell of bubbling yeast (which is like the smell of puppy pee).

*

Mum wears a neat grey uniform – a dress with silver buttons and epaulets and the letters 'BSAP' on the sleeve.

'What's that for?' I finger the letters.

'British South African Police.'

'But we're Rhodesian.'

'Mmm.' She tucks her hair under a peaked hat and looks in the mirror, lips crooked the way people look when they are pleased with themselves. 'How do I look?'

'Pretty.'

She flashes me a rewarding smile. I am kicking-legs bored on her bed.

Mum tugs a pair of nylon tights onto humid-hot legs and slips into a pair of black lace-up shoes, which look like school shoes.

'Are you a policeman?'

'A police reservist.'

'Oh.'

We drive into Umtali. Mum stops to buy lunch. A sausage roll and a chocolate-covered sponge-cake mouse each from Mitchells the Bakery on Main Street, with a Coke for me.

The police station is out towards the African part of town, in the Third Class district which is less than the Second Class district (with the Indian shops and mosques) and less again, by far, than the distant First Class district where the Europeans shop and live.

There is a small grey duty room for the police reservists, with a wooden desk under a window at which Mum sits. She has brought a book. She sighs, slips off her shoes, and rubs her nylon-covered feet together while she reads. Against the other wall is a thin, narrow bed for the person who will be on duty all night. I sit on the floor nibbling the delicious, flaky, greasy luxury of my sausage roll, working my way through the pastry to the salty meat in the middle. I am in an agony of knowing that the sausage roll will come to an end. But I am also fat with the knowledge that I will have the chocolate mouse next and then my Coke. I make my lunch last, lick by lick, sip by sip, as long as I can. On the wall above the bed there is a chart with the army alphabet on it. After I have finished my lunch I press my back against the cool metal frame of the bed (my belly swollen) and stare at the wall quietly for a long time until the words are completely in my head: 'Alpha, Bravo, Charlie, Delta, Echo, Foxtrot . . .' all the way to 'Zulu'. I pretend that I have twenty-six horses named after the army alphabet and gallop them around on the bed, my fingers jumping wrinkles and dodging water hazards. Under my breath, 'Come on, India. Chtch, chtch. Up we go, boy.'

Next to the bed there is a map of Manicaland with lots of tiny lights dotted here and there.

'What are the lights for?'

'That shows where people live.' She points to where we live; our dot almost spills into Mozambique.

'Why lights, though?'

'If someone gets attacked then they press the alarm on their Agricalert and the light will go off here and I can tell who is getting attacked.'

'What then?'

'I call up the army guys and they go and rescue whoever it is.'

'What if they're all dead by the time the army guys get there?'

'Don't ask silly questions.' She goes back to her book.

So I go outside and stare at the jail, which is behind the police station. It is a small grey two-celled building. The cells don't have windows but there are little slots on the door and in front of the door there are two fenced off yards, like the yards at the SPCA where we sometimes go to rescue dogs to add to the pack. I squint against the sun long enough and peer deeply enough into the doors, and I am rewarded by the startled eyes – very white and staring from the depths of the jail – of an actual prisoner. I smile and wave, the way some people try and get a reaction from a bored animal at a zoo, to see if anything will happen. The eyes blink shut. The face disappears.

I sit under the frangipani tree on the spiky, drying police station lawn with its ring of whitewashed stones and aloe vera flower beds, and I poke pieces of grass into ant lion traps to see the little ant lions leap up with sharp claws in anticipation of an ant meal which I, and my little piece of grass, are not. Then one of the African sergeants comes out of the police station with trays of food for the prisoners. I lower myself onto my belly, flat against the speckled shadows of the frangipani tree. I don't want to be told to 'go inside now'. The sergeant opens the dog-run gate and bangs on the grey cell doors. The hatches open. The sergeant slides the trays halfway into the mouths of the slots, and they are swallowed into the police cells.

And then Mum comes out and says, 'Bobo!' And then, 'There you are. Look, you're all dusty.' She glances towards the prison cells. 'Come inside now. It's time to rest.'

I have to lie down on the prickly grey army-issue blanket for rest time. Mum puts her feet up on the edge of the bed and reads her book. The sound of her breathing, her nylon-covered-foot-rubbing-foot, her gently shuffling pages, and the gathering force of hot-yellow sun are stupefying. And then I am asleep.

In the late afternoon, Mum has finished her book and still no one has been attacked, although I have woken up from my afternoon sleep (dry-mouthed and eyes stinging) and lain on my side for ages staring at the little lights on the map, hoping.

The flies are buzzing hotly against the windows and the sun has sunk below the level of the corrugated-tin roof and is sliding breathlessly against the wall with the army alphabet on it (fading Alpha through Golf and Hotel). There is a knock on the door and the police station's maid comes in with the tea tray (a plate of Marie biscuits, two chipped mugs, sweet powdered milk reconstituted in a plastic jug, a tub of white sugar, and a small government-issue metal pot for the tea so that Mum immediately asks for more, in anticipation of her second cup).

Mum pours out the tea into the two chipped mugs. Their handles are greasy.

'I hope the prisoners haven't drunk out of these cups.'

'I'm sure they have their own plastic mugs.'

'What about the other Affies?' I mean the black policemen, the police station's maid.

'I'm sure they are not allowed to drink out of the same mugs as us.'

'Good.' I dip my Marie biscuit into my tea and watch crumbs float on the hot, greasy surface.

When we have drunk our tea, Mum reads to me. I lie on the cot under the army alphabet chart. She reads C. S. Lewis's *The Lion, the Witch and the Wardrobe*. Lucy is in the land where it will never be summer, snow crunches underfoot. The sultry afternoon, pale with light-washing sun and the faint hum of traffic from the road that passes the police station all wash into the background. I am transported to a cool snowy world with fawns and witches and Peter and Susan and Edmund and Aslan. I shut my eyes and spread myself out so that my sweating skin can cool; the world of Narnia is more real and wonderful than the world I am alive in.

*

'Olé!' Mum sings at the club on Saturday night. 'I'm a bandit. I'm a bandit from Brazil. I'm the quickest on the trigger. When I shoot I shoot to kill . . .' She cocks her hip when she sings and sometimes she climbs up onto the bar and dances and shrugs her shoulders, slow-sexy, eyes half-mast, and sometimes she falls off the bar again. But she can't shoot straight. At target practice she shuts her eyes and her mouth goes worm-bottom tight and she once put a round in the swimming pool wall and another time she shot a pattern, like beads on a string, across the bark of the flamboyant tree at the bottom of the garden. But she has never shot the target in the head or the heart where you are supposed to shoot it.

She taught the horses not to be scared of guns. She burst paper bags at their feet for a whole morning. She popped balloons all afternoon. And the next day she shot guns right by their heads until they only swished their tails and jerked their heads at the sound, as if trying to get rid of a biting fly. So the horses lazily ignore gunshot when we're out riding, but they still bolt if there's a rustle in the bushes, or if a cow surprises them, or if they see a monkey or a snake, or if a troop of baboons startles out of the bush with their warning cry, 'Wa-hu!'

Dog Rescue

Dad and Pippin

Although Mum actually shot an Egyptian spitting cobra once, and killed it. But that was for real, when her dogs were threatened, which is more serious than target practice.

We are sitting at the breakfast table eating oat porridge. Mum is ignoring my string of questions. She is reading a book and the radio is on. Sally Donaldson hosts *Forces Requests* and plays songs sent in by loved ones for the boys in the bush.

'Yesterday, all my troubles seemed so far away,' I sing along.

Mum says, irritably, 'Shhh,' and turns the radio down.

If I peer around the huge stone-wall flower bed Mum has erected to stop bombs and bullets from coming in the dining-room window, I can see that Flywell has brought the horses up for our morning ride. I look at Mum. She is absorbed in her book. We won't get out for a ride until it's too hot and then we'll ride until the afternoon, riding through lunch, past the time when my stomach turns and knots with hunger and my throat is burning with thirst and the sun will burn the back of our necks. I will complain of thirst and Mum will say, 'You should have had more tea at breakfast.'

I kick the legs of my chair. Mum says, without looking up, 'Don't.' And then, 'Eat up.'

But I've already eaten up. 'Can I have some more?'

'Ask July.'

But before I can get to the kitchen to ask July if there's more porridge, there is a scramble of dogs from under the dining-room table, claws scrabbling on the cement floor before they find purchase and race yapping into the pantry, which is between the kitchen and dining room. Mum looks up from her book. 'What have you got?' she asks the dogs.

Three of the dogs retreat sheepishly from the pantry and suddenly Mum says, 'Oh hell,' because she can see from their faces and from the sound of their voices that they're barking at a snake. And then the maid starts to shout, 'Madam! Madam!' from the kitchen door and pointing. She has her hand over her mouth. 'Madam! *Nyuka!*'

Mum and I stand at the entrance to the pantry and stare in at the snake. Its neck is caped, as wide as a fan, and it's swaying and tall.

Mum shouts, 'Stand behind the table.' She calls the dogs. Shea and Jacko, Best Beloved Among Dogs, are still barking at the snake. 'Come!' shouts Mum. She's loading the magazine. I hear the bullets go in, *clicka-click.* 'Come here!' Suddenly the snake rears back and snaps forward and sets out into the air a thin mist of poisonous spray and the dogs come reeling back out of the pantry, yelping and blind, staggering from the pain. Mum lifts the gun to her shoulder. She squeezes her eyes shut and eases back on the trigger. There's an explosion of glasses and bottles and tins and a wild chattering of bullets. Mum has the Uzi on automatic. She empties an entire magazine towards the snake and then there is dust, the splintering of still-falling glass, the whimpering dogs. Violet, July, and I cautiously creep up behind Mum. The snake is splattered in a red mosaic on the back wall of the pantry along with sprayed beer, and the lumpy contents of tinned beef, tomato sauce, peas. Flour has exploded and has settled peacefully onto the chaos in a fine lacy shroud.

'Madam,' says July admiringly, 'but you got him one time!'

By now Shea and Jacko's eyes have swollen up like tennis balls. Mum screams for milk and July brings the jug from the paraffin fridge in the kitchen. She pours the milk into the dogs' eyes and they yelp in pain. Mum says, 'We have to take them in to Uncle Bill.'

We are not supposed to leave the valley without an armed escort because there are land mines in the road on the way to Umtali and terrorist ambushes and Dad is on patrol, so we are women-without-men which is supposed to be a weakened state of affairs. But this is an emergency. We put the dogs in the car and drive as fast as we can out of the valley, up the escarpment to the dusty wasteland of the Tribal Trust Land and round the snake-body road which clings to the mountain and spits us out at the paper factory (which smells pungent and rotten and warm) so that when we drive past it as a family Vanessa holds her nose and sings, 'Bobo farted.'

'Did not.'

'Bo-bo fart-ed.'

Until I am in tears and then Mum says, 'Shuddup both of you or you'll both get a hiding.'

And now we race past the petrol station that marks the entrance into town and we tear past the gaudy string of Indian stores in the Second Class district where we don't shop. We bump through the tunnel under the railway line which advertises cigarettes, 'People say Players, Please,' and hurry through the centre of town, the First Class district, where we *do* shop. Uncle

Bill's veterinary practice is on the other side of town, past the high school. The dogs are crying softly to themselves. Shea is on Mum's lap and Jacko is on the passenger seat with me.

Uncle Bill says, 'You drove in alone?' He sounds angry.

'What else could I do?'

He glances at me, presses his lips shut, and says, 'All right. Let me have a look.'

Aunty Sheila says, 'Bobo, would you like to come with me?'

I wouldn't like to go with Aunty Sheila. She has rock-hard bosoms encased in twin-set sweaters. She has hair like a grey paper wasps' nest.

Mum says, 'What do you say, Bobo,' in a warning voice.

So I say, 'Yes please Aunty Sheila,' and she takes me into her perfect sitting room, which leads off the waiting room of the surgery. She tells me to sit-there-and-wait-and-don't-touch-anything and she goes into the kitchen and comes back with a tray of tea and a plate of food, for which I am grateful, having missed lunch. I am not allowed to eat on the chairs, which are carefully kept clean, with crocheted doilies on their arms. I must sit on the polished floor with the china plate on my lap. Aunty Sheila says, 'I don't have children, I have dogs.'

She has a rash of small spoiled dogs, who are allowed on her beautiful armchairs (unlike me), and some larger dogs who live outside.

I finish my tea and the plate of biscuits and stare at my empty plate meaningfully until Aunty Sheila says, 'Would you like another . . .'

And I say yes, quickly, before she can change her mind.

'You're a hungry little girl,' she says, hardly able to disguise her distaste.

'It's because I have worms in my bum,' I say, helping myself to a pink vanilla wafer.

We can't take the dogs home that night. They have to stay with Uncle Bill. When we fetch them a few days later (coming into town in a proper convoy this time), only Jacko is still a little bit blind in one eye.

When Dad comes back from patrol, Mum shows him the pantry and tells him about the snake.

Dad frowns at the shot-up chaos of the pantry, and he says to me, 'My God, your mother's a lousy shot.'

But he wasn't there to see how wide the snake's neck was, how it swayed and wove and how its head snapped forward towards the dogs. 'I think she's a jolly good shot,' I say loyally.

Vanessa

Van

Anyway, Vanessa will save us if we ever get attacked. She is the conversation-stopping beauty in our family. Some old men try and kiss her and ask about her boobs and one of them did to her what Fanie Vorster did to me, only it was worse. But Vanessa can take care of herself. The man was called Roly Swift and he lived with his wife in Umtali. Mum and Dad left us with Roly Swift one morning while they had work to do. Roly's wife was with Mum and Dad who said, 'Be good for Mr Swift while we're gone.'

Roly was drunk before lunch, and he started to follow Vanessa and me around the house and he kissed me and tried to squash me up against the passage wall. Vanessa said, 'Leave my sister alone.' Roly laughed at Vanessa and then he tried to kiss her and put his hands under her skirt and Vanessa pushed him away but Roly only tried to hold her tighter. He was laughing although the look on his face was not happy and he was doing something under Vanessa's skirt which made her face go red.

She said, 'Leave me alone!' There were tears in her voice.

Roly pulled Vanessa into a bedroom from which I heard the sounds of scuffle, and then Vanessa emerged, her hair untidy and her clothes in disarray. She grabbed me by the hand. 'Quickly, let's run.'

We ran outside.

Vanessa said, 'Come.'

'But what about Mr Swift?'

'What about Mr Swift? Nothing about Mr Swift.'

She marched me across the road and knocked on the door of a little white neighbouring house.

'We need to stay here,' she told the astonished lady who opened the door.

The astonished lady let us into her house reluctantly. I was holding Vanessa's hand.

Vanessa cleared her throat and said in a big, brave voice, 'We haven't had lunch yet.'

We were fed lunch and allowed to stay in the white neighbouring house until Mum and Dad came back and then we crept over to their car, which was parked in the Swifts' driveway, keeping our heads down – as if we were under attack – so that Roly wouldn't see us. Mum and Dad were talking to Roly in brightly natural voices as if Everything Was Normal even though Roly had to say that we had run next door and Everything Wasn't Normal. But he didn't say why we had run away.

'Ah,' said Dad, when he saw us suddenly appear in the car, 'there you are.'

There we were. There was a bad taste in my mouth and a sick feeling in my stomach. We climbed into the car, we sullied goods, and Mum and Dad drove stiffly away, grinning at Roly like skeletons. Vanessa tried to tell Mum and Dad what had happened and they said, 'Don't exaggerate.' Vanessa has a way of looking far away when Mum and Dad won't listen. She looks far away now, as if she doesn't care about anything.

She has inherited our paternal grandmother's enormous eyes; a pale, almost glassy blue and she can hood her eyes like a cat and go very still and deep and distant. She has very long, blonde thick hair, which she wears in a wrist-thick braid down her back. She has full lips and a very proud, very African carriage (shoulders held back, languid steps, bordering on lazy) and she has stopped listening. Like an African.

Mum says, 'Why don't you bloody people listen?' to the cook and the maid and the groom and the gardener and they are silent and you can tell they are not listening even now.

Vanessa and I, like all the kids over the age of five in our valley, have to learn how to load an FN rifle magazine, strip and clean all the guns in the house, and, ultimately, shoot-to-kill. If we are attacked and Mum and Dad are injured or killed, Vanessa and I will have to know how to defend ourselves. Mum and Dad and all our friends say, 'Vanessa's a Dozy Arab.' But I know that they are wrong. Mum and Dad say that Vanessa won't be able to shoot a gun. They says that she's too placid. They don't know Vanessa. She's not a Dozy Arab. She's a Quiet-Waiting-Alert Arab. She's an Angry Arab.

I want to be like an army guy, so I clean and load my dad's FN and my mum's Uzi with enthusiasm, but the guns are too heavy for me to be anything but a stick insect dangling from the end of a chattering barrel. I have to prop the gun up against a wall to shoot it, or its kick will knock me over. I am allowed to shoot my mum's pistol, but even that cracks my wrist, and my whole arm jolts with the shock of its report.

Vanessa has to be forced to strip and clean the gun. She is slow and unwilling even when Dad loses his temper and shouts at her and says, '*Fergodsake* don't just stand there, do something! Bunch-of-bloody-women-in-the-house.'

Van: Zomba Plateau

Vanessa gets her cat-hooded, African deadpan, not-listening eyes.

'You have to learn how this thing is made,' says Dad. 'Come on, take the bloody thing apart.'

Vanessa moves slowly, reluctance personified.

'Now you must put it back together,' says Dad, looking at the gun.

Vanessa blinks at Dad. She says, 'Bobo can do it.'

'No. You must learn.'

'I'll do it. I'll do it,' I say. I want to do it to show my dad that I'm as good as a boy. I don't want to be a bunch-of-bloody-women-in-the-house.

'Vanessa must learn.'

But Vanessa resolutely refuses to put the thing back together again. She has it in pieces on a sheet in the sitting room and she won't make it right again. Dad gives up.

I say, 'I'll do it. I'll do it.' Dad is as impatient with my overeagerness as he is with Vanessa's undereagerness. We can't win.

Dad says, 'Go on, then.'

I am tongue-sticking-out and trying-to-do-it-right. I put the gun back together.

Set up at the end of the garden, on the other side of our scorpion-infested pool, is an enormous cardboard cutout of a crouched, running terrorist, kitted out in Russian-issue uniform and brandishing an AK-47; around his heart is a series of rings, like a diagram in a biology book. The baboons that steal the corn and run from the gong in the watchman's hut look like this terrorist, with a long dog's nose and a short, square forehead.

Dad shows Vanessa what to do. He crouches down to her height. 'Lift the barrel of the gun onto the wall like this. Steady yourself, legs apart. Hold your chin away from the butt, squeeze the trigger – count one-Zambezi, two-Zambezi – release.' I hold my hands over my ears and shut my eyes. The sound of the gun cracks the air and hits me above the belly. That's where gun sounds go, thumping the air out of you with their shout.

Dad hands Vanessa the gun 'The kick will knock your teeth out if you're not careful,' he says. 'Use the wall to hold the gun. All right? Don't worry about hitting the target, just try not to put a hole in the swimming-pool wall.' We laugh.

I said, 'Ja, Van, don't shoot a scorp hey. Ha, ha. Or a frog.'

Dad says, 'That's right. Let's just see if you can fire off a round without falling backwards.'

Vanessa takes the gun and her eyes go surface-cold, like water on the dam in the winter.

'No, not like that,' says Dad, 'here, use the wall.' He moves behind her to adjust her arms. He wants to get the gun onto the top of the wall, but before he can touch her Vanessa squeezes the trigger. Dad steps back, startled. The gun kicks up. Mum says, 'The child will break her jaw.' Vanessa is not listening to us.

She shoots at the target again. She has shot the running

baboon-terrorist once clean through the nose and once clean through the heart. She hands the gun back to Dad.

'Good shot, Van!' we are all shouting at the same time.

'Where did you learn to do that?' says Dad.

I am hopping up and down and pointing at the target. 'You killed him! Look, you killed him!'

Vanessa's expression stays flat and blank, but she looks at the target for a long time. And then she turns away from us with a slight frown and I want to hang on her hand but she shrugs me off, impatient.

I say, '*Jeez* man, Van. You donnered him. You killed him one time!'

Mum says, 'Don't say that, Bobo.'

'What?'

'Don't say "*donnered*". It isn't proper English. It's slang.'

'Okay.' And then, '*Jeez* man, Van!'

Vanessa looks resigned and not at all triumphant. I wish she would smile and be pleased about shooting the terrorist.

I say, 'Let me have a go, hey. Can I have a go? Look, Van, watch me.'

But she has turned away and is going inside. A couple of the dogs follow her.

Missionaries: 1975

Mum, Dad and Bobo

My second sister – my mother's fourth child – was born on 28 August 1976.

*

Early in October 1975, when the first rains had already come but were still deciding what sort of season to create (over-full, with floods and swollen, dead cows in our river, or a sparse and teasing drought), a small plague of two missionaries descended upon us.

They had driven from Salisbury, through Umtali, and down to the valley, to the farthest house they could find with people in it in the whole of Rhodesia, which was Mum and me lying on her bed at two o'clock in the afternoon listening to Sally Donaldson on the radio. Dad is away in the bush, fighting gooks. Vanessa is at boarding school. Mum and I are waiting for *Women's Hour* to come on.

It's eye-ball-burning hot. I lie on my belly and let my legs wag lazily back and forth, my head in the crook of my arms where my forehead is pressing a sweaty band into the skin there. Mum is reading to herself. It is so hot that the flamboyant tree outside cracks to itself, as if already anticipating how it will feel to be on fire. The dogs are splayed out on the floor, wherever they can find bare cement, panting and creating wet pools with their dripping tongues. Our throats are papered with the heat; we sip at cups of cold, milky tea just enough to make spit in our mouths. The sky and air are so thick with wildfire smoke that we can't see the hills, they are distant, gauzy shapes, the same colour as the haze, only denser. The colour is hot, yellow-grey, breathless, breath-sucking colour. Swollen clouds scrape purple, fat bellies on the tops of the surrounding hills.

Suddenly, there is the claw-scrabbling alarm of dogs, raised from sodden, deep, two-o'clock-in-the-afternoon heat into full alarm. They rush outside, into the yard, kicking up a cloud of terracotta behind them, barking with their thirsty, hoarse summer voices.

'What now?' says Mum. She slings her Uzi over her shoulder, checks that the safety catch is on (although she keeps her finger against the catch, prepared to change that setting at a moment's notice) and scuffles her feet into the thick, black sandals, made from strips of used tractor tyres, which we both wear. We call them *manutellas*. They are good farm shoes. There is not a thorn in Africa that can get through their soles, and they are cool in the heat and it doesn't matter if they get wet, muddy, or covered in oil. Their only fault, as farm shoes, is that they leave our ankles and the tops of our feet exposed to the place where a snake is most likely to bite.

'Right before *Women's Hour*, too,' says Mum.

The dogs are still barking. Especially Bubbles, who is an unfortunate mix, half Labrador and half Rhodesian ridgeback. He's the colour of a lion, with lion-yellow eyes and a mean, snaky way of walking, like a lion. Bubbles can kill baboons. He's the only dog I know that can kill a baboon. Baboons are huge, as big as a small man when they stand on their back legs. And they have long, pointy teeth and they work in troops. They flip their prey onto its back and tear its stomach out. Bubbles runs away from us sometimes for a day or two and comes back leg-hanging exhausted and with scratches on his belly, but otherwise very pleased with himself. There are dead baboons in his wake.

The fox terrier, the dachshund, the German shepherd, the two black Labradors, and the springer spaniels come back into the house to see what is taking us so long. Bubbles alone keeps up a fierce rally of deep-throated barks outside.

Mum calls, 'I'm coming, I'm coming. Who is it?'

I follow her outside. The dogs scramble for position behind me.

A vision: two men climbing out of a white station wagon. They are wearing button-down white shirts tucked neatly into pulled-up-high creased shorts, plus pulled-up socks and proper lace-up shoes. They have dark glasses but they are not wearing hats. I don't know many men who wear dark glasses. The men I know squint into the sun. If they have sunglasses, they use them to chew on while they stare into the distance, into the hope-of-rain, or the threat-of-terrorists, or the possibility-of-a-kudu.

Mum shades her eyes from the sun and walks slowly, suspiciously, toward the car. I stay behind her. Mum's finger plays lightly over the top of the safety catch on her gun. 'Yes? Can I help you?' We can't trust anyone anymore. Not even white men.

It is only then we see that both men are armed with thick shiny black Bibles.

Mum shuffles her gun behind her back. 'Oh shit, Jesus creepers,' she mutters, and then, more loudly, 'Hello.'

The men approach. Our pack of dogs growl, hackles raised, around their ankles, swarming. One of the men, blond and overweight (overweight for the heat, overweight for a war, over-weight for a poor farm this far from the city) comes forward, his Bible outstretched, hand extended. He introduces himself and his partner: 'And we're here to tell you about the Lord.' He's American. I start to giggle.

Mum sighs. 'Well, come in for a cup of tea, anyway,' she says.

The other man is fat, too. As he turns to follow Mum into the house I see that his shorts have gathered into the crack of his bum; his legs extend baggy and grey and hairy like elephant's legs from the too-pulled-up shorts. His shirt is stuck to his back with sweat, two wet rings extend from under his armpits. I giggle some more.

Mum says, 'Bobo, go and ask July to make us a tray of tea, please.'

I find July asleep on the cool, damp patch of cement behind the laundry.

'There are some bosses from God,' I tell him, poking his rib with the toe of my *manutella*, 'come all the way from town for tea.'

'Eh?' July jumps to his feet.

'*Faga moto*,' I tell July. Which means, literally, 'Put fire,' but figuratively, 'Get moving.'

July glares at me. 'You are too cheeky,' he tells me.

'Hurry! Hey! Hurry. They are waiting.' I am anxious to make the most of our afternoon's surprise. We don't have fresh visitors very often. Especially not since the land mines and ambushes got worse.

'Tea's coming,' I say, and sit on the floor with my back to the dead-ash-smelling fireplace where I can observe everyone well. The sitting room is stifling: the sofa and chairs breathe out heat; humid, heat-saturated air billows in the windows. The dogs start to pace restlessly in front of the missionaries, who are sitting in the dogs' chairs. The fox terrier glares; the Labrador-ridgeback is growling softly, looking baboon-murderer indignant. The springer spaniels make repeated attempts to fling themselves up on the visitors' laps, and the missionaries fight them off, in an offhand, I'm-not-really-pushing-your-dog-off-my-lap-I-love-dogs-really way.

The blond American says, 'We've come to share the teachings of Christ with you.'

'How kind.' Mum pauses. 'We're Anglican.'

Which makes the missionaries glance at each other.

July brings the tea. He smells strongly of green laundry soap and of freshly smoked *gwayi* – raw, coarsely chopped native tobacco. The cups are greasy and unmatched, and all but one are chipped. Mum hands out the chipped mugs to the guests and to me; she keeps the best mug for herself. On a plate are slabs of homemade bread with slices of curling butter and cucumbers balanced on them. The cucumbers have been liberally sprinkled with salt and they are beading water.

Mum asks me, 'Will you hand out the sugar?'

The missionaries sit with their cups of tea balanced in mismatched saucers on their laps, where there is a precariously good chance a zealous spaniel might, at any moment, send the cup flying. I offer them sugar and then a slice of salty cucumber and bread, which they are too polite to refuse and too polite to know how to eat. The bread is days old and crumbling; the dough for the bread was a mix of corn and wheat to make the flour last longer. The visitors are disarmed. They can't get to their Bibles now, what with the tea and the dogs and the toppling bread.

The tea makes us sweat. Mum says that's why tea is good for you. If you drink a cup of tea and eat something salty in the middle of the afternoon, you won't get heat exhaustion. The sweat will cool us down. The sweat runs down the back of my legs, tickling. The salt will replace the salt we lose in sweat. I munch my bread; the dogs become more frantic in their efforts to climb onto our laps. They lick crumbs from my hands. I pour a little tea out in a saucer for the dachshund.

'I've never seen a dog drink tea,' says Elephant Bottom.

Mum fixes the man with cold surprise, 'How extraordinary,' she says.

The missionaries wilt.

Mum finishes her tea. 'Anyone for a second cup?'

The missionaries smile, shake their heads. The blond one clears his throat. He is starting to squirm on the sofa, like a dog when they're rubbing worms out of their bum on a rug, or on the furniture, which we call sailing. 'Oh, look, Mum, Shea's sailing!' And Mum says, 'I'll have to worm the whole lot of them again.' Then Elephant Bottom starts to writhe, too. They put down their cups of tea, disburden themselves of their pecked-at salty-cucumber bread, and stand up, as if to leave. Already. I am disappointed. I was hoping for battle. I was hoping to see these two men *fight the good fight*.

'Well thank you . . .' says Elephant Bottom, and makes for the door, followed by his partner. Mum and I notice, at the same time, that both men have pink welting fleabites down the backs of their soft, white, fatty legs. I start giggling again.

Mum has tried and tried to kill the fleas, but fleas are as tough as dirt. Fleas cling to dog hair until the last moment and drown like flecks of pepper in the scum on top of the milky poisonous wash that Mum mixes up in a drum in the backyard once a month. A few brave, knowing fleas jump onto Mum's arms while she's washing the dogs (holding them by the scruffs of their necks with her lips pressed together so that she won't get any of the poison in her mouth when the dogs struggle and shake) but she crushes them between her nails and they pop and die, usually before they can bite her. I have fleabites up and down my arms and on my legs because of the dogs; they are small, familiar red bumps – almost friendly – and are less irritating than the swollen lumps from mosquitoes, or the burning place where a tick has bitten and which needs to be watched in case of infection. My fleabites are tiny, the kind of bites you get when you are used to fleas so they don't bother you so much anymore. The missionaries' bites – even new as they are – already look irritated and itchy and plaguing because these men are evidently not accustomed to fleas.

Mum says, 'So nice of you to drop by.' And regrets it instantly because the missionaries seize on this: 'Will you pray with us before we leave?'

So we gather in the red-dusty yard with the dogs, who are now restless for their afternoon walk, milling around at our feet. The missionaries hold out their hands. 'Let's hold hands,' says the blond one.

Mum looks icy, but she holds out her hands. She says, 'Hold their hands, Bobo.'

I slouch with embarrassment, but take the offered hands reluctantly. We hardly ever hold hands in our family and we never hold hands with strangers. *Sis*, man. Mum is glaring at me fiercely. From my vantage point, I can see July and Violet and the gardener gathered under the kitchen door and peering out at us with undisguised amusement. Violet is giggling behind her hand.

The men start to pray. They pray and pray for ages. Our hands swap sweat, start slipping, and are reclutched. I cannot concentrate on the words the men are saying because I am thinking how slithering our hands have become. Elephant Bottom says, 'Would you like to pray?' It is a few moments before I realize that he is talking to me.

'What?'

'You can ask God for anything you want.'

I speak quickly, before my chance to communicate directly with God is taken away. 'A baby brother or sister,' I say. 'I want a new baby in the family. Please.'

Everyone laughs uncomfortably except me.

At that moment Bubbles lifts his leg on the blond missionary's leg and lets forth a thick yellow stream of alpha-male-dog pee and our prayer session direct-line-to-God is abruptly terminated.

*

Ten months later, Olivia Jane Fuller is born in the hospital in Umtali. Which goes to show, some prayers are answered. Olivia is my fault. She is the direct result of my prayer. I am secretly, ecstatically proud.

In January 1977, when Olivia is five months old, I join Vanessa at boarding school.

Olivia: January 1978

Olivia

It's during the Christmas holidays when everything is green-growing with the rainy season. The roads are slick with rutted mud. Mum and Dad have taken Vanessa into Umtali to buy some new school shoes and catch up with farm shopping. They leave Olivia and me at Aunty Rena's.

Aunty Rena has a store on her farm. It is called the Pa Mazonwe store and it is sweet with treasures. There are bright nylon dresses hanging from the beams in the roof among the gleaming silver-black bicycle wheels. On the far right of the store, there are wads of thick grey and pink blankets which have a special itchy smell to them and the smell makes you think of the feeling of catching rough skin against polyester. And there are crates of Coca-Cola and bolts of cloth. Next are boxes of tea and coffee and Panadol and Enos Liver Salts and cigarettes, sold either by the box or by one stick, one stick.

And then comes the explosion of incandescent sweets: the butternut rocks wrapped in transparent paper with blue writing on it; bubble gum with gold foil inside a pink, bubbled wrapper; jars of yellow thumb-sized synthetic apricots and black, sweet gobstoppers which reveal layers of different colours when sucked. And next to the sweets, the bags of Willards chips and the rows of limp penny cools, which are cigar-shaped plastic packets of sugared water and which we drink by biting a corner of plastic off and squirting the warm nectar into the backs of our throats.

On the right, by the door which leads to Aunty Rena's clinic, are the stacks of Pronutro and baby food, powdered milk, sugar, salt, and hessian bags filled with dried kapenta – a tiny salted fish, complete with eyeballs and tail – which give the whole store its salty, sharp flavour. Under glass at the end of the counter are tinny gold earrings and spools of multicoloured thread and cards of bright, shiny buttons. On the veranda, an old tailor sits whirring swaths of fabric through his fingers, his pedalling eating up the shapeless cloth and turning it magically into puff-sleeved dresses and button-down shirts. His treadle-treadle is a rhythmic, constant background noise along with the store's small black radio, its back hanging open to reveal batteries and wires, which plays the hip-swaying African music which I am supposed to despise but which is impossible for me not to listen to with guilty pleasure.

'Keep an eye on your little sister,' says Mum.

'I will,' I say, swinging in the gap in the countertop through which only the privileged are allowed.

'Do you love your little sister?' asks Aunty Rena.

I love Olivia more than anything else I can think of but I say, 'Not really.'

The grown-ups laugh.

While I am being mesmerized by the glut of treasures in the store and by the customers who are coming up to the counter, cautiously, to carefully spend their monthly wages, Olivia must have tottered out of the store and wandered out the back where the ducks splash in a ankle-deep, duck-shit-green pond. Aunty Rena is in the small, thatched, white-washed hut out at the front of the store doling out rations to the Mazonwe labourers; some of their monthly wages came in the form of salt, mealie-meal, dried fish, tea, soap, sugar, and oil.

'Give these buggers money and they'll only spend most of it on Chibuku,' says Dad. Chibuku is the lumpy, sorghum-brewed beer on which the African men get drunk on payday.

Duncan, Rena's younger son, and I are in the store to watch the Africans buy what they have not received as part of their rations: thread, sweets, batteries, buttons. I am still swinging from the gap in the counter where the wood is worn soft-smooth and soft-greasy by so many hands.

The African women keep their money in a folded wad in their dresses, against their breasts, so that it is soft and creased and warm when they lay it out on the counter to count it. One bag of flour, one box of matches, and then, after a voluptuous hesitation, a single cigarette and one Coke. Their children clamour for boiled sweets.

It is almost lunch before anyone notices Olivia is missing.

She is floating face down in the pond. The ducks are used to her body by now, paddling and waddling around it, throwing back their heads and drinking the water that is full of her last breaths. She is wearing a purple and white vest that Mum had tie-dyed during one of her artistic inspirations to dress us differently from all the rest. When we turn her over, her lips are as violet as her eyes, her cheeks are grey-white. Aunty Rena puts her on the floor in the clinic and pumps duck shit out of her lungs. The green slop is pumped up onto the grey concrete and lies around her head, halolike. My whole happy world spins away from me then – I feel it leave, like something warm and

Mum, Olivia and Van

comfortable leaving in hot breath – and a chill settles onto the top of my stomach. Even my skin has gone cold with shock.

I will never know peace again, I know. I will never be comfortable or happy again in my life.

> *Oh my darling, oh my darling,*
> *Oh my darling Clementine,*
> *You are lost and gone forever.*
> *Oh my darling Clementine.*

After half an hour Aunty Rena sinks back on her heels. She has been pressing soft-dead, green water from Olivia's mouth and breathing air into her nose and mouth in slow, hopeless rhythm. Now she says, 'Olivia's dead.' And then she says, 'My God, it's the second one.'

I say, 'Please do something, Aunty Rena. Aunty Rena, please.'

She says to Duncan, 'Take Bobo to the house.'

'What will you do with Libby?' She can't be dead. This can't be the end of her life. Just like that. There hasn't been a bomb or a gun or a terrorist-under-the-bed. She was alive in the morning. She is still supposed to be alive.

'She's dead,' says Aunty Rena, and pulls a sheet up over Olivia's head.

I say, 'Let me feel.' I press my fingers against Olivia's wrist, as I have seen Aunty Rena do, and hold my breath. 'I think I feel something,' I say hopefully.

Aunty Rena looks away, 'Take Bobo to the house,' she says again.

Duncan takes me to his room and shows me his comic books. Desperate Dan, Minnie the Minx, Roger the Dodger. I say, 'I just want Olivia back.'

He says, 'She's dead.'

'I want her back,' I insist.

'She's well and truly dead.' He knows about death because of his kitten-killing experiments. He has drowned and burned and buried kittens before. That way, he says, he'll know what it's like when his turn comes to be drowned or burned. He says, 'Drowning is better than a cat in the fire.'

I say, 'Maybe she'll get better.'

'You don't get better from being dead.'

I cry violently into Duncan's pillow until he sighs and fetches me some loo paper. 'Here,' he says, handing me the paper, 'blow your nose.'

I wipe my nose on my arm. 'My brother also died,' I tell him, screwing the paper into a damp ball in my fist.

'You don't have a brother.'

'*Ja*, but he's dead. Before I was born, he died.'

'Then he wasn't really your brother.'

'Yes, he was.'

'Not if he's a dead brother. Dead before you were alive, I mean.'

'He was still in our family. Then he died. If he didn't die he would still be in our family.'

'How'd he die?' he asks, challenging me.

'Because Mum and Dad took Vanessa for lunch when he was in the hospital.'

'You don't die from that.'

'He did.' I start to cry again.

Duncan says, 'Stop crying.'

I cry harder.

He says, 'I'll read to you.'

I keep crying.

'I'll read to you only if you stop crying.' And then, his voice rising with impatience and edged with panic, 'Stop crying hey.' He puts his arms awkwardly around my skinny, worm-swollen frame. 'Please, Bobo. Please stop crying.'

'Okay.' I sniff and push Duncan away. I scrub my face vigorously with the back of my arm. 'There,' I say, 'I've stopped crying.'

I sit with Duncan for a long time. He reads his comic books to me, trying to do all the voices. I can't hear what he's saying but I can hear cars and grown-up voices outside and the Staffordshire terriers barking. I can hear the cook going on about his happy, normal day in the kitchen, counting eggs, making bread, cooking supper. Then Duncan's sisters come and they say to me, 'You have to be brave.'

I nod.

The sisters take me outside to a car and someone drives me to the Dickinsons' farm which is next door to our farm but no one tells me why we are going there. I say, 'Where are Mum and Dad?'

Someone says, 'They're coming.'

I shrink my head into my chin. 'They're going to kill me,' I say.

'What? They won't kill you.'

I nod and start crying again. 'I let Olivia drown.'

'It wasn't your fault.'

I look out of the window at the spiky-topped fields of pineapples that the Dickinsons grow. The pineapple fields have dissolved into orange and green blurs through my tears. It was my fault. It was definitely my fault. I kick the seat in front of me out of sheer, trapped misery. I wish it was me lying dead, instead. I am going to be in trouble for the rest of my life.

Olivia is lying on the spare bed at the Dickinsons' house. Someone has washed all the duck shit off her face and has combed her dark curls where the algae have been clinging. Her hair has never had comb marks in it, in life. In life her hair was a soft, brushable halo. Mum used to brush out the brown-shining curls with a light-bristled blue brush. I think, *Then she's really dead.*

There are some flowers from Cierina Dickinson's garden on the pillow by her head. I stare and stare at her face. I wanted her to be alive. I was the one who prayed her into life that day with the missionaries. Now it is my fault she is dead. I had looked the other way and Olivia's life flew out of her body because I wasn't taking care of it. Here she is, her skin a blue-grey pallor, lying on the Dickinson's spare bed with summer violets around her head and she is not breathing.

Then Rena's two daughters, Anne and Ronelle, appear. Ronelle takes me by the shoulders and says, 'That's enough,' and she and Anne take me for a walk.

Anne says, 'You won't see her again. She's gone to Jesus.'

Which is a lie. She has not gone to Jesus. Her body is still on that bed. Jesus has not *suffered her to come unto Him.* I press my lips together. My throat hurts because there will never be enough crying to get rid of the sorrow inside.

Mum and Dad come back from town and I run down the driveway where I have been walking with the Viljoen sisters to meet them. Dad catches me in his arms. He is crying silently, both his cheeks are wet, and his face is drawn and grey. He dries his tears on my neck and says, 'You're so brave, Chookies.'

But I feel as if he won't say that once he finds out that Olivia is dead because of me. She's dead because I haven't been paying attention. I think, *He'll probably hate me then.* But I don't tell him what has happened. The lump in my throat makes it hurt to swallow.

That night Vanessa and I sleep in Mum and Dad's room, except none of us sleep. It is the first time in my life that I have lain awake all night from beginning to end. I listen to Mum's soft, drugged sobs. Aunty Rena has given her some pills, 'You need to take these to help you sleep.' Dad is a hump in the dark, perched up against the wall. He smokes one cigarette after another, the red glows of their cherries travelling steadily to his lips. Vanessa is very quiet next to me on the floor, very still. I know she has gone deep and still and inside herself. I whisper her name into the acrid-smoke-smelling density of our collective grief, but she won't answer.

She knows, I think to myself. *She knows I killed Olivia and she hates me now.*

And she'll hate me for ever.

The next morning I go into Olivia's room and look in the cot. The bed is still rumpled from her body from the morning before. Her toys are spread about on top of her sheets. Her pyjamas are folded up on her pillow. Mum has buried her face in Olivia's bedclothes and when I come in, she looks up at me. She says, in a smothered voice, 'It still smells of baby.'

For a long time after that, Mum was very quiet most of the time. The Burma Valley farmers pool their money and write us a cheque so that we can go on holiday, maybe to South Africa to the beach, they say. But Dad won't cash the cheque. He says, 'We're all hard up. They're hard up, too.' He frames the cheque and hangs it in the sitting room. He says, 'Let's drive around Rhodesia for a holiday. We'll take tins of food and sleeping bags. It won't cost much.'

So we bury Olivia in a little baby-sized coffin in the cemetery where the old white settlers are lying in their big, proud graves with moss-covered white gravestones and permanent pots of flowering plants and careful, exclusive fences which are there for show and do nothing to stop the monkeys running onto the graves. And after Olivia is buried, we drive to the nearest house; all the families in the Burma Valley in their most careful, sad clothes driving in a long segmented snake of sad-slow cars to an Afrikaner's house, and we eat the sweet greasy *koeksisters* and pound cake and scones that the Afrikaner women have been baking all morning and we drink sweet milky tea until someone finds a bottle of brandy and some beers and starts to hand those around. Which gives us the courage to have a small church service in the only way we know how as a community: drunk and maudlin. Alf Sutcliffe pulls out his guitar. He doesn't know church songs, so we sing, 'You picked a fine time to leave me, Lucille' and 'Love Me Tender' until even the grown men, even the tough old Boer farmers, are wiping away tears with the backs of their hands.

A few days after the funeral, we pack ourselves into the green Peugeot station wagon and drive up and out of the valley. But we couldn't drive away from the memories of the baby who lay under the soft, silent pile of red-fertile soil cut into a barely contained cemetery against the edge of the valley floor where mostly old people lie rotting gently in the rains and drying to dust in the dry season.

No one ever came right out and said in the broad light of day that I was responsible for Olivia's death and that Olivia's death made Mum go from being a fun drunk to a crazy, sad drunk and so I am also responsible for Mum's madness. No one ever came right out and said it in words and with pointing fingers. They didn't have to.

Afterwards

Mum

My life is sliced in half.

*

The first half is the happy years, before Olivia dies.

Like this: Vanessa and the older neighbour children are sitting with their feet dangling over the windscreen; their legs are speckled with nuggets of red mud. We are sitting behind the big brothers and sisters – we minor offspring – and we are using them as a shield against the slinging flicks of mud and the fat, humid wind, which grows colder as the evening comes.

'Sing,' Dad shouts at us, threatening to catapult us from the roof by steering the car into a sliding halt, 'sing!'

We are hilarious with half-fright, half-delight, the way Dad drives. Olivia is on Mum's lap in the front seat, screaming with excitement. Her sweet, baby happiness comes up to us on the roof in snatches.

'He's *penga*!' says one of the big brothers.

And then someone starts, 'Because we're' – pause – 'all Rhodesians and we'll fight through thickanthin!' and we all join in.

And Dad shouts, 'That's better!' and presses the car forward, freckling the big brothers and sisters with newfound mud.

We throw back our heads. 'We'll keep this land' – breathe – 'a free land, stop the enemy comin' in.' We're shout-singing. We'll be Rhodesian forever and ever on top of the roof driving through mud up the side of the mountain, through thick secret forests which may or may not be seething with terrorists, we'll keep singing to keep the car going.

'We'll keep them north of the Zambezi till that river's runnin' dry! And this great land will prosper, 'cos Rhodesians never die!'

The spit flies from our mouths and dries in silver streaks along our cheeks. Our fingers have frozen around the roof rack, white as bones. We are ecstatic with fear-joy.

*

The second half of my childhood is now. After Olivia dies.

After Olivia dies, Mum and Dad's joyful careless embrace of life is sucked away, like water swirling down a drain. The joy is gone. The love has trickled out.

Sometimes Mum and Dad are terrifying now. They don't seem to see Vanessa and me in the backseat. Or they have forgotten that we are on the roof of the car, and they drive too fast under low thorn trees and the look on their faces is grim.

We are not supposed to drive after dark – there is a curfew – but the war and mosquitoes and land mines and ambushes don't seem to matter to Mum and Dad after Olivia dies. Vanessa and I sit outside at the Club while Mum and Dad drink until

Dad

they can hardly open the car door. We are on the tattered lawn, around the pond where Olivia drowned (fenced off now, and empty for good measure). Mosquitoes are in a cloud around our ankles and Mum and Dad do not care about malaria. We are sunburned and thirsty, bored. We lie back on the prickling grass and watch the sky turn from day to evening.

We drive home in the thick night through the black, secret, terrorist-hiding jungle on dirt roads and Dad has his window down and he is smoking. The gun is loaded across his lap.

Vanessa and I have not had supper.

So Mum and Dad buy us more Coke'n'chips for the drive and tell us to sit in the backseat with the dog, who has been forgotten about in the car all afternoon and who needs a pee.

We let Shea out for a pee.

Mum is fumbling-drunk and Dad, who is sharp-drunk, is getting angry.

'Come on,' he says to Shea, aiming a kick at her, 'in the bloody car now.'

'Don't kick her,' says Mum, indistinctly protective.

'I wasn't kicking her.'

'You were, I saw you.'

'Get in the bloody car, all of you!' shouts Dad.

Vanessa and I quickly climb into the car and start to fight about where Shea should sit. 'On my lap.'

'No, mine.'

'Mine. She's my dog.'

'No, she's not.'

'*Ja*, she is. Mum, is Shea my dog or Bobo's?'

'Shuddup or I'll give both of you a bloody good hiding.'

Vanessa smirks at me and pulls Shea onto her lap. I stick my tongue out at Vanessa.

'Mum, Bobo pulled her tongue at me.'

'I did not.'

Mum turns around and slaps wildly at us. We shrink from her flailing hand. She's too drunk and sad and half-mast to hit us.

'Now another sound from either of you and I'll have you both for bloody mutton chops,' says Dad.

That's that. Mutton chops is not what we want to be. We shut up.

Vanessa and I eat our chips slowly, one at a time, dissolving them on our tongues, and the vinegar burns so we swallow Coke to wash down the sting. We each feed Shea three or four chips. She missed her supper too.

Dad drives wildly, but it's not children-on-the-roof-wild which is fun and scary all at the same time and we're singing and the saliva is stringing from our mouths in thin silver ribbons. This is the way a man drives when he hopes he will slam into a tree and there will be silence afterward and he won't have to think anymore. Now we are only scared.

Mum has gone to sleep. She is softly, deeply drunk. When Dad slows down to take a corner, she sags forward and hits her forehead damply on the dashboard and is startled, briefly, awake. The car is strong with the smell of cigarette smoke and stale beer. Burped-and-farted beer. Breathed-out beer. In the dark we watch the bright red cherry from Dad's cigarette. It lights his face and the lines on his face are old and angry. Vanessa and I have finished our Coke'n'chips. Our tummies are full-of-nothing-aching-hungry. Shea is asleep on Vanessa's lap.

If we crash and all of us die it will be my fault because Olivia died and that made Mum and Dad crazy.

*

That's how it is after Olivia dies.

Vacation

Bus stop

The house is more than we can stand without Olivia. The emptiness of life without her is loud and bright and sore, like being in the full anger of the sun without a piece of shade to hide under.

Dad has said we'll go on holiday.

'To where?'

'Anywhere. Anywhere that isn't here.'

So we drive recklessly through war-ravaged Rhodesia.

A green Peugeot rattling along the desolate black strips of tar with toilet paper flying victoriously from the back windows (where Vanessa and I were seeing how long it could go before it tore off and lay behind us on the road like a fat, white run-over snake, twisting in agony). As the roads of Rhodesia uncurled in front of our new, hungry sorrow, we sang, 'One man went to mow, Wenttomowameadow,' and 'One hundred baboons playing on a mine field. And if one baboon should accidentally explode, there'll be ninety-nine baboons playing on a mine field.'

And when we stop singing, Dad shouts, 'Sing.'

So we sing, 'Because we're' – pause – 'all Rhodesians and we'll fight through thickanthin, We'll keep this land a free land, stop the enemy comin' in. We'll keep them north of the Zambezi till that river's runnin' dry. And this great land will prosper 'cos Rhodesians never die.'

And we sing, '*Ag pleez*, Daddy won't you take us to the drive-in? All six, seven of us eight, nine, ten.'

Until Mum says, 'Please, Tim, can't we just have some quiet? Hey? Some peace and quiet.'

Mum is quietly, steadily drinking out of a flask that contains coffee and brandy. She is softly, sadly drunk.

Dad says, 'Okay, kids, that's *enoughofthat*.'

So we sit on each side of the back seat with the big hole in the middle where Olivia should be and watch Mum's eyes go half-mast.

We are driving through a dreamscape. The war has cast a ghastly magic, like the spell on Sleeping Beauty's castle. Everything is dormant or is holding its breath against triggering a land mine. Everything is waiting and watchful and suspicious. Bushes might suddenly explode with bristling AK-47s and we'll be rattled with machine-gun fire and be lipless and earless on the road in front of the burned out smouldering plastic and singed metal of our melting car.

The only living creatures to celebrate our war are the plants, which spill and knot and twist victoriously around buildings and closed-down schools in the Tribal Trust Lands, or wrap themselves around the feet of empty kraals. Rhodesia's war has turned the place back on itself, giving the land back to the vegetation with which it had once been swallowed before people.

And before the trappings of people; crops and cattle and goats and houses and business.

And then, through deep-quiet, long-stretching-road boredom and quite suddenly, and as surprising as the Prince battling madly through briars to reach a sleeping woman he has never met, two white figures appear on the road. They aren't princes. Even from afar we can tell they aren't princes. They look stained grey-brown in filthy travellers' clothes with unruly hair sticking up with grease and dirt. They aren't Rhodesians either, we can tell, because they are walking along the road and white Rhodesians don't walk anywhere on a road because that's what Africans do and it is therefore counted among the things white people do not do to distinguish themselves from black people (don't pick your nose in public or listen to muntu music or cement-mix in your mouth or wear your shoes hanging off at the heel). One of the walking white men sticks out his thumb as we approach.

Mum slumps forwards damply as Dad slows down. Dad gives her an anxious look. Mum feels his glance and smiles crookedly. She says, 'Why are you slowing down?'

'Hitchhikers.'

'Oh.'

Dad says, 'Well, I can't bloody well leave them on the side of the road, can I?'

'I don't see why not. It's where we found them.' Mum, who picks up every stray animal she ever sees.

Dad says, 'Stupid bloody buggers.'

*

At this point in our journey, when we see the hitchhikers, Vanessa has built a barrier of sleeping bags and suitcases between us so that she doesn't have to look at me because, she has told me, I am so disgusting that I make her feel carsick. We have run out of the toilet paper we had brought for the trip. It now lies strewn in our wake or clings, fluttering, to thorn trees by the sides of the road. We have played I Spy until we accused each other of cheating.

'Mu-uuum, Bobo's cheating.'

'I'm not, Vanessa is.'

'It's Bobo.'

I start crying.

'See? She's crying. That means she was cheating.'

Mum turns around in her seat and swipes ineffectually at us, slow-motion drunk. Until now she has been spending an agreeable hour looking at herself in the rearview mirror and trying out various expressions to see which most suits her lips. Now she says, 'Anything more from either of you and you can both *getoutandwalk.*'

Like a hitchhiker.

And now this. The two mazungu figures looming out of the hot rush of road.

'We don't have room for hijackers,' says Vanessa pointing at the pile between us and the back of the car, which is already stuffed to overflowing with suitcases and sleeping bags.

'Hear that, Tim, ha ha. Vanessa calls them hijackers.'

Dad stops and shouts out the window. 'Where are you going?'

'Wherever you're going,' says the little blond one in an American accent.

'We don't have a plan,' says Dad, getting out and trying to make room for the two men among our luggage, among the sleeping bags, between Vanessa and me.

'That's fine with us,' says the little one.

'Not us,' mutters Vanessa.

The hitchhikers squeeze into their allotted spaces and Dad drives on through the empty land.

The little one says, 'I'm Scott.'

'You're a bloody idiot,' says Dad.

Scott laughs. Dad lights a cigarette.

The big, dark one says, 'I'm Kiki.' He has a thick German accent.

Mum turns around and smiles expansively to make up for Dad's unfriendliness. 'I'm Nicola,' she says, and then the effort of staring back at our new passengers obviously does not mix with coffee and brandy because she pales, hiccups, and turns abruptly to the front.

'I'm Bobo,' I say. 'I'm eight. Nearly nine.'

Dad says, 'Did you know there's a war on?'

'Oh, ja. Ve thought it vould be a good time to travel. Not too many other tourists.'

Dad raises his eyebrows at our hitchhikers in the rearview mirror. He has sky-blue eyes that can be very piercing. He blows smoke out of his nose and flicks ash out of the window and his jaw starts to clench and unclench so I know it will be a long time before he speaks again.

So I say, 'And that's Vanessa, she's eleven, nearly twelve.'

Our avocado-green Peugeot heads into the sunset, towards the Motopos Hills. We stop to pee behind some bushes and Mum gives us each a banana and a plastic mug of hot, stewed tea from the thermos flask. We're all reluctant to get back into the car. Kiki sleeps, Scott reads. Dad smokes, Mum looks at herself in the side mirror. I am reduced to staring out of the windows. Reading my collection of books (I have brought a small library to accompany me on my journey) is making me carsick, and the pungent rotting-sausage smell emanating from Kiki's socks doesn't help. The effort of being confined in a small space is making Kiki sweat. With six of us in one station wagon, Kiki has to lie with his nose pressed against the roof, on top of the suitcases and sleeping bags in the rear of the car. His feet poke out on either side of Scott and me.

On the stretches of road that pass through European settlements, there are flowering shrubs and trees – clipped bougainvilleas or small frangipanis, jacarandas, and flame trees – planted at picturesque intervals. The verges of the road have been mown to reveal neat, upright barbed-wire fencing and fields of army-straight tobacco, maize, cotton, or placidly grazing cattle shiny and plump with sweet pasture. Occasionally, gleaming out of a soothing oasis of trees and a sweep of lawn, I can see the white-owned farmhouses, all of them behind razor-gleaming fences, bristling with their defence.

In contrast, the Tribal Trust Lands are blown clear of vegetation. Spiky euphorbia hedges which bleed poisonous, burning milk when their stems are broken poke greenly out of otherwise barren, worn soil. The schools wear the blank faces of war buildings, their windows blown blind by rocks or guns or mortars. Their plaster is an acne of bullet marks. The huts and small houses crouch open and vulnerable; their doors are flimsy pieces of plyboard or sacks hanging and lank. Children and chickens and dogs scratch in the red, raw soil and stare at us as we drive through their open, eroding lives. Thin cattle sway in long lines coming to and from distant water and even more distant grazing. There are stores and shebeens, which are hung about with young men. The stores wear faded paint advertisements for Madison cigarettes, Fanta Orange, Coca-Cola, Panadol, Enos Liver Salts ('First Aid for Tummies, Enos makes you feel brand new').

I know enough about farming to know that the Africans are not practising good soil conservation, farming practices, water management. I ask, 'Why?' Why don't they rotate? Why do they overgraze? Where are their windbreaks? Why aren't there any ridges or contours to catch the rain?

Dad says, 'Because they're *muntus*, that's why.'

'When I grow up, I'll be in charge of *muntus* and show them how to farm properly,' I declare.

'You're quite a little madam,' Scott tells me.

'I'm a jolly good farmer,' I tell him back. 'Aren't I, Dad, aren't I a good farmer?'

'She's an excellent farmer,' says Dad.

I smirk.

Vanessa sinks further into herself. She waits until I look over at her and wipes the smug look off my face with one, mouthed word: 'Freak.'

Chimurenga: 1979

Bo and Burma Boy

The young African men whom we used to see sloped up against the shebeens in the Tribal Trust Lands have disappeared as the war has intensified. They have left their homes and have headed into neighbouring countries to join the guerrilla military camps there. On a clear day we can see where there are new trails snaking up through the rocky scrub into the hills where the mine fields are. Now, when those young men come back from Mozambique or Zambia, picking their way across the mine fields and scrambling down into jungles or flat, hot savannah, they don't go home to their villages but stay in the bush to fight the war of liberation.

As we dust our way through the Zimunya TTLs on our

way from the farm into town, we see only the women, the elderly, and young children. They shrink from our gaze, from our bristling guns. Some of the bigger children run after us and throw rocks at the car. Their mothers shout but their words are snatched away by dust, sucked up in the fury of our driving.

The guerrillas come back into Rhodesia from their training bases under cover of darkness and hide in the bush in secret camps. The camps are easy to disassemble if Rhodesian forces are nearby. Ghost camps. Sometimes, my sister and I find the ghost camps on the farm; cold fires, empty tins, smashed bottles, bits and pieces of broken abandoned shoes. The grass is crushed in small circles, like the circles left by sleeping animals, when they are gone. The wind blows dryly though the hills. The traces of the camp are covered with dust, leaves, grass.

If we perch on rocks around the ghost camps we can look out and see what the guerrillas must have seen when they were camped here. We see that they have watched us, that they must know where we go every day, our favourite walks, the way we ride. They can see me running down to the dairy first thing in the morning, and Mum and me leaving the house (too late to be back before it is dark) for our evening walk. They have seen Vanessa alone in the garden painting and reading. They have seen Dad striding down to the barns or kicking up sand as he scuds off on his motorbike. Still, they have not swooped from the hills and killed us, leaving us lipless, eyelidless, bleeding, dead.

The guerrillas only come back into the villages from their bush camps at night. They come to hold *pungwe* (political rallies) and to recruit *mujiba* (young boys) and *chimwido* (young girls) to bring supplies to their bush camps. Under the black, silent, secret, careless African skies, they urge children, barely older than my sister, to come back into the bush with them, to join them in their fight for independence. They tell the *mujiba* and the *chimwido* to supply information about the movements of the Rhodesian forces.

The *mujiba* and the *chimwido* are the small, dark, moving shadows in the thick jungle terrain. They are the high, crying voices, like hooting owls, on the still night air. They are the scurry of activity in the bush on the sides of the road. They can secrete themselves in culverts, in hollow trees, behind small rocks. Now the war has grown calmly violent, secret, earnest.

Over a million African villagers are forced to live in 'protected villages' surrounded by barbed wire and guarded by Rhodesian government forces so that there can be no more pungwe. Children of fighting age are kept at gunpoint. Toddlers, the elderly, and women crouch under the watchful eye of their captors. They are allowed to fetch water. They are fed. But the captives, too, are watching. Shading their eyes against the sun, they stare into the hills, which rustle suddenly with movement: a chain of swaying grass and bushes. The Rhodesian forces look quickly over their shoulders, but they see nothing. Only the grass moving in the wind. What the old women and the small children and the mothers see are familiar bodies (soldier brothers, sisters, fathers, aunts) in a column, moving quickly over rough ground. The women pull their babies to their breasts, sink back on their heels, and wait for liberation.

The untended crops in the TTLs wither in the hot sun, curl up, and blow away. The African cattle hunch, starving, untended, until at last they push through the fences of neighbouring commercial farms run by whites, where the grazing is fat and cultivated.

The long-horned, high-hipped village Sanga cattle spread ticks to our pampered, pastured cows, who instantly succumb to heartwater, redwater, and sweating sickness and whose bellies swell with the babies of the native bullocks. They run in the hills behind our house, unhandled, until they become wild. At night we hear them roaring to each other, not the gentle pastoral calling of our domestic cattle in the home paddocks, but the noise of wild animals in the hills, kraaling against leopards and baboons for the night or calling in randy, unrequited shouts.

*

Dad is away more and more, fighting. The material of his uniform wears thin, like wings, across his shoulder blades. The skin on his shoulder is bruised in a stripe, where his FN rifle hangs. Mum runs the farm now. When Dad is away, we are given a Bright Light – an armed man deemed unworthy to fight the actual war, but worthy enough to guard European women and children – to take care of us. Our Bright Light is called Clem Wiggens. He has tattoos from head to toe; his eyelids read 'I'm' and 'Dead'. His feet are labelled 'I'm Tired' and 'Me Too'. He comes to breakfast late, rumpled, having slept soundly through his watch. He has fiery red eyes, wafting marijuana. He is kind to the dogs, but if we ever get attacked, Mum says, 'it's just one more kid to take care of.' Sometimes she tells him to go and check up on the other women-without-men and *their* children. And so he leaves us and sits all day on *another* woman's veranda and drinks gallons of *her* tea and stares with undisguised lust at *her* maids.

*

Mum and I are having breakfast. Vanessa is painting on the veranda. The cook comes with a tray of toast and an announcement: 'Philemon wants to see you, madam.'

I follow Mum outside, to the back door. The dogs, hoping for a walk, are at our feet.

'Yes, Philemon?'

'The wild cattle came into the home paddock last night, Madam,' says Philemon. 'They are jumping the dairy cows.'

'Oh, hell.' Mum bites the inside of her lip.

'They will make the cows sick,' says Philemon.

'I know. I know that.'

Philemon waits, dropping to his haunches and rolling tobacco in a square of newspaper.

Mum sniffs. 'I'll see what I can do,' she says.

She whistles up the dogs, orders me to put on my tackies for a walk, and stalks down to the paddock with my air gun tucked under her arm and her Uzi, as usual, slung over her front (where it is starting to rub permanent grey marks on her clothes). I am trotting breathlessly behind her.

'What are you going to do?' I ask, hopping over a patch of paper thorns and ducking under the barbed wire as Mum strides through the Rhodes grass toward the native cows, colourful and raw-boned against our square-rumped red cows.

'Shoot the buggers in the balls,' she says.

'Oh.'

'See?' she says, as we came up to the native cattle, who are grazing near our cows, but in their own distinct group, like newcomers at a party. 'They're getting at my little heifers.'

'Oh.'

She says, 'Get away from my nice cows,' and aims a shot at the offending bullocks' rear ends with my air gun. She misses.

'Bugger it.'

'We need Vanessa,' I say. But Vanessa is in the middle of another art project, which means she won't be off the veranda for days now.

Mum edges closer to the native cows, who move mildly away from her, swishing their tails and keeping their heads steadfastly low in the high, tangled Rhodes grass. 'Now,' Mum says, raising the air gun to her shoulder and letting go with a pop. Nothing happens.

'Did I miss?'

'Which one were you aiming for?'

'Any of them. Did I hit one?'

'I don't think so.' I frown into the high summer sun, a big ball of red hanging through the haze of wildfires, over the yellow fig tree on the edge field. 'It's hard to tell in this light.'

Mum hands me the gun, 'You have a go,' she says.

I break the gun, slip a pellet into the barrel, take aim and fire.

But the native cattle are tough. The pellets from my air gun ping off their unyielding hides even at close quarters.

'Damn it,' says Mum. She picks up a clod of earth and throws it feebly toward the offending cows. 'Go away!' she screams. 'Go home!' The clod of earth falls to the ground not far from our feet and crumbles in a little sighing breath of dust. Some egrets, startled, fly out of the grass, like a tattered white picnic cloth being shaken out of the earth, and then settle again at the cows' feet.

Mum's shoulders sink, and her face folds, defeated.

I say, 'They're quite fat, some of them.'

'On our grazing.'

We start to walk back to the house, up past the diesel-smelling workshop and the sharp-tobacco-smelling barns. Mum is silent and angry, stomping along the road.

*

The next morning when I come to breakfast Mum is already two-thirds of the way through her pot of tea.

I sit down and wait for July to bring me a bowl of porridge. I order two fried eggs with toast.

Mum says, 'Eat up,' looking over my shoulder and out of the window. 'The horses are ready.'

I am surprised. Usually Mum dawdles through breakfast, listening with half an ear to the radio if it is the news or *Story on the Air* and reading a book propped up on the toast rack while simultaneously dealing with the constant flow of requests that come from labourers at the back door, via the trembling hand of the cook, who is greeted with a hostile 'What is it now?'

'Malaria, madam,' says July, or 'Sick baby', or 'Snake bite', or 'Accident with fire'.

But this morning Mum tells July, 'I am not seeing anyone. Tell them to go away. They can come tomorrow.'

The cook hovers, distressed, 'But madam . . .'.

'But nothing. I mean it,' says Mum. 'They won't die if they wait another day.'

She shoulders her Uzi and pulls on her hat. 'Come on, Bobo,' she says. 'You'll have to leave the rest.'

I stare in dismay at my half-eaten bowl of porridge and my promising plate of eggs and toast.

'But – '

'We've got work to do.'

'What?'

'We're going to round up every bloody stray cow on this farm,' she says, 'and have a cow sale.'

*

That day Mum and I ride up into the foothills on game paths and tracks that the terrorists have used. These paths are already strangled with fresh growth, with the promise of a new rainy season coming, the quick green threads of creepers stretching over old, dry tracks, swallowing footpaths, and demonstrating how quickly this part of Africa would reclaim its wild lands if it were left untrodden. The horses struggle over rocks, their unshod hooves slipping against the hard ground as we climb ever higher into the mountains. Mum rides ahead on her big bay thoroughbred, an ex-trotter rescued from an abusive home and made rideable again under Mum's patient training. I am on my fat chestnut pony, Burma Boy, a bad-tempered and ill-behaved animal; bucking, bolting, kicking, and biting regularly – all of which, Dad says, is good for me. The dogs swarm, noses down, through the bush ahead of us, yelping with excitement when they put up a hare or mongoose and bounding hysterically through the bush if they catch sight of a duiker or wild pig.

By late morning, we are on the border of our farm in the

high, thick bush, as close to Mozambique as I have ever been on a horse.

'Keep your eyes peeled for buffalo bean,' says Mum.

I start to itch at once and look ahead nervously. Buffalo bean is a creeper boasting an attractive purple bloom in the spring, followed by a mass of beans that are covered in tiny velvet hairs, which blow off in the wind and can lodge in your skin. The hairs can stimulate a reaction so severe, so burning and persistent, that it has been known to send grown men mad, tearing into the bush in search of mud in which to roll to alleviate the torture. I am also compelled to crouch, my head pressed against Burma Boy's neck, to avoid the strong, elaborate webs that spread taut across our path. In the middle of these bright, tight webs there are big red- and yellow-legged spiders waiting hopefully for prey to fall. Burma Boy's ears are laced with the silvery threads.

Mum is following the native cattle trails, fresh manure and tracks and freshly disturbed bush; she pushes on and on, occasionally getting off her horse to inspect the ground and then riding on with more confidence. 'They've gone this way. See?' The cows have stayed close to the springs that feed out of the mountains and run through these foothills to come down into the rivers in the heart of our farm.

'Look,' says Mum fiercely, 'bloody cows! Look!' She points at the damaged stream banks and kicks Caesar on with fresh determination, her face set in a scowl. The horses are straining, wet with sweat and frothing white under the tail and mane. Even the dogs have stopped following their noses and bounding ahead after wild game scents; they are beginning to follow closely on the horses' heels, tongues lolling. I say, 'Are we nearly there yet?' I am starting to get thirsty and we have brought nothing with us to drink.

Mum says, 'Stop whinging.'

'I'm not whinging. I was just *saying*.'

'Start looking for mombies.'

The cattle that have stayed up this high are wild. As quickly as we cover their fresh tracks, they move on, staying ahead of us, out of sight and almost beyond earshot. Mum says, 'I'm going to go around. You stay here, and catch them if they come down.' She pushes Caesar forward into the thick bush with the dogs scrambling behind her, and soon disappears from sight. For a while I can hear her and the dogs as they make their way through the bush, and then there is silence. I hold my breath and listen. I am surrounded by the high, whining noise of insects – their frantic spring singing in dry grass – and by the occasional shriek of an invisible bird. Burma Boy puts his head down and starts to pull at the thin, bitter dry grass. It is very hot and still and I am enveloped in the salty steam sent up by Burma Boy as he sweats; my fingers sting against the leather reins and my eyes burn. Sweat drips down from my hatband and flies swarm onto our stillness to take advantage of the moisture, crawling over my eyes and lips until I swat them away. I am very thirsty now.

'Mu-um.' My voice sounds high and thin in the heat.

I wait. There is no answer. I hold my breath and then call again, louder, 'Mu-uum!' Still no answer. I look around, suddenly imagining that terrorists might crawl up on me at any moment and take me by surprise. I wonder where Mum has gone; she has the gun with her. I wonder if she will hear me if I am attacked by terrorists. I close my eyes and take a deep breath. What will Burma Boy do if we are suddenly surrounded by terrorists? Bolt, no doubt. And I will be scraped off on a tree and lie winded and wounded on the ground waiting for Mum to come and rescue me. I wonder how she would find me again in this thick bush. I'd be dead by then. Shot. Eyelids chopped off and fried, no ears, no lips. Dead. Burma Boy would be home. They would have a funeral for me, like the funeral we had for Olivia. They would say how brave I was. I start to cry. I would be buried, next to my fried eyelids, lips and ears, in a little coffin. There would be a hump of fresh earth, crawling with earthworms, piled over me in the little settlers' cemetery. Tears stream down my face. The *Umtali Post* will write a moving article about my death.

'Mum!' I shout, genuinely frightened.

Burma Boy throws up his head at my alarm.

'It's okay,' I say shakily, crying and running my hand down his wet neck. 'It's okay.'

I start to imagine that perhaps Mum, Caesar, and the dogs have been caught by terrorists themselves. Maybe Mum is lying in a bloody puddle, eyelidless and lipless, with the dogs licking helplessly, lovingly at her lifeless hands. I will be brave at Mum's funeral. The *Umtali Post* will write an article about me, lost and alone in the bush, while my mother lay dead surrounded by her faithful dogs and loyal horse. I turn Burma Boy around. 'Do you know the way home?' I ask, letting him have his head. But he, after looking around for a few moments, placidly puts his head down and starts to eat again.

It feels like a long time during which I alternated between quiet, dry panic and noisy, copious weeping before I hear Mum and the dogs coming through the bush. Mum is singing, like the herdsmen taking the cows to the dip, 'Here dip-dip-dip-dip dip! Dip, dip-dip-dip-dip dip!' And in front of her there are a dozen multicoloured cows, running with heads held high, wild and frightened, their eyes white-rimmed, their long, unruly horns slashing at the bush. Burma Boy throws up his head, startled, and shies. I pull up the reins. Mum says, 'Get behind me.'

I start to cry with relief at seeing her. 'I thought you were lost.'

'Out the way,' she shouts, 'out the way! Get behind!'

I pull Burma Boy around.

'Come on,' says Mum, riding past me, 'let's herd this lot down.'

I say, 'You were so long.'

'Catch the cows as they come through.'

But the cows are not used to being herded and are unwilling

and frightened participants. They break loose frequently and Mum has to circle back to bring the herd into order. She has identified the leader, a tall-hipped ox with a very old, almost worn-through leather strap around his neck that once must have held a bell. All the cows are dripping with ticks: their ears are crusted with small red ticks and their bodies are bumped with the raised grey engorged adults, which look ready to drop off. Mum says, 'If we can keep the leader going, the rest might follow.' But it still takes us more than an hour to move the cows less than half a mile. I start to cry again.

'What's the matter now?' says Mum irritably.

'I'm thirsty,' I cry, 'I'm tired.'

'Well, you go on home, then,' says Mum. 'I'm bringing these cows down.'

'But I don't know the way.'

'*Fergodsake*,' says Mum between her teeth.

I start to cry even harder.

She says, 'Give Burma Boy his head, he'll take you home.'

But Burma Boy, given his head, is content to follow Caesar and graze happily at this leisurely pace. 'Look, he won't go home.'

'Then *ride* him.'

I kick feebly. 'I'm thirsty,' I whine.

Mum is unrelenting. 'So let's get these cows home. The sooner we get these cows home the sooner you'll have something to drink.'

We ride on for two more hours. I slouch over in my saddle, letting myself rock lazily with Burma Boy's tread. I make no attempt to herd the cows.

Mum scowls at me with irritation: '*Ride* your bloody horse.'

I flap my legs and pull weakly at the reins. 'He won't listen.'

'Don't be so bloody feeble.'

Fresh tears spring into my eyes. 'I'm not being feeble.'

Mum says, 'If you would help, we'd get home a lot sooner.'

We ride on in hostile silence for another half an hour or so. Then I say, 'I think I have buffalo bean.' I start to scratch fretfully. I am so thirsty that my tongue feels dry and cracking. 'I'm going to faint, I'm so thirsty.'

Mum circles back to catch a stray cow.

'Mu-uuum.'

She isn't going to listen. It is no good. It is clear that I am not going to get home until the cows are safely fenced up in the home paddocks. I pull Burma Boy's head up and circle him back to the lagging cows, straggling at the rear of the herd. 'Dip, dip-dip-dip-dip dip,' I sing, my voice dry on the hot air. 'Dip, dip-dip-dip-dip-dip-dip.'

One of the cows tries to run out of the herd and break for the bush. I dig my heels into Burma Boy's sides and spin him around, catching the cow before she can escape.

'That's it,' says Mum, 'that's better. Keep it up.'

It takes until late afternoon to get the cows down to the home paddocks, by which time the cows' flanks are wet with sweat, their horn-heavy heads are low and swinging; they are tripping forward without thought of a fight. I have stopped snivelling, but am hunched over the front of my saddle trying not to think about how thirsty I am.

'There,' says Mum, wiping the sweat off her top lip as she shuts the gate behind the wild cows, 'that's not a bad day's work.'

I shrug miserably.

'Don't you think?'

'I s'pose.'

Mum swings up on Caesar again and pats him on the rump. 'You know, we're descended from cattle rustlers, you and me,' she tells me, her eyes shining. 'In Scotland, our family were cattle rustlers.'

I think, *At least Scotland is cool. At least there are streams of fresh water to drink from. At least Scottish cows don't lead you into buffalo bean.*

*

The next day Mum sends the cattle boys into the nearby villages. She says, 'Tell the villagers I have their cows. If they want their cows back, they can come and get them.' She pauses. 'But they'll have to pay me for grazing,' she says slowly. 'Understand? Lots and lots of money for grazing and for taking care of their cows. Hey? *Mazvinzwa?* Do you understand?'

'Eh-eh, madam.'

No one comes to collect their cows. Mum dips the cows, deworms them, brands them with our brand, feeds them up on the Rhodes grass until their skins are shiny and they are so fat it seems as if they might burst, and then sends them on the red lorry into Umtali, to the Cold Storage Corporation, to be sold as ration meat. With the proceeds, she buys a plane ticket for Vanessa to visit Granny and Grandbra in England and she pays for the rest of us to drive down to South Africa on a camping holiday where we are flooded out of our tent on the second night on the West Coast and subsequently spend a damp, drunken fortnight in a grey fishing village trying to avoid hostile Afrikaners and waiting for the sun to come out.

That is the year I turn ten. The year before the war ends.

Violet

Violet

Pru Hilderbrand is like a mum out of a book. When we go to her house we get home-made lemonade and slices of home-made whole-wheat bread with slabs of home-made butter on it. Her three little boys do not have itchy bums and worms and bites up their arms from fleas. Pru doesn't like to drink beer or wine and she hates the Club. Her children have finger painting and Lego and the house smells of disinfectant and clean sheets. There are always fresh-cut flowers from her soft-green, rocky garden in the summer and dried flowers cut from the highlands in the winter. Next to the fireplace, there are clay pots with newspapers and magazines and big, cushioned chairs, and there are soft, secret places in that house for a child to feel comfortable and safe. There are quilts on the beds and tea is a proper meal on the veranda with a bowl of brown sugar and the salt is in a little pottery pot in the middle of the table and it is in little granules, not grains, and you sprinkle it on your food with a tiny wooden spoon. Pru plays cricket with us on the lawn.

So, we have spent all afternoon at the Hilderbrands', who have a squash court and a pool which is in the belly of some rocks and held in by a small concrete wall which is invisible because the pool is fed by a small spring and the water is allowed to slosh over the concrete wall like a waterfall. After we've been swimming, Pru makes us dry ourselves (she has fresh-smelling crisp towels in the changing rooms, which rub our skins raw) and she lets us play on the lawn until it is almost time for the sun to set and then she says to the mums and dads that we should leave now because of the curfew.

We have the furthest to drive, all the way to the other side of the valley, so no matter how fast we drive we'll break curfew, we'll be home after dark.

We shudder up the washboards on the ribby Mazonwe road in the dull light of a thick African sunset and then, as we turn up the Robandi farm road, it is dark. African night comes like that, long rich sunsets and then, abruptly, night. The cooler night air is releasing the scents trapped by a hot day; the sweet, warm waft of the potato bush; the sharp citronella smell of khaki weed; raw cow manure; dry-dust cow manure. We bump over the culvert at the bottom of our road (in which the big snake lives) and head up towards the house, which is a pale, unlit mass in the evening light.

Dad stops at the security gate, which is locked; he gets out with the FN slung over his shoulder and stops, listening, for a moment before making his way to the gate. Today he hesitates longer than usual.

'Everything okay?' says Mum.

'Just thought I heard something.'

'Did you?'

Dad doesn't answer.

The cook has instructions to lock the gate when he has fed the dogs, before he knocks off for the night. Mum slides over into Dad's seat, she has the car in reverse, ready to fly backward down the driveway and leave Dad to his own devices if we find ourselves under attack. It takes Dad a long time to get behind his own shadow from the headlamps of the car and unlock the padlock. He opens the gate and Mum drives quickly into the yard. Dad follows us on foot to the house.

Mum says, 'I'll see what July left out for us for supper.'

Dad still has a sweaty shirt on from his game of squash. He says, 'I'll change my shirt before we eat.'

But when he goes to the cupboard, he has no shirts.

And when Mum goes into the kitchen there is no supper. And the pots and pans and plates and knives have been pulled onto the floor and there is the chaos of a recent scuffle among the debris.

Now we all have candles and we run around the house shouting to each other the growing list of things that are missing.

'All my clothes!' shouts Vanessa.

'And mine.'

'Oh shit, Tim, they've taken everything.'

We hold candles up to all our cupboards. They are all bare. Our clothes, food, bedding.

'My rings!' shouts Mum. And there is real panic in her voice. 'Tim, my rings!'

At the beginning of every planting season Mum has to give her rings to the tobacco man who lets us have money to grow another crop and he gives Mum back the rings at the end of the season when we have sold the tobacco. Now we have no rings and we will not be able to plant tobacco at the beginning of the rains.

Then Dad says, 'Wait.' He says that he heard something when he was unlocking the gate. 'Remember?'

'What kind of sound?'

A moaning sound, he says. 'I'm going to see what it was.'

Mum says, 'Get backup. Don't go in on your own.'

But Dad has already hurried outside.

Mum says to Vanessa and me, 'Take a candle and go to your room.'

We go to our room and Vanessa says, 'I know, let's play cards.'

We play twos 'n' eights.

Dad is outside and we can hear him shouting, 'Nicola!'

Mum runs outside and the dogs scrabble down the length of the shiny-slick cement floor after her. We abandon our game of cards and follow the dogs.

Dad has Violet, our maid, in his arms. To begin with it looks as if she is not wearing any clothes but then Mum holds up the paraffin lamp and we see that Violet is wearing a dress that is stuck perfectly to her body and that she is viscous and shiny with blood, as if someone has poured oil on her, or wrapped her tightly in black plastic.

'Is she breathing?'

'I don't know.'

Her blood looks so gleaming, it doesn't seem possible she can be dead. Her blood is running and alive and keeps replenishing itself over the sleek lustrous skin of her dress, like a new snake's skin.

Mum says, 'Here,' and opens the back of the Land Rover. Dad slides Violet's body into the back; it makes a noise like a wet sponge. Mum has rolled out a grey army-issue blanket and slid it under Violet. The blanket is soon black with blood.

Mum says, 'Go inside, you kids.'

Vanessa says, 'Come on, Bobo.'

Dad says, 'I'm going to catch the bastards that did this.'

'Call for backup.'

'Come on, Bobo,' says Vanessa again.

Dad goes inside to get more ammunition and Vanessa goes

inside so that she won't have to watch. But I want to see what Mum is doing. I want to see everything.

I say, 'Mum, can I do anything?' but she does not answer.

I have a special Red Cross certificate from school. I can stabilize a broken limb or a broken neck and bandage a sprain. I can dress a bullet wound. I can make hospital corners on a bed. I know how to find a vein and administer a drip, but I am only allowed to do this if All the Grown-ups Are Dead. I can do mouth-to-mouth and CPR, and I have practised on the kids at school who are also signed up for the Red Cross class.

*

Red Cross first-aid classes are held in the old music room at the end of the kindergarten block. I practise giving mouth-to-mouth resuscitation. It is the closest I have ever come to someone's mouth, having it open like that, breathing into the soft, red, ripe cave of someone else's body. I practise on a small girl called Anne Brown. My tackie lips feel as if they might suffocate her, hovering above hers.

'Close her nose, tilt her chin.'

I feel the way her nostrils stick with mucus as I squeeze them closed. The skin on her nose feels sweaty, greasy and bobbly.

It's very hot in the small classroom where we have pushed the desks aside to make room for a hospital bed and bandages, bodies, stretchers. I lean over Anne. Small beads of sweat have sprung up on her top lip, like a mustache.

'Have you checked her mouth for vomit?' asks the nurse teacher.

Anne opens her mouth obligingly. I scrape my finger around her mouth.

'Don't forget, you're supposed to be unconscious, Anne. Don't help Bobo.'

Anne sinks her teeth unhelpfully onto my finger.

When I have resuscitated her, she looks flushed and breathless, closer to death than when I started. My finger is purple with perfect Anne Brown–shaped teeth marks.

*

Mum has scissors from her first-aid kit that she keeps in the back of the Land Rover. She is cutting the dress off Violet. In the bright, white hissing-blue light of the paraffin lamp we can see that Violet has been sliced, like rashers of bacon, all the way up her thighs, across her belly, her arms, her face.

Mum slaps the inside of Violet's arm, looking for a vein. She says over and over again, under her breath, 'Hold on, Violet. Hold on.' She has forgotten, or has stopped caring, that I am watching. Dad has come outside again. He has his FN rifle strapped across his back and he says, 'I'm going down to the compound.' He gets on his motorbike.

Mum looks up from Violet's body and pushes hair out of her eyes with the back of her hand, which means a smudge of blood up her nose and above her eyebrow. She says, 'I wish you'd wait for backup.'

But Dad kicks his motorbike alive, and I watch the red taillight wind down the hill and around the corner, humping as it goes over the big culvert at the corner, and then the sound of the two-stroke engine is absorbed by the night.

'Hold on,' says Mum to Violet, into the silence left by the disappearing roar of Dad's motorbike. She says, 'Don't die. Hold on.' The lamp hisses and there are the usual singsong, rasping calls of frogs from the pool. The dogs scratch and whine as they stretch and recurl themselves into comfortable positions and there is the rhythmic slip-slap of some of the dogs licking their balls. Usually Mum says, 'Hey, stop that!' when she hears them licking their balls, but not now.

Dad comes back from the compound. Mum has emptied one drip into Violet's arm. While the drip has been emptying into the nearly flat vein, Mum has scrambled to the front of the Land Rover and turned on the mobile radio. She has called for backup. She says, 'HQ, HQ. This is Oscar Papa 28, do you read?'

There is a small, crackling pause. Then, 'Oscar Papa 28 this is HQ. Reading you strength five. Go ahead. Over.'

'We need mobile medics. We have one African female in critical condition. Over.'

'Have you been under terrorist attack? Over.'

'Negative. It appears to be . . . domestic in nature. Over.'

There is a hissing pause of disappointment, and then the voice comes back at us. 'Sending mobile medic team to Oscar Papa 28. Over.'

'Thank you. Over and out.'

Dad comes back. He says, 'It was July.'

Mum straightens up and stares at Dad. 'What?'

'The boys haven't seen him since this morning. He's not in his hut.'

'Fucking kaffir,' says Mum.

'The boys are coming with me. I'm going to catch him.'

'The boys' are Dad's most loyal labourers. Duncan is the boss-boy. He has a handsome open face, with a long nose and wide-set eyes. Cephas is a small squat man whose father, Chibodo, is our witch doctor. Chibodo has very long nails and is very, very old. He smells as old as an ancient tree, like burnt bark. He doesn't talk very much, but when he opens his mouth he has only a few teeth (black and brown pegs) and his tongue looks very pink, thin and alive and wet. He sits at night in the watchman's hut, right up against the hills, and watches the maize, scaring off the baboons that come to steal corncobs. He has an old plough disk hanging from a tree which he beats with a simbe, like the old woman in the TTL who warns terrorists when a convoy is coming. Cephas has learned secrets from his father: he can track animals that have passed by days before. He can smell where terrorists have been, see from the shift in the landscape where they are camping. He can put his mind inside the mind of any other living thing and tell you where it has gone. He can touch the earth and know if an animal has passed that way. But he can't tell you why. Philemon, the cattle boy, can read tracks, but he can't read tracks as well as Cephas. Philemon is the one who can quiet a cow in labour and sing the calf into life when it is born too sick to stand. Cloud is the man from the workshop who whittles wood with a lathe into salt and pepper pots, spice racks, egg cups. He smells of the shiny paint he sprays onto the wood and his eyes are always burning red from the ganja he smokes.

'I'm going into the hills. He'll be trying to get to Mozambique.'

'He's armed,' says Mum. July has stolen knives. 'And he's not alone. He couldn't carry all that stuff on his own. You'll need backup.'

Dad says, 'I'll be okay.'

'At least call.'

Dad radios for backup but no one will come with him. This is not a military emergency, it's only a robbery. We have not been attacked by terrorists. Dad's friends tell him not to go into the hills. There are terrorists in those hills, and the hills themselves are unsafe: they are edged by mine fields.

Dad settles on his haunches and smokes. Violet moans.

The men – Dad's 'boys' – arrive on foot. I see them running steadily up the hill to the house; they have lit the branches of a tree for light. They have a conference with Dad and decide to wait until just before first light before leaving for the hills. They don't want to run into a terrorist camp by mistake. Dad gives the men a packet of cigarettes each. They are talking in low, intense voices to each other in Shona; their words are like water over rocks, bubbling, soft, incessant. Dad packs food and water, a shovel, a hatchet, matches, and a gun. They will drive as far as they can into the hills and then walk towards Mozambique from there.

Before first light, before Dad leaves, the mobile medics arrive. By the time they reach the house, Violet has had three drips, one in one arm and two in the other, and her eyes have fluttered open once or twice, but each time the pain washes over her again and drags her back deep into a blessed, dark, empty place. Near death.

Mum says, 'For God's sake, hold on. You can make it.'

The first medic, a man, hops out of the Land Rover, gun slung over his shoulder, and comes over to look at Violet. He turns away and vomits behind the flower bed in which our gardener has allowed some cannas to live. The second man comes out. He waves a cigarette at Dad.

'Howzit?'

Dad says, 'Okay.'

The medics swarm around the back of the Land Rover. Mum crawls out. Her hands and clothes are covered with blood. 'She's going to make it,' she says.

The medics stare. 'Shit, I dunno, hey. She looks pretty bad,' says one.

Another says softly, 'Jesus Christ!'

The medics roll Violet onto a stretcher. She is soft and heavy. The stretcher sags under her weight. They put her into the back of their Land Rover.

Mum says, 'Will you have a drink?' It's almost light. 'Or a cup of tea?'

They accept tea out of tin cups and drink it quickly as the eastern sky softens with dawn. And then they drive away and we never see Violet again. We hear later that she got out of hospital and went back to her village. Afterwards the *Umtali Post* writes a story, 'Farmer Saves Maid's Life'

Mum says, 'The farmer had nothing to do with it. It was the farmer's wife.'

The sky is starting to streak vigorously now, pink-grey. Dad and his gang head off for the hills.

Mum says, 'Why don't you take the dogs, at least?'

Dad shakes his head. 'Too much noise.'

Mum goes into her bedroom but she does not sleep. Vanessa

and I don't sleep. We stay on our beds, with the dogs, and our eyes sting and our mouths are dry. It is breakfast time but there is no one to feed us. Violet is sliced and bleeding in the back of the medics' Land Rover, heading for hospital; July is running for Mozambique with all our clothes and money and Mum's rings. Mum is not talking. Dad has gone to kill July.

'Let's play cards,' says Vanessa.

'I can't. I'm too hungry.'

'I'll make you some Pronutro,' says Vanessa, 'then will you play cards with me?'

'Okay.'

Vanessa mixes the powdered soybean meal into a paste with some milk and sprinkles sugar on the top for me. She puts the kettle onto the woodstove for tea. The fire has gone out and we try to make another one but the fire from the newspapers we shove into the stove's mouth generates only a thick, oily, black smoke.

Vanessa says, 'We'll have to wait for tea.' She finds some bottles of Coke, which we are ordinarily only allowed on Sunday, and opens one.

'We'll get into trouble, hey.'

'We'd better share,' she says, pouring the contents of the bottle into two plastic cups. Warm Coke and Pronutro for breakfast. It feels like camping.

We sit opposite each other on the dining room table. Vanessa patiently builds a barrier around me because she can't watch me eat. She puts the milk jug in front of my face and sits back down and says, 'Not enough.' She fetches a coffee can and some boxes and bottles from the pantry. From behind the barrier she says, 'I can still *hear* you. You should try and eat more slowly.' But I'm too hungry to slow down, I hurry food into my drum-tight empty stomach, which swells with the pasty, cold porridge and the warm Coke.

Then Vanessa brings the cards and dismantles the barrier, and we play war.

Dad's story comes out in bits and pieces, and I catch it from the stories told around the bar at the Club. And sometimes, when I'm older, around campfires in Malawi and Zambia, there will be quiet after supper when we are full and heavy and drinking and staring into the fire. And Dad will be smoking a cigarette and suddenly he will clear his throat and say, as if it were still relevant, 'Best damned tracker I ever saw was that Cephas.' And he tells me the story of that night.

Dad and his 'boys' – the men – park near Ross Hilderbrand's old farm. Before the war, there were white farmers all over these hills. They were high enough above the hot, steamy valley to grow coffee in thick red soil. But the farmers here were intimidated by their proximity to the border and they were attacked by terrorists and their labour abducted and taken to Mozambique. All those farmers have left the area. Now, quick-growing bougainvillea and Mauritius thorn have started to hang thickly from the verandas of those old farmhouses. In the gardens, cannas have spread over the edge of their beds and the grass has grown like long untidy hair and the windows have had rocks thrown through them. Bats shit on the floors and hang upside-down from the ceilings, where yellow-brown stains from rat pee spread like tea spills above them. The whitewashed sitting rooms where dinner parties (with proper place settings and flowers on the table and servants in white uniforms, stiff with desperate civilization) took place are creeping green with mould. The irrigation ditches that fed the cow troughs are swollen with buffalo bean.

Cephas is the lead tracker; he takes off at a run, watching the ground steadily, not hesitating, reading soft signs in the dew-crushed earth which tell him secrets. The other men hang back and let Cephas lead until he is steadily, confidently on the track. He has found the place, he says, where the men have gone. He says, 'There are two.'

To begin with Dad can't see how Cephas can tell which way July and his companion have gone – and he is not sure how Cephas can be so sure of himself – but then they find things that the cook has dropped. A cooking pot, a dress, some packaged food. July or his companion is wearing Dad's gumboots. When the men come to a muddy place, they can see the tracks clearly. And then they find the gumboots, discarded in the grass. Cephas laughs: 'His feet are getting pain.' July is not used to gumboots. He is given a new pair of Bata tackies every year but he chops the toe out of them and ties the laces loosely so that his dry-cracked feet will fit in them even when they swell in the heat.

When the men come to a river, wide and deep enough that it would soak them to their waists, they hesitate. Cephas shakes his head. 'They didn't cross here,' he says, and then he sees that there is an old bridge upstream. The path that used to lead to and from the bridge has long ago been swallowed by thick ground cover. Small shrubs and baby trees have started to fill in the swath cut by the cleared old growth. Cephas says, 'They saw the bridge, too.' He holds up his hand and the men drop behind him. He has gone crouched and his energy is forward and is like something you can almost feel – like wind when it moves the leaves and grass. He creeps over the bridge silently and the other men follow him and then suddenly Cephas stops and shakes his head. In one sweep he retraces his steps back to the middle of the bridge and jumps up and down on it.

'They are under here,' he says. 'See? This bridge should bend. It does not bend.'

Dad's 'boys' scramble into the river and pull July and his companion out from under the bridge, where they have been hanging on to the old, half-rotten beams with their fingernails. They haul them onto the bank. For some minutes Dad's boys beat the thieves, kicking them and punching them, until Dad says, 'Let's get them back to the car.'

*

Dad radios Mum from the car. 'Oscar Papa 28, Oscar Papa 28, this is Oscar Papa 28 mobile. Do you read, over?'

Mum runs from her bedroom, but Vanessa and I have heard the Agricalert crackle into life, too. 'Tim? Oscar Papa 28 mobile? This is Oscar Papa 28. Are you all right? Over.'

There is a pause and then Dad's voice, hissing with static, 'I got the bastards. We found your rings. Over and out.'

Mum shouts, 'Wa-hoo!'

And Vanessa and I spontaneously perform our version of a Red Indian War Dance around the veranda, 'Wa-wa-wa-wa,' we skip on alternate legs.

By the time Dad comes back with July and his companion, both the cook and his accomplice have swelling eyes and lips and hard bonelike lumps on their faces. Vanessa and Mum and I are standing in the yard. When Mum sees July get out of the car, she runs at him. She is screaming, 'Fucking kaffir! Murderer!' She starts to beat him but Dad pulls her back.

He says, 'Let the boys deal with him.' He nods to the 'boys'. The militia who have come to arrest July and his companion turn and look the other way.

Dad's 'boys' kick July and in one soft sound, like a sack of mealie meal hitting concrete, he buckles to his knees. And then they kick him again and again. July curls himself up and covers his head with his hands but the feet find holds to flip him back on his belly and prise open his arms to expose his belly and ribs, which I can hear cracking like the branches of the frangipani tree. His skin splits open like a ripe papaya.

Then Dad says, 'That's enough, hey.'

But they don't stop.

Dad says to the militia men, 'You'd better pull them off before they kill the fucking bastard.'

The militia men break the 'boys' from the tight scrummage of kicking. They put July and his accomplice in the back of their white pickup. The accomplice folds over himself like a collapsible chair, but July grips blindly to the edge of the truck, perching on bloodied legs. He has been handcuffed and his eyes are almost shut with swelling. As the militia drive off down the road, he makes one last attempt to escape, flinging himself from the moving car and hitting the dirt road; it seems impossible he doesn't burst on impact. Two of the militia men explode out of the front of the truck and then dust kicks up and the white truck and the men and July vanish from view for a moment. When the dust clears, they are dragging July behind the truck by a rope. He runs, his legs spinning like an egg whisk, until he is jerked off his feet and then he is pulled twisting behind the vehicle until it reaches the end of the driveway. After that, the militia men throw him in the back of the truck and he does not try to jump out again.

Selling

Bubbles, Bobo and Vanessa

What I can't know about Africa as a child (because I have no memory of any other place) is her smell; hot, sweet, smoky, salty, sharp-soft. It is like black tea, cut tobacco, fresh fire, old sweat, young grass. When, years later, I leave the continent for the first time and arrive in the damp wool sock of London-Heathrow, I am (as soon as I poke my head up from the intestinal process of travel) most struck not by the sight, but by the smell of England. How flat-empty it is; car fumes, concrete, street-wet.

The other thing I can't know about Africa until I have left (and heard the sound of other, colder, quieter, more insulated places) is her noise.

At dawn there is an explosion of day birds, a fierce fight for territory, for females and food. This crashing of wings and the secret language of birds is such a perpetual background sound that I begin to understand its language. A change in the tone, an increase in the intensity of the birds' activity, will break into my everyday world and I will know that there is a snake somewhere, or I will look skyward (the way a person might automatically, almost subconsciously, check their watch against the radio's announcement of time) and confirm a hovering hawk.

In the hot, slow time of day when time and sun and thought slow to a dragging, shallow, pale crawl, there is the sound of heat. The grasshoppers and crickets sing and whine. Drying grass crackles. Dogs pant. There is the sound of breath and breathing, of an entire world collapsed under the apathy of the tropics. And at four o'clock, when the sun at last has started to slide west, and cool waves of air are mixed with the heat, there is the shuffling sound of animals coming back into action to secure themselves for the night. Cows lowing to their babies, the high-honeyed call of the cattle boys singing 'Dip! Dip-dip-dip-dip' as they herd the animals to the home paddocks. Dogs rising from stunned afternoon sleep and whining for their walk.

The night creatures (which take over from the chattering, roosting birds at dusk) saw and hum with such persistence that the human brain is forced to translate the song into pulse. Night apes, owls, nightjars, jackals, hyenas; these animals have the woo-ooping, sweeping, land-travelling calls that add an eerie mystery to the night. Frogs throb, impossibly loud for such small bodies.

There is only one time of absolute silence. Halfway between the dark of night and the light of morning, all animals and crickets and birds fall into a profound silence as if pressed quiet by the deep quality of the blackest time of night. This is when we are startled awake by Dad on tobacco-sale day. This silence is how I know it is not yet dawn, nor is it the middle of the night, but it is the place of no-time, when all things sleep most deeply, when their guard is dozing, and when terrorists (who know this fact) are most likely to attack.

Dad shakes my shoulder. 'Come on, Chookies.'

I startle awake, in the quick, gasping, suddenly alert way of all people who have lived in a war (and for which there is no cure, ever, not even now).

'It's okay, it's okay,' says Dad (who naturally suffers a more extreme version of this where's-the-danger response to being shaken awake).

Vanessa is awakened by my quiet panic. 'What?' Her urgent hiss reaches across to the jumping black shadow of Dad against candlelight.

'Time to get up.'

'Oh.' She sinks back into her pillow.

'Here's tea.' Dad props Vanessa up and hands her a cup of hot-milky-sweet tea.

'Come on, Bobo, tea.' But I am already out of bed and dressed.

I have slept with my pyjamas pulled over my best-for-the-tobacco-sale-day clothes. All I have to do is drink my tea. I have already put several books into a bag, along with my toothbrush, a change of clothes, and a torch that has ceased to work (the batteries have leaked and killed it). I am sitting in the plastic, damp-dog smelling car, eyes stinging with tiredness, long before the rest of my family. I kick my feet against the back of Dad's seat with anticipation.

When we turn onto the main road, Mum will hand us a banana and a boiled egg and we will be allowed sips of tea from her steaming cup (just one sip at the bottom, so we don't spill) and then we will sleep until we reach Rusape, where the high morning sun will stroke us alert.

Today, we will arrive at the tobacco floors in Salisbury in time for the free breakfast that is provided for all farmers and buyers and Tabex personnel. Today, I will eat until I feel sick.

I will eat until my belly bloats with the joyful, unaccustomed nausea of too-much. And the food is egg (fried, scrambled, omelettes), sausage, fried tomatoes, chips, bacon, and dripping-butter toast. There are several varieties of boxed cereals: Cocoa Puffs, Honey Pops, Cornflakes, Pronutro, muesli. There is Zambezi mud porridge, oats and meali meal porridge. There are huge bowls of fruit salad and silver trays of cheese and crackers. I eat some of everything and fill my plate again and I am still reluctant to leave the food but Dad says, 'Come on, Chooks, leave it now. You'll make yourself sick.'

And then we make our way onto the auction floors to our two or three lines of tobacco (soldiered between similar lines belonging to other farmers). The bitter-smelling, hessian-wrapped blocks of leaf-laid-upon-leaf have miraculously made the journey from Robandi to here. They have been graded, tied into hands, and packed: primings, lugs, tips, droughted, spotted, scrap. We stand, ill with food, next to our crop. Mum takes my shoulders in a fierce, ringless grip. She alone did not eat breakfast. She drank tea in quick, nervous gulps and glanced repeatedly at the clock that hangs above the door leading to the wide, plane-hangar-sized auction floors.

The buyers walk the line of our tobacco.

Mum tightens her clutch. She whispers, 'Here they come.'

Dad nonchalantly stands, resting on one leg, like a horse at rest. He looks away, as if the buyers are a common, bland species of bird on an otherwise more exciting safari.

Mum hisses, 'Try and look hungry, kids.'

I suck in my belly as far as possible and open my eyes as wide as they will go, so that they will seem hollow and needy. Vanessa sinks her head to her chest and shrinks with not-wanting-to-be-here.

Mum turns a fierce, fixed, terrifying smile on the buyers. Her look says, 'Give us a good price and you will be rewarded with my love for all time. Please give us a good price. Please.'

Waves of her anxiety sink down into my belly and churn with the too-greasy excess of my recent breakfast.

None of us look at the other farmers and their families, who are also hovering with palpably jittering nerves over their bales.

The bales are torn open, leaves are pulled up and smelled; the thin-veined crop is rubbed between thick fingers (fingers flashing with gold bands, which are among the many things that tell the buyers from the farmers: no farmer I know wears rings). A price is scrawled on a ticket. Dad waits until the buyers are out of earshot and then whispers to Mum in a soft, warning voice, 'Steady. Hold it,' in the way he would talk to a fretful animal.

Now Mum, Vanessa and I watch Dad's hands as he walks the line. If he agrees with the price we have been offered for each bale, he hesitates, fingers hovering briefly above the ticket, and then walks on, leaving the ticket intact. That tobacco will be taken away to cigarette factories: famous, well-travelled Rhodesian burley all the way from our lucky farm.

If Dad disagrees with the price the buyer has offered, he tears the ticket. Those bales will be rewrapped, loaded onto lorries, and brought back to unlucky Robandi. Dad will wait to sell them later in the season, when perhaps the buyers will be more hungry for tobacco. Those bales will sit in the grading shed, open to the air, where blasts of steam will keep the leaves in a fine balance between soft and mouldy. They will anger Dad whenever he sees them. Mum will spend hours, until her fingers burn with the sticky yellowing residue of the leaves, resorting and rebaling the leaves in the superstitious belief that a new presentation might bring a healthier price.

If Dad starts tearing tickets and his face becomes folded and deep, we feel ourselves become quiet and wishing-we-weren't-here. But if he is walking quickly over the line of tobacco, leaving the tickets pristine, beautiful whole rectangles of yellow, we are giddy. Vanessa and I start to run between the bales, exuberant, silly, loud, and Mum doesn't say, 'Shhh girls! Behave yourselves!' And then Dad has walked the line and, without looking at the other farmers, he takes Mum by the hand and he says, 'Come on, Tub.' Vanessa and I fall into line behind Mum and Dad. His fingers are wrapped round hers. By the end of today Dad will have gone to see the fat man with the wet lips from Tabex and Mum will have her rings back, and when we get home to Robandi she will polish them in Silvo to remove the tarnish of shame and disuse.

Dad doesn't smile, or concede any kind of victory in front of the buyers. He waits until we are in the car and then he says to Mum, 'Fair price.'

Which means that, in addition to our yearly and unavoidable checkup at the dentist, there will be a new set of clothes, a new pair of shoes, a visit to the used-book store, tea and scones with strawberry jam and clotted cream at the tea room in Meikles Department Store. We will spend the night in the delicious luxury of a friends' town house with its irrigated garden, clipped lawn, tiled white shiny kitchen, properly flushing loos, and (most wondrous of all) television. When our tobacco sells well, we are rich for a day.

But whether the tobacco sells well or badly, when we arrive at Robandi it will be back to rations and rat packs.

School

Off to school

Vanessa goes away to school when I am four. Packets come for me from the Correspondence School in Salisbury. Cloud makes me a small chair and table at the woodwork shop and paints them blue and the table sits next to Dad's desk on the veranda. In the morning, after breakfast, I sit down with Mum and the wad of papers from Salisbury and I write my 'Story of the Day' and I learn to colour, count, paint. Once a week after lunch, Mum turns on the radio and we listen to *School on the Air* and I throw beanbags around the sitting room and pronounce ('Say after me') the colours of the rainbow and the names of the shapes, and I walk like a giant and ('Now, then, very softly') like a fairy and Mum lies on the sofa and reads her book.

But the afternoons are long and hot and buzzing with fat flies and lizards lying still on the windowsills, and Mum is resting, and my nanny – my nanny of the moment; they seem to change like the seasons – has gone off for lunch. So I recruit children (picanins, I call them) from the compound and force them to play 'boss and boys' with me. Of course, I am always the boss and they are always the boys.

'Fetch *mahutchi*!'

'Yes, boss.'

'Quicker than that! Run. Boss up! Boss up! Come on, *faga moto*!'

The children run off and fetch an imaginary horse for me.

'Now brush him!' I shout. 'No, not like *that*. Like *this*. Hell man, you guys are a bunch of Dozy Arabs.' And I push the children away from the invisible horse to demonstrate the action of a currycomb, a body brush, hoof pick.

My nanny comes back from her lunch and she presses her lips at me. She claps her hands at my 'boys' and shoos them away, like chickens. They run down the drive, holding their mouths with insolent laughter, and shout insults back to me in Shona.

'Why did you send my boys away?'

'They are not your boys. They are children like you. Girls and boys.'

I've told her that if she shouts at me I will fire her. But now I say, 'I was only playing.'

'You were bossing.'

'So?'

She says, 'Are you grown-up?'

I frown and push out my worm-pregnant belly.

She says, 'When you can reach your hand over your head like this' – and she reaches a hand up, over the top of her head, and covers the opposite ear – 'then it means you are grown. Then you can boss other children and you can fire me.'

'I can fire you if I like. Anytime I want, I can fire you.'

'*Aiee.*'

I reach my hand over the top of my head but it only reaches halfway down the other side.

'See?' she says.

In the later afternoon, after the laundry has been washed and hung up in bright flags at the back of the house, my nanny stands under the tap at the back of the house and rubs green soap on her legs. She doesn't wash the soap off again, so her legs stay shiny and smooth and the colour of light chocolate. If she leaves her legs without soap, I can draw pictures on her dry skin with the sharp end of a small stick and the picture shows up grey on her skin. If I fall, or hurt myself, or if I'm tired, my nanny lets me put my hand down her shirt onto her breast and I can suck my thumb and feel how soft she is, and her breasts are full and soft and smell of the way rain smells when it hits hot earth. I know, without knowing why, that Mum would smack me if she saw me doing this.

My nanny sings to me in Shona. '*Eh, oh-oh eh, nyarara mwana.*'

'What song is that?'

'A song for my children.'

'What does it say?'

She tuts, sucking on her teeth. 'You are not my children.'

*

And then, the year I turn eight, I am too old for a nanny anymore. I am ready for boarding school. I get my own trunk with my full, proper name, 'Alexandra Fuller,' printed on the top.

'But I thought my name is Bobo.'

'Not anymore. You're Alexandra now. That's your real name.'

Dad takes a photograph of us leaving the farm for my first day of big school in January 1977.

Vanessa is almost as tall as Mum. I am holding the Uzi,

pressing out my belly to help catch the weight of it. We are standing in front of Lucy, the mine-proofed Land Rover.

*

Chancellor Junior School is an 'A' school, for white children only. This means we have over one hundred acres of grounds: a rugby field, a cricket pitch, hockey fields, tennis courts, a swimming pool, an athletics track, a roller-skating rink. After independence, the skating rink is turned into a basketball court and half the athletics track is turned into a soccer pitch. (Basketball and soccer are things white children do not do, like picking your nose in public, mixing cement with tea and bread in your mouth, dancing hip-waggling to African music.)

We have our very own extensive library and more than enough books to go around. We have more than enough very well-trained (only white) teachers to go around, including a remedial teacher for the remedial kids, whom we call retards. The retards have their own room at the end of the block (all of them together, regardless of age) and they have to sit in front of everyone else in assembly, even in front of the Standard Ones. And no one plays with them at break or after school and they are excused from athletics practice.

We have music teachers, art teachers, sewing teachers, wood-work teachers, a Red Cross teacher, a tennis coach, a cricket coach, a rugby coach, and an athletics coach, who also teaches us how to swim. Our matrons are white. They're old, and crazy, but they're white.

The groundsmen and cleaners are black, supervised by a drunken old white man who keeps whisky and peppermints in the broom cupboard.

The cooks are black, supervised by an old white lady who has spectacularly high hair and who sits in the cool room outside the kitchen drinking tea and reading books with pictures of ladies (whose boobs are about to pop out of their dresses) fainting into men's arms on the covers.

The maids who do our laundry are black and are supervised by the senior girls' matron, who is deaf and so tired she spends most of the day half asleep with the radio on in her sitting room. Her room smells of old lady and mothballs.

The boardinghouse we call a hostel, a massive redbrick colonial building that was an army barracks once. It sleeps two hundred children. Forty kids per dormitory, each with a foot-locker in which we keep the set of clothes for the week; one set of school uniform and one set of play clothes to last seven days, new brookies and socks daily.

Milk of magnesia, administered by our hook-nosed matron every Friday, keeps us regular. Although the fish, also administered on Friday, usually takes care of any constipation we may have been suffering from.

We wash our hair on Saturday mornings and periodically we are doused with a scalp-stinging mixture that is supposed to kill lice.

The boys are punished with stripes – a leather strap, which hangs in the teachers' common room. Afterwards, we ask to see the pattern of welts on their bums and we ask if they cried and although their faces are streaked and we have heard their shouts of pain they shake their heads,

The girls are hardly ever beaten. For our punishments, we are made to kneel on a cement floor for half an hour. Or write out lines: 'I will not talk after lights out. I will not talk after lights out,' four hundred times. Or memorize passages from the Bible: 'Let us walk honestly, as in the day; not in rioting and drunkeness, not in chambering and wantonness, not in strife and envying. But put ye on the Lord Jesus Christ, and make not provision for the flesh to fulfil the lusts thereof.'

The two hundred boarders are mostly children from farms around Umtali, and the two hundred day scholars are townies and we despise and torture them, luring them up into the pine forest, where we attack them and steal their packed lunches. We are better athletes and worse students and tougher fighters than the day-bugs. It is rare that we allow a townie into the rarefied circle of friends and alliances and conspirators that makes up the boarders' gang. But every morning we meet, in class lines, in the Assembly Hall to sing.

> *Morning has broken, like the first morning,*
> *Blackbird has spoken, like the first bird.*

And a chosen senior kid reads from the Bible, mumbling nervous words. We pray for the army guys. We say the 'Ah Father'. And then we go back to our classrooms and stand behind our desks and say another prayer, also for the army guys. Some of the kids, whose dads or brothers have been killed in the War, cry every morning. Their soft sobs are part of the praying.

There are not very many townies with dead dads. Most of the dead dads are farmers; killed on patrol, or in an ambush, or by a land mine, or during a farm attack.

On Wednesday before lunch we take Scripture Class from a teacher with hairy legs and sandals (which gives our regular teacher a break to go and smoke cigarettes and drink tea in the teachers' lounge). On Saturday, another woman (also with hairy legs and sandals, so that I come to associate Christian women with these particular characteristics) comes to the boardinghouse from the Rhodesian Scripture Union and we have to sit in the prep room while the sun and the fields call to us from outside. She tells us Bible stories and makes us pray and hold hands and sing the kind of songs which require clapping and hopping up and down. On Sunday we walk in snaking lines toward our various churches; Vanessa and I are Anglicans; my best friend is Presbyterian ('Press-button'). There are also Dutch Reformed, Catholics ('Cattle-ticks'), and a fistful of Baptists and Methodists.

But all denominations, all the time, focus prayers and singing and scripture on the War and we all ask God to take care of our army guys and keep them safe from terrorists and we assume that God knows this means (without us actually coming right out and saying it) that we want to win the War.

Independence

Independence Arch

Which is why it is such a surprise when we lose the War.

Lost. Like something that falls between the crack in the sofa. Like something that drops out of your pocket. And after all that praying and singing and hours on our knees, too.

Ian Smith rings the Independence Bell thirteen times, one ring for every year since the Unilateral Declaration of Independence from Britain. He and his wife, Janet, raise their glasses in a toast to 'the faithful' one last time.

Even then we have a hard time believing it's over. That we are giving in after all this time. That we're not fighting through *thickanthin* after all.

'Everyone that asketh receiveth; and he that seeketh findeth.'

We lost, they found. *Our-men.*

*

Independence, coming *readyornot.*

In March 1978, Bishop Abel Tendekayi Muzorewa of the African National Council makes an agreement with the white government and forms an interim government, which combines the weakest of the African political parties with the most determined of the old white guard and in June 1979 he wins elections, which may or may not have been free and fair (depending on who you are, and the colour of your skin). We buy T-shirts to replace our old RHODESIA IS SUPER T-shirts. These new T-shirts read, ZIMBABWE-RHODESIA IS SUPER and we say, 'Especially Rhodesia.' But the war carries on and more and more people die and the fight is fiercer and more angry than before.

Now the whites are fighting everyone who is not white and the Africans have splintered into political groups and tribal factions and fight each other, on top of also fighting the whites.

So Muzorewa, who is (after all) a Christian man and a Methodist, does a most un-African thing. He gives up power after only six months. He hands Zimbabwe-Rhodesia and the whole damned mess back to the British. In London, December 1979, it is decided that once again we are a British colony except this time, the British mean to give us independence under majority rule. None of this mix-and-match, pick-your-own-muntu style of Rhodesian government.

There is a cease-fire and we have to take Dad's FN rifle and Mum's Uzi and all Dad's army-issue camouflage to the police station. We keep the rat packs and eat the last of the pink-coated peanuts and stale Cowboy Bubble Gum and we dissolve and drink the last of the gluey coffee paste. The policeman who collects the guns writes our name in a book and apologizes, 'I'm sorry, hey.' He doesn't say what he is sorry for.

There are *freeanfair* elections in February 1980, just before my eleventh birthday, and we lose the elections. By which I mean our muntu, Bishop Muzorewa, is soundly defeated. He wins three paltry seats. One man, one vote. We're out.

On April 18, 1980, Robert Gabriel Mugabe takes power as Zimbabwe's first prime minister. I have never even heard of him. The name 'Rhodesia' is dropped from 'Zimbabwe-Rhodesia'. Now our country is simply 'Zimbabwe'.

Zimba dza mabwe. Houses of stone.

Those who live in stone houses shouldn't throw stones for fear of ricochet.

*

The first to go are the Afrikaner children.

The day Robert Gabriel Mugabe wins the elections the Afrikaner parents drive up to the school, making a long snake of cars like a funeral procession, to collect their kids. The kids, fists held tightly by stern-bosomed mothers, are taken to their dormitories, where we are not ordinarily allowed until five o'clock bath time. The matrons have to get the maids to bring stacks of trunks down from the trunk room. The Afrikaner mothers pack. The Afrikaner fathers stay, leaning against their cars, smoking and talking quietly to each other in Afrikaans. There is a sense of history in their carriage; *we've done this before and we'll do it again.*

We have learned about the Great Trek in school.

*

The 'Groot Trek' of 1835, when more than ten thousand Boers, the Voortrekkers, left the Cape Colony and came north. They left the paradise of the Cape because they were fighting with their Xhosa neighbours and because they were dissatisfied with the English colonial authorities, who had forbidden the slave trade and who believed in equality between whites and nonwhites. So many men, women, and children died during the Great Trek, their bodies draped gorily over wagon wheels and under wagon wheels and next to horses in the illustrations in our history books. They died because they believed that the British policy of Emancipation destroyed their social order, which was based on separation of the races. They saw white predominance as God's own will.

So, now the Little Trek.

*

But the next day some of the English Rhodesians are driven away too. There is only a handful of us left at supper that night; no more than twenty children in a dining room designed to hold ten times as many. My sister has already moved from Chancellor Junior School to the Umtali Girls' High School. So she is not around for me to ask, 'Where are Mum and Dad?'

Tomorrow, the children who have gone to 'B' schools, for coloureds and Indians, will be here. The children from 'C' schools, for blacks, will be here too. Tomorrow, children who have never been to school, never used a flush toilet, never eaten with a knife and fork, will arrive. They will be smelling of wood smoke from their hut fires.

Tomorrow child soldiers will arrive. They can track their way through the night-African bush by the light of the stars, these *mujiba* and *chimwido*. They are worldly and old and have fixed, long distance stares.

Eating with your mouth closed and using a knife and fork properly can't save your life.

It only takes a minute to learn how to flush a toilet.

But still Mum and Dad don't come and fetch me away.

Instead, the first black child is brought to the school. We watch in amazement as he is helped out of a car – a proper car like Europeans drive – by his mother, who is more beautifully dressed than my mother ever is. She smiles as she leads her son, confidently, head held high, one high-heeled foot clacking smartly past the next high-heeled foot, through the tunnel that leads around the sandbags and into the boys' dormitory.

We won't be needing those sandbags any more.

This woman is not a *muntu* nanny. This child is not a

picanin. He is beautifully dressed in a brand new uniform. The uniform is not a worn and stained hand-me-down like the one I wear.

We wait until the mother and father of this little black child drive away, spinning up gravel from the back wheels of their white-people's car as they leave. And then we make a circle around the little black boy. The boy tells us he is called Oliver Chiweshe.

I have not known the full name of a single African until now. Oliver Chiweshe. Until now I only knew Africans by their Christian names: Cephas, Douglas, Loveness, Violet, Cloud, July, Flywell. I am learning that Africans, too, have full names. And not only do Africans have full names, but their names can be fuller than ours. I try and get my tongue around Joshua Mqabuko Nyongolo Nkomo; Robert Gabriel Mugabe; the Reverend Canaan Sodindo Banana; Bishop Abel Tendekayi Muzorewa: these are the names of our new leaders.

I say, 'That's a nice name.'

'Actually, my full name is Oliver Tendai Chiweshe,' says Oliver, emphasizing his middle name. He speaks beautifully accented, perfect English.

We say, 'Was that your father who dropped you off?'

Oliver looks at us with pity. 'That was my driver,' he tells us, 'and my maid.' He pauses and says, 'Daddy is in South Africa this week.'

We are stunned by this news. 'Why?'

'Business,' says Oliver complacently.

'And then he'll come back?'

'*Ja*,' says Oliver.

That night at supper, Oliver sits alone. None of us will sit next to him. We wait to see if he eats like a *muntu*. We wait to see if he cement mixes. But he has perfect European manners which are quite different from Mashona manners. He takes small, polite bites. He puts his knife and fork down on the edge of his plate between mouthfuls. He sips his water modestly. At the end of his meal, he pats the top of his lip with his napkin and puts his knife and fork together.

I turn to my neighbour and hiss, 'I hope I don't get *that* napkin when it comes back from laundry.'

'*Ja*, me too, hey.'

Within one term, there are three white girls and two white boys left in the boardinghouse. We are among two hundred African children who speak to one another in Shona – a language we don't understand – who play games that exclude us, who don't have to listen to a word we say.

Then our white matron leaves and a young black woman comes to take her place. She is pretty and firm and kind. She does not smoke cigarettes and drink cheap African sherry in her room after lights out. She redecorates the matron's sitting room with a white cloth over the back of the worn old sofa and fresh flowers on the coffee table, and she gets rid of all the ashtrays. A sign goes up on the door of her sitting room: No SMOKING PLEASE. YOUNG LUNGS GROWING.

Some of the new children in the boardinghouse are much older than us, fourteen at least. They already have their periods, they have boyfriends. They laugh at my pigeon-flat chest.

We sleep so close that, even with the lights out, I can make out the shape of my neighbour's body under the thin government-issue blanket. I watch the way she sleeps, rolled onto her side, too womanly for the slender child's bed. Her name is Helen. Her warm breath reaches my face.

Helen, Katie, Do It, Fiona, Margaret, Mary, Kumberai.

Some of the children at my school are the children of well-known guerrilla fighters. We have the Zvobgo twin sisters for instance, whose father, Eddison, spent seven years in jail during the war for 'political activism'. He is a war hero now and very famous;' he is in the new government.

There are, it turns out, no white war heroes. None of the army guys for whom I cheered and prayed will be buried at Heroes Acre under the eternal flame. They will not have their bones dug up from faraway battlefields and a driven in stately fashion all the way to Harare for reburial.

We eat elbow to elbow. We brush our teeth next to each other, leaning over shared sinks, our spit mixing together in a toothpaste rainbow of blue and green and white. We shit next to each other in the small, thin-walled booths.

That year, there is a water shortage and we have to conserve water.

Now we must pee on top of each other's pee. One cup of water each every day with which we must brush our teeth and wash our faces in the morning. We have to share bathwater. I am reluctant. Then the new, black matron says, 'Come on, stop this silly nonsense. Skin is skin. In you get.'

While our new matron watches, I climb into the bathwater, lukewarm with the floating skin cells of Margaret and Mary Zvogbo. Nothing happens. I bathe, I dry myself. I do not break out in spots or a rash. I do not turn black.

*

The year I turn twelve, Mum and Dad drive me to Harare, where I write an entrance examination to get into a prestigious, girls-only private high school, and much to everyone's surprise I pass the examination and am accepted into Arundel High School, known by its past and current inmates as the Pink Prison.

Losing Robandi

Mum on Caesar

Rhodesia has more history stuffed into its make-believe, colonial-dream borders than one country the size of a very large teapot should be able to amass in less than a hundred years. Without cracking.

But all the history of this land returns to the ground on which we stand, because all of us (black, white, coloured, Indian, old-timers, newcomers) are fighting for the same thing: tillable, rain-turned-over-fresh, fertile, worm-smelling soil. Land on which to grow tobacco, cattle, cotton, soybeans, sheep, women, children.

In Rhodesia, we are born and then the umbilical cord of each child is sewn straight from the mother onto the ground, where it takes root and grows. Pulling away from the ground cause death by suffocation, starvation. That's what the people of this land believe. Deprive us of the land and you are depriving us of air, water, food, and sex.

*

The British South Africa Company's 1891 Mining Regulations allowed white settlers to peg out farms of up to three thousand acres.

The Lippert Concession tricked King Lobengula of the Matabeles into allowing the settlers land.

In 1894 a British Land Commission declared itself unable to remove white settlers from native land.

In 1898 the British government set up 'sufficient' areas for the exclusive occupation of the African people.

In 1915 the boundaries of the 'Native Reserves' were set up.

In 1920 a Southern Rhodesia Order-in-Council assigned 21.5 million acres (of a possible 96 million acres) for the sole use of Africans.

The 1923 Morris Carter Commission recommended division of land among the races.

The Land Apportionment Act of 1930 divided the country: 21.5 million acres for 'Native Reserves'; 48 million acres for occupation and purchase only by Europeans; and 7.5 million acres for occupation and purchase only by Africans. Seventeen and a half million acres were unassigned.

The Land Apportionment Act was amended in 1941, 1946, and several times in the 1950s and 1960s and the Native Reserves were renamed Tribal Trust Lands.

The Rhodesian government built its policy of racial segregation on the Land Tenure Act of 1969, (repealed in 1979 under growing international and internal pressure).

The Tribal Trust Lands Act was replaced by the Communal Land Act in 1982.

*

'To us the time has now come for those who have fought each other as enemies to accept the reality of a new situation by accepting each other as allies who, in spite of their ideological, racial, ethnic, or religious differences are now being called upon to express loyalty to Zimbabwe. That's what the new 'ZANU (PF)' government announces at the end of the war.

'I'll show them peace and re-bloody-conciliation,' says Mum.

Piss and reconciliation, we call it.

*

Our farm is designated as one of those that, under the new government, may be taken away (for nothing) or bought (at whatever nominal price) by the government for the purpose of 'land redistribution'.

This is how land redistribution goes.

First, the nice farms, near the city, are given to Prime Minister Robert Mugabe's political allies.

Then, the nice farms far from the city are given to those politicians whom Mugabe must appease, but who are not best-beloved.

After that, the productive, tucked-away farms are given to worthy war veterans – to the men, and a few women, who showed themselves to be brave liberation strugglers.

Then farms like ours – dangerously close to existing mine fields, without the hope of television reception and with sporadic rains, unreliable soil, a history of bad luck – are given to Mugabe's enemies, whom he is pretending to appease.

Our farm is a gift of badlands, eel-worm-in-the-bananas, rats-in-the-ceiling.

Our farm is a gift of the Dead Mazungu Baby.

Our farm is gone, whether we like it or not.

Dad shrugs. He lights a cigarette. He says, 'Well, we had a good run of it, hey?'

But already, landless squatters from Mozambique have set themselves up on our farm. Before our farm has been officially auctioned, and the old crop has been pulled in, before the new owners can set foot on the road that leads, ribby and washed away, up to the squat barracks house that Mum painted peach, years ago, to try and cheer us up, before our footsteps are cold on the shiny cement floors of the veranda, the squatters come.

No one invited the squatters to come and take over the farm and other farms close to the border. The squatters are mostly illiterate, unlikely to have been war heroes, but hungry. They are belly-hungry, home-hungry, land-hungry.

They have made themselves a camp up in the hills above the house, they have chopped down virgin forest and planted maize. Their cattle drink straight from hillside springs, crushing creek banks into red erosion, which comes out, in the end, like blood in our tap water.

Mum says, 'I'll show them land re-bloody-redistribution.'

Dad says, 'Too late now.'

Mum grits her teeth and talks between them, so that the words are sharp and white-edged. She says, 'It's not theirs yet. It's still our farm.' She pours brandy straight into a glass and drinks it without pretending to be doing anything else. Straight brandy without water, Coke, lemon. She says, pointing her finger at Dad, 'We fought for this land, Tim! We fought for it,' and she makes her hand into a fist and shakes it. 'And I'm not letting it go without a fight.'

Dad sighs and looks tired. He stomps out his cigarette and lights another.

'I'll go and show those buggers,' says Mum.

'Take it easy, Tub.'

'Take it easy? Take it easy? Why should I take it easy?'

There is a baby, our fifth, swelling in her belly.

Mum started to throw up just after Christmas. She puked when she smelled soap, petrol, diesel fumes, perfume, cooking meat. Which is how we knew she was pregnant again.

I had prayed so hard for another baby, this one might have been conceived out of my sheer willpower.

Now Mum says, 'These bloody *munts* make me feel sick.'

Which is not, apparently, anything to do with morning sickness and everything to do with losing the war.

She has closed down the little school which we used to run for the African children. 'They can go to any school they like now.' But there is no transport for the children, so they hang around under the big sausage tree near the compound, where their mothers have told them not to play. Mum will no longer run a clinic from the back door for the labourers or anyone else who happens through our farm and is ill or malnutritioned.

Now she says, 'Don't you have your *comrades* at the hospital? We're all lovely socialists together now, didn't you know? If you go the hospital, your *comrades* will treat you there.'

'But, madam . . .'

'Don't "But, madam" me. I'm not "madam" anymore. I'm "comrade".'

'You are my mother . . .'

'I am not your bloody mother.'

'We are seeking health.'

'You should have thought of that in the first place.'

The sick, the swollen-bellied, the bleeding, the malarial all sit at the end of the road, past the Pa Mazonwe store, and wait for a lift into town, where they will wait hours, maybe days, for the suddenly flooded, socialized health care system to take care of them.

*

Mum's belly makes it hard for her to get on her horse. She makes Flywell hold Caesar next to a big rock and she hops from the rock into her stirrup and eases herself up. Then she arranges her stomach over the pommel and kicks Caesar on.

'Wait for me!' I yank at Burma Boy's head. He is ear deep in some yellow-flowered black jacks. Mum doesn't even turn around. She whistles to the dogs, one short, sharp note. She is in a dangerous, quiet rage this morning.

We ride up, past the barns and past the turnoff to the cattle dip and past the compound where our labourers live in low-roofed redbrick houses or elaborately patterned huts. We ride up past the small plots where the labourers are allowed to grow their crops of cabbage, rape, beans, and tomatoes and up the newly blazed trails that lead to the new village erected by the squatters.

There is the acid-sweet smell of burning wood on damp air as we follow the patted-down red earth into the squatter village. We can hear the high, persistent wail of a small child and, as we get closer, the frantic yapping of dogs. The squatters have built three mud huts in a circle around a wood fire over which a pot of sadza is bubbling. The curly-tailed African dogs run out at our pack and start to growl, their hackles raised high on bony backs.

'Call your dogs!' Mum shouts into the raw new village (the bush poles that have been cut to make the huts are still bleeding and wet; the thatched roofs smell green – they will not stop water from leaking into the huts when it rains).

The squatters are standing in a row in front of their huts. The baby that has been crying stops now and looks at us in silent astonishment. He is hanging from his mother's back. The other women have slung their small children onto soft, ready hips. The men stand in a row, chins high, mouths soft and sullen. One of the children is coughing, eyes bulging, hair fuzzed a tell-tale protein-deficient red: *kwashiorkor* hair. He is naked except for a pair of threadbare shorts through which I can see his shriveled penis and the tops of his stick-thin legs.

Mum circles around the huts; Caesar spins up the newly stripped earth as he paces. I pull Burma Boy up under one of the huts and sit, crouched into my saddle, watching.

'This is our land!'

The squatters stare back, their expressions not changing.

Mum spurs Caesar on, charging into the impassive group of men, women, and children. The African dogs yelp and flee, cowering, into the dark mouths of the huts. One of the young children, too big to be on a hip but too small to be far from his mother, screams and follows the dogs. The mother with the baby on her back is holding a gourd, used for carrying water or beer. She suddenly, in a rage of bravado, runs at Mum, shouting in a high, tremulous, singing voice, and strikes Caesar on the nose with the container. Caesar backs up, but Mum spins him around again, digs down into her saddle, legs tight. 'Come on,' she growls, and then as Caesar surges forward, his nostrils wide and red-rimmed with surprise, Mum screams at the woman, 'Don't you hit my horse! You hear me? Don't you hit my bloody horse . . .'

Mum charges at the squatters repeatedly, kicking Caesar fiercely and running indiscriminately at the women, the children, the men. And then she turns her horse onto the freshly planted maize field and begins tearing through it, between the still-bleeding stumps of the newly cut msasa trees. 'You fucking kaffirs!' she screams, 'Fucking, fucking kaffirs.'

Some of the men break from the huddle around the huts and start to run after Caesar, shouting and waving their badzas and machetes. The children are all crying now. The women wrap the children in their arms and skirts and shield their faces.

'You bastards!' screams Mum. 'You bloody, bloody bastards. This is our farm!'

One of the men starts to hurl clumps of earth at Mum. They fall damply against Caesar's flank. He shies away, but Mum hunches down and clamps her legs onto him so that the breath comes out – *umph* – and she charges again and again at the squatters. The women scream and run into the huts with the children, shutting the flimsy bush-pole doors behind them. The men stand their ground, heaving whatever comes to hand at Mum and her horse. They are shouting at us in Shona.

I shout, 'Come on, Mum!' Scared. 'Mu-uuum.'

Still she wheels Caesar around again and again; the white

froths of sweat gathering in balls on his neck and flecking out from between his hind legs.

I stand up in my stirrups and scream as loudly as I can, 'Mum! Let's go.'

I start to cry, pleading, 'Mum-umm, please.'

Finally the fight seems to bleed out of her. She turns to the men one last time and shakes her riding crop at them. 'You get off my farm,' she says in a beaten, broken voice, 'you hear? You get the hell off my farm.'

*

Mum has come back from the ride pale and with a light film of sweat on her top lip. She doesn't talk. When we get back to the yard, she slips off the horse, sliding down the saddle on her back, and then grimaces, holding her belly. She lets Caesar wander off, still saddled, reins looped and dragging on the ground, to graze in the garden. I shout for Flywell, frightened by the look of Mum.

Mum pours herself a glass of water and goes into her room. When I go in there, the curtains are drawn and it sounds as if Mum is breathing through her voice.

'Are you all right?'

'Uh-huh.'

'Can I get you some tea?'

'That would be nice.'

So I order the cook to make tea and I bring Mum a cup but she does not drink it.

When Dad comes in from the fields, he goes into the bedroom and stays there. I hear them talking softly to each other. It sounds as if Mum is crying.

*

Vanessa says, 'Why don't we make a cake for Mum?'

I shake my head, 'I don't feel like it.' I go to my room and lie on my bed, staring at the ceiling. It is a hot, sleepy afternoon and I am tired and salt-stinging from the excitement of the morning. My eyes are closing. Puncho, a rescued dog who has attached himself to me, sidles up to my head, licks my face and settles himself happily next to me on the pillow. Sleepily, I start to search under his ears for ticks.

Suddenly, Puncho leaps off the bed, his hackles up, barking in high excitement, and I can hear the other dogs scrambling off the veranda and bursting outside with a volley of barking. An instant later I hear Dad shout, 'You bloody baboons!'

I spring off my bed and run onto the veranda. Mum comes running out of her bedroom, still pale and holding her stomach. 'Quick,' she says, pressing herself against the front door, a simple wooden affair on a hook latch, but without a lock or bolt, 'lean on the door.'

'What's going on?' I ask, pinning my shoulder up against the door.

'Shhh,' Mum hisses. She looks around wildly to see what dogs we have inside. 'Hey Puncho!' Puncho is whining, his nose pressed to the bottom of the door. 'Hsss,' she says to Shea and Sam, 'bark! Sound fierce.'

I can hear Dad shouting on the other side of the door but I cannot hear what he is saying.

'Who is it?'

'Soldiers,' says Mum.

'Army guys?'

'No, not army guys. Soldiers.'

Mum and I are losing the battle of the door. There are two of us leaning with all our might against the door, but it is being pushed from the other side by three grown men. Suddenly, our resistance proves too feeble and the door collapses inward, sending Mum and me sprawling and a clatter of soldiers in on top of us.

I fall as I have been taught. Curl into a ball and cover your head. I bring my arms up and close my eyes. I take a deep, shaky breath.

I am going to die now. I wait. Does a bullet feel red hot coming into you? Do you feel it slicing into your flesh? Will I be dead before I feel pain?

Mum says, '*Fergodsake,* Bobo, get off the floor.'

I open my eyes.

The Zimbabwean army soldiers are standing with their backs against the door. They are staring down at me.

I sit up and find that I have not been shot. The soldiers' eyes are blazing red, and they smell strongly of *ganja* and native-brewed beer. Now that they have pushed our feeble wooden door open and have us at gunpoint, they look a bit sheepish.

Mum says, 'Up!' And then she looks at me strangely. 'Bobo, where's Vanessa?'

'Making a cake.'

'Vanessa!' Suddenly Mum is screaming, 'Vanessa!' and pushing her way past the three soldiers at the door. 'Get out of my way you stupid bloody – Vanessa!'

Vanessa is still in the kitchen, where fright has turned into her habitual seeming-calmness. Two soldiers are observing her from a polite distance, guns aimed casually at her belly, while she pours batter into a cake tin, scrapes the side of the bowl, puts the cake in the oven.

'Are you all right?' screams Mum, rushing toward Vanessa.

'Fine.' Vanessa points to the cookbook lying open on the greasy-topped kitchen table. 'It says forty minutes in a medium oven for the cake.' The woodstove is belching smoke. 'Would you say that is a medium oven?'

Mum is almost sobbing. 'Oh, God,' she says. She catches her breath sharply and holds the edge of the table.

'Are you all right, Mum?'

Mum nods. The soldiers look from Mum to Vanessa and back to Mum, uncertainly. They wave their guns, 'Come on, come on. Outside,' says one of them. They herd Vanessa and Mum out onto the veranda.

'Don't let me forget. Forty minutes,' says Vanessa.

Dad is negotiating with five or six more soldiers on the veranda. They are the new Zimbabwean army, fresh out of guerrilla troops. They are still war-minded. They are still war-trigger-happy.

'You called us baboons.'

'You jumped into my bedroom window. That is not a civilized thing to do, that is a baboon thing to do.'

The soldiers stare belligerently at Dad. There is a long, shuffling silence.

At last Dad says, 'Look, either shoot me or put your fucking guns down and let's talk about this sensibly.'

I want to say, 'Dad was only joking about shooting him. And don't be touchy about being called a baboon. I'm their kid and they call *me* Bobo. Same thing.'

One of the soldiers says, 'Ah, comrade . . .'

Dad says, 'And there's another thing. You can call me Mr Fuller or Silly Old Bugger or Old Goat Fuller or any damn thing you like but comrade . . . never! You can never call me comrade.'

The soldiers look at Dad in astonishment.

'I'm not your comrade.' Dad takes the tip of one of the soldier's guns and moves the barrel out of the way. He says, 'Didn't anyone teach you not to point these things at live targets?'

The afternoon turns into a thick mellow evening, the light filters syrup-yellow and as the heat of the day melts away, so does the anger in the men. The soldiers grow tired; some of them sprawl on the top of the wall, slouched over the barrels of their guns and watch, eyes hooded, as Dad speaks to the soldier who seems to be in charge. Vanessa and I sit on the steps with the dogs, picking ticks out of their coats and popping the little gray and red bodies on the stone flags. Mum is very pale, breathing in quick shallow breaths. At last the soldier in charge stands up and stretches. 'Okay, okay. Let's leave this incident to sleep now. You just keep your wife under control from now on,' he tells Dad. 'This is Zimbabwe now. You can't just do as you please from now. From now it is we who are in charge.'

They drive away. We watch them until their lorry humps over the culvert at the bottom of the drive.

Dad says, 'You okay, Tub?'

Mum nods. She says, 'Let's have a drink.'

Vanessa says, 'Oh no! My cake.'

That night we go out to the Club. While Vanessa and I sit on the black plastic chairs in the smoky bar sipping Cokes and crunching on salt and vinegar chips, kicking our heels against the chair legs, Mum and Dad drink and tell the story of their day's adventure. By the time deep night has come and the nocturnal creatures have started to sing and croak and screech, Mum and Dad are drunk and Vanessa and I are curled up in the back of the car, staring out of the windows at the slowly swinging bright stars as they make their way across the cloud-scudding sky. We are eating our third packet of chips and sipping on dumpy-sized bottles of Coke.

'Did you think you were going to die?' I ask Vanessa, carefully licking a chip to get the salt off it before I put the whole thing into my mouth.

'What?'

'Did you think we were going to be shot by those Affies?'

Vanessa yawns and scrunches up her chip packet. 'Have you finished your chips?'

'No.'

'Give them to me.'

'No!'

'Do you want a Chinese bangle?'

I stuff the remaining chips into my mouth. My eyes sting and tears roll down my cheeks with the effort of it. Vanessa scrambles over the seat and squashes my cheeks together until the food squeezes out of my mouth.

I start to cry. 'I'm telling on you,' I weep. 'I'm telling Mum and Dad.'

Vanessa snorts. 'Go ahead,' she says.

*

Robandi is put up for mandatory auction under the new land distribution programme. It is sold, in the loosest sense of the word, to a black Zimbabwean. The money that changes hands in this exchange doesn't even touch the sides of our pockets. Everything from the farm is given to the Farmer's Co-op, from which we had borrowed money to buy the farm in the first place.

Robandi never belonged to us, and it doesn't belong to the new Zimbabwean farmer. It belongs to the mortgage company. They, alone of everyone, seem unmoved by the fierce fight for land through which we have just come.

Devuli

The Fullers: Devuli

On a recent map entitled 'Comfort-Discomfort Belts', Devuli Ranch is shown in the area of Zimbabwe that is shaded with tight red lines. This means that it is an uncomfortably hot place bordering on oppressive. 'Health and efficiency suffer,' the map's legend says.

The older maps, drawn up in the 1920s, are more blunt. On these old maps, the area in which Devuli Ranch sits has stamped across it in bold black letters, '**Not Fit for White Man's Habitation.**'

Dad bends over a map and shows me: 'See?' He lights a cigarette and points with the two fingers which hold the cigarette at the ranch. Blue smoke floats over the flat, yellow, red-lined patch of map.

There are no towns anywhere near the ranch, and only one thin road leads past it, described on the map as a strip road. I point this out to Dad.

He says, 'Great, isn't it?' He takes a deep pull on his cigarette and shows me. 'Look at the rivers.' There are three rivers running through the ranch.

'Well, that looks watery,' I say, more hopefully.

Dad snorts, 'It just *looks* that way. Dry as a bloody bone.'

'Will we grow tobacco?'

'Cattle,' says Dad. 'I'm going to find their cattle.' His thumb covers hundreds of miles and he moves it slowly across the bottom of the map. 'All this, see? That's where the cattle are. They think.'

The herd went wild during the war. They've started to range and roam like wild herds of eland or kudu. Dad is going to find, herd, dip, vaccinate, dehorn, castrate, cull, and brand a few thousand head of wild Brahman cattle.

'Will we be the only white people?'

'Almost. There's the ranch manager and his wife.'

'Are there any kids?'

'Not white kids.'

'Oh.'

'You can help me round up the cattle.'

'Okay.' I am not enthusiastic.

'There are wild horses, too.'

'Oh. Can we train them?'

'Perhaps.'

'How long will we live there?'

Dad smokes and squints up his blue eyes. He says, 'I've told them if they give me a year, I'll give them their herd back.'

'And then?'

'We'll cross that river when we get to it.'

The Turgwe, Save, and Devure rivers flood once or twice each year, each flood within a few weeks of the last. A great wall of water gushing brownly through the scrubby low mopane woodland makes a roaring sound like a thousand Cape buffalo galloping over hollow ground. Floating carcasses of large animals are caught, legs poking up among washed-away trees. Smaller animals, still alive, cling wide-eyed to the branches of the barrelling trees, bodies hunched, wet faces pinched with fear. By morning, the flood is over. The rivers lie almost still, swollen, sluggish. And then the rivers dry into smaller and smaller pools, stinking and lurking with scorpions, until nothing is left of them but glittering white sand.

The Africans and animals who have learned to live down here near the ranch, in the low veldt, dig deep wells into the dry riverbeds until they reach the black, dank water that lies there. For nine months out of every year, these warm, barely ample wells feed everything that is alive within a fifty-mile radius.

Which will, very shortly, include us.

Between these three rivers lies Devuli Ranch. Seven hundred and fifty thousand mostly flat acres of scrubby, bitter grass, mopane woodland, acacia thorn trees, thorny scrub, and the occasional rocky outcrop. The cattle have not been touched for ten years – almost the entire war. There are second-, third- and fourth-generation Brahman cows running wild on the ranch.

Brahman cows are the wildest of all domesticated cattle, notoriously jumpy and hard to handle even when they do have frequent human contact. They are strangely feral-looking, with their elaborate humped shoulders and sweeping dewlaps and floppy ears. And these cows have been alone so long that they have become hardy and prone to spooking, like prey animals.

For there is also an abundance of leopard in the kopjes. Kopje, Afrikaans for 'head'. That's how these small hills look, like buried black giant heads in the hot sand. The leopards are as still as dappled blankets rumpled against the grey rock; their flanks beating in the heat like fluttering leaf-shadows. They watch the young spring Brahman calves by day and they hunt by night. Leopards kill at the throat, one efficient, powerful bite to the jugular. Which is why they can hunt alone.

We bring our new cook, Thompson, with us from the farm, and our nanny, Judith, who has recently changed her name to Loveness. They step out of the car and their faces twist with disgust.

'It's alone,' says Judith/Loveness.

'Alone what?' asks Mum.

'All alone.'

Thompson says, 'Too much sand, madam.'

Cephas, our tracker, has also come with us from Robandi and it is as if his feet have hit the earth on which he was meant to walk when he steps out of the car. His whole body seems to twitch with excitement in the stupefying heat. The rest of us blink at the shiny, flat, scrubby landscape and feel thirst. Cephas scans the horizon, his nostrils grow wide, and he feels Life.

'They drink blood,' he tells me.

'Who?'

'Leopards.'

'Why?'

'For fun. Leopard beer.' He laughs.

Cephas has been designated the family's tracker. For most of the time, while I am at school, he is tracking wild cattle for Dad and wild game for the pot. During the holidays, I can go anywhere on the ranch, as long as Cephas is with me – he tracks to make sure we are not walking into a leopard's tree or the place where a snake likes to sleep. And in this landscape, which is turn-around-the-same no matter which way you face (more mopane and scrub and acacia), Cephas makes sure we don't get lost.

*

Within a tall security fence near the entrance to the ranch, there are several houses for white people, although all but two are abandoned. The ranch manager and his wife live in one house.

They kill leopards and Vanessa and I skulk close to their house and see the stretched-out skins on wire racks at the back of their yard. We tell Dad.

We say, 'They're poaching leopards.'

Dad says, 'Oh, hell.'

'Oh, hell, what?'

'Don't say "hell".'

'*You* did.'

'Do what I say, not what I do.'

We live in a small, white house surrounded by bare sandy ground and, for shade, two acacia trees. In the garden, left over from the war, is a snake-infested bombproof bunker which is accessed through a heavy metal door in the floor in my room. There is a generator at the workshops, which provides a spluttering, surging electricity for us from six in the evening until ten at night. At ten o'clock the lights dim once, to warn us to climb into our beds or light candles, and then in a minute the whole place is plunged into darkness and the kind of shattering silence that comes after a generator has been shut off.

To my relief, I discover that we do not have to rely on the rivers for water. We receive thin, saline water from a borehole within the security fence. There is just enough for baths and flushing the loo, and for pots of tea, but hardly enough to keep a few struggling vegetables in the garden. During the long, hot, dry months, we find miraculous isolated dams in the far reaches of the ranch. They are almost forgotten-about reservoirs constructed forty years earlier by the original cattlemen who settled this place.

The house is surrounded by a gauze-covered veranda on which there is a meat safe to keep recently shot impala carcasses, and bins where we store horse feed. The meat safe is an old one, a wooden-framed closet with metal gauze on all sides to allow for a cross breeze. The carcasses grow an oily translucent skin, which protects the meat below from going off too quickly, although we must still eat the entire animal within a week.

We eat impala at each meal. Fried, baked, broiled, minced.
Impala and rice.
Impala and potatoes.
Impala and sadza.
Tinned beans.
Tinned peas.
Tinned peas and beans with impala.
Bran flakes for breakfast if we're lucky, oat porridge if we're not.

We drink thin, animal-smelling milk, which comes from a small herd of skinny beef cows. These are cows caught and tamed from the wild herd. The milk they give is reluctant.

We eat Mum's cottage cheese, which hangs from mutton cloth dripping into a basin in the hot kitchen.

And fresh rolls of bread made by Thompson every morning and baked in the woodstove and which we also sell to the ranch labourers from a little store in the compound. Five cents for a bun. Twenty cents for a bun and a Coke.

Last thing at night we are allowed a glass of milk with Milo in it – a crunchy, sweet, supposedly chocolate-tasting powder. But nothing can disguise the taste of the reluctant milk.

Mutare General

Mum and Dad

The doctor in Mutare is old – old for anybody. He is especially old for a doctor and especially old for an African. But he doesn't have the luxury of retirement to look forward to. There aren't enough doctors in Africa. Those who choose to become doctors here don't do it for the money or because they want to do good. They do it because they have to heal, the way most people need to breathe or eat or love. They can't stop. As long as they are alive, they will never not be a doctor. They can be old, or alcoholic, or burnt-out, but they will always be a doctor.

Even if a doctor decides to leave and stop being a doctor, people will still come to him from miles around to present severed limbs, labouring sisters, children flinging themselves backwards, rigid with cerebral malaria.

A shit, carefully wrapped in a mealie leaf, is brought on the back of a bicycle through October heat and presented with proud, agonizing care at a clinic. 'Here look! I am with blood when I go.'

This is the place where educated eight-year-old farm children are taught how to stabilize a broken limb, perform CPR, deliver a baby.

'The mother should not push or bear down until the child is beginning to move down into the birth canal, and she feels she has to push.'

Dr Mitchell, the doctor in Mutare, is old and bent and very white, bordering on grey. No European African manages such white skin in Africa unless he is up before dawn, works in an office all day, and comes home after dark, seven days a week.

Mum starts having problems with the pregnancy. She says her problems are caused by the stress of independence. Losing the war. Losing the farm. She has heart palpitations and she is carrying too much fluid in her womb. She has started to look yellow. Her red hair has turned black and then grey from all the medication she takes and all the stress she is under. She bleeds and cramps. And Dad says, 'Let this one go.'

'What?'

We hear them fighting.

'It didn't have a good start.'

Mum is sobbing, 'He, heee, heeeeee.'

'Come on, Tub. Maybe this one isn't meant to happen, hey?' He sounds gentle with her.

'Heeee, heeeee.'

Dad gets up in the dark, lights a candle and a cigarette. I hear him sighing, walking down the corridor, and the bitter-acrid smell of tobacco smoke curls into my room. I shut my eyes tight and close my fists and want to hold on to the baby in Mum's belly.

'Let's not let this one go,' I say to myself.

Dr Mitchell says that if Mum wants the baby then she needs to lie down all day and night and be close to a hospital just in case. If she wants the baby.

Mum wants the baby.

Vanessa and I want Mum to have the baby.

So she goes into the hospital in Mutare with her too-much-fluid-in-the-womb and her heart palpitations which she says feel like butterflies escaping into her throat. She takes a pile of books. Her friends from the Burma Valley bring her magazines and chocolates and sometimes beer. She lies down for weeks and weeks in the hospital.

Every day Mum watches from her window in the maternity ward.

Here is the line of Africans with their sick, dying, malarial, malnourished children and their severed, broken, bleeding limbs. Here they have come with their swollen wombs. And they have brought their curled bodies like tadpoles, small on the drying lawn, where they leak dysentery and diarrhoea. Some of them are Africans who would have come to our clinic. Or to the Mazonwe clinic. Or to any one of hundreds of clinics that used to be run by farmers' wives on remote farms across the area. Now they wait for a lift into town and after that they wait in the slow, yellow, fly-crawling sun. There aren't enough nurses or beds and there isn't enough medicine for all of them. Mum sighs and turns onto her side and her face falls long and old and yellow into the government-issue sheets (left over from the days of Rhodesia, but beginning to thin and tear). She starts to cry again.

Loo Paper and Coke

Van and Bobo on a kopj

Dad takes Vanessa and me with him while he's out looking for stray wild cattle and fencing the vast, unfenced ranch. We drive for two days to reach this particular herd. Dad is in the front, smoking, alone with his thoughts. Vanessa and I are in the back of the Land Rover with the dogs and the African labourers, bumping with our skinny bottoms on the spare tyre and singing against the loud scream of the diesel engine cutting through roadless land, 'If you think Ah 'm sexy and you want my body . . .' The Africans are crouched, quiet, gently rocking with the sway of the Land Rover. We travel for two days like this, blowing out tyres on camel thorns, climbing over fallen trees, churning through dried-out flash-flood riverbeds.

'Come on,' Dad shouts, 'everyone *getoutandpush*!'

And we leap over the edge of the back, all of us tumbling, scrambling for earth under numb muscles, hurrying before the Land Rover loses what little momentum it has. And we shout in Shona, '*Potsi, piri, tatu, ini*!' One, two, three, four!

And 'Push!'

'Ah, ah, ah!'

The men start to sing. '*Potsi, piri, tatu, ini*!'

The Land Rover bites. The dogs are out, too, herding, barking at the back tyres. 'Yip-yip.'

The Land Rover finds edible ground and surges forward; we cling to the tailgate, jostling for a place. Dad won't stop in case he gets stuck again. We climb aboard while the Land Rover spins ahead.

Dad stops on level, solid ground and we all get out to pee. The men congregate at the front of the Land Rover, Vanessa and I crouch behind the back wheels.

She says, 'Keep boogies for me. Make sure they aren't spying.'

So I keep boogies. And when she has finished I say, 'Keep boogies for me,' and she nonchalantly climbs back into the Land Rover. 'Hey, that's not fair. I kept boogies for you.'

'So?'

'Then keep boogies for me.'

'You're just a kid, you don't count.'

I pee quickly, crouching, looking over my shoulder. The sweet smell of pee steams up to me from the burning sand, sand hot enough to evaporate pee on contact.

Dad has a compass. He looks at the sun, lights a cigarette. He gets down on his haunches and looks through the trees for a straight passage, wide enough for the Land Rover to fit between the trunks of the thickly-growing mopane.

The men, who have been saving their own cigarettes, stick by stick from one payday to the next, relight old stompies and take two or three drags, holding the smoke deep in their lungs before exhaling, and then carefully pinching the end off their cigarettes, saving them for later.

Cephas has found impala tracks while we are waiting for everyone to pee and to stretch the kinks out of their bones. He shows Dad, without talking, his shoulders shrugging casually in the direction of the thick bush.

'Fresh?' asks Dad.

Cephas reads the ground the way we read a map or a signpost. 'They passed this way within one hour.'

'Can we catch them?'

'They are moving slowly.' Cephas points to newly pinched shrubs. 'Eating.'

So Dad says, 'You girls want to come or stay here?'

The sun is starting to fall into its own fiery pool of colour behind the mopane trees and the air is releasing night smells. Vanessa and I know that in less than an hour we are going to be bunched-up, shivering cold.

'Stay here, thank you, Dad.'

'Keep the dogs, hey?'

'*Ja*.'

We hold the dogs by the scruff of the neck until Dad is out of sight.

Dad shoulders his .303. He lights a cigarette. Cephas starts to run ahead, darting, ducking, zigzagging. It's as if he's sniffing the ground. Dad follows, his quick strides swallowing ground.

Vanessa and I hunker down next to the Land Rover with the dogs. We have both brought books, but the books need to last us for weeks while we are in camp. We have been in charge of our own packing. Dad said, 'You girls are old enough now to pack for yourselves.'

We have packed teabags, powered milk, sugar, and bran flakes for breakfast. Zimbabwean bran flakes taste like barely crushed tree bark. We have tins of baked beans and fish in tomato sauce for lunch. We have brought two shirts, two pairs of shorts, two pairs of brookies, and a jersey each. We already realize that we have forgotten to pack loo paper.

Dad has packed cigarettes, brandy, bullets and his gun.

Vanessa pulls out the packet of cards. 'Want to play war?'

'Okay.'

She deals. We play in the failing evening light, which is going in fast stages from mellowing yellow-red into dusky grey, filtered through the trees. The sun sets below the horizon and it is suddenly dark-black. The moon has not yet risen. We put the cards away. The temperature drops from strangling heat to goose-pimple cold in a matter of minutes. The men climb out of the back of the Land Rover and build a fire, to the west of the vehicle, using the body of the car as a windbreak. They slump on their haunches and stretch out their hands to the fire, resting elbows on knees. They relight their stumps of cigarettes and start to talk, their voices rising and falling like wind coming from a distance.

Vanessa and I hunch beside the men, arms outstretched to the warmth of the fire. The men shuffle aside to make room for us, offer us a pull off their carefully smoked cigarettes, and laugh when we shake our heads.

We wait for Dad.

When the men get hungry they boil water and add a fistful of cornmeal into a pot for sadza. Into another pot they throw beans, oil, salt and sliced dry meat for the relish. One man gets up and fills a small bowl with water from the drums in the back of the Land Rover. The water bowl is passed around and we all wash our hands. Now we eat, squashing balls of hot sadza with the fingers of our right hands and scooping up a little of the gravy onto the ball of meal. The men eat communally from dishes that sit in the middle of us, everyone eating slowly, eyeing their neighbours, careful not to take too much. Each man finishes when he is full, washes his hands from the small bowl. The men relight their cigarettes.

By the time Dad and Cephas return, the moon has risen in

the east and is hanging low over the trees, sending a silver light over the faces around the fire. Cephas comes first. He is walking effortlessly with an eighty-pound impala ram slung over his shoulders, the little black-socked feet caught in his fists. Dad follows with the gun. The impala has been field-dressed; the stomach and guts have been left in the bush for hyenas, jackals and the morning-circling vultures.

Dad has killed the impala with one shot to the heart. I insert my forefinger into the passage where the bullet has gone. It is still warm and wet with quickly robbed life. There is a tinny smell of blood, and there are animal smells that waft up from the carcass – the smells this ram carried with it in life: dust, rutting, shit, sun, rain. Live ticks still suck from the dead animal, clustered where the skin is most soft, near the animal's ears and genitals and on its stomach. Its eyes bulge hugely under eyelashes as long as my finger.

Cephas hangs the impala from a tree and slits its throat, and blood gushes out onto the ground where the dogs are waiting, tongues hanging.

We pull out sleeping bags and set up to sleep around the fire. Dad heats up some baked beans for supper, which he washes down with brandy and warm, silty-tasting water. We can hear the hyenas starting their evening scour: '*Waaaa-oooop!*' '*Waaaa-oooop!*' The dogs, blood-spattered and bellies distended, growl and press themselves against our sleeping bags.

'*Waaaa-ooooop!*'

*

The next morning we are up before dawn. It is too cold to sleep. The men stoke the fire and boil water for tea. Dad smokes. We curl stiff-cold hands around our tin cups and suck on the milky sweet tea until the sun startles up over the horizon, flooding pink light through the trees to our camp. It is almost immediately warm. In an hour it will be so hot that sweat will run in stinging rivulets into our eyes and dust will stick onto fresh sweat. For now, it is cool enough. Food and tea, wood-smoke flavoured, are sweet comfort. The mourning doves begin their sad call, *'Wuwu-woo. Wuwu-woo.'* The Cape turtle dove is crying, *'Kuk-KOORR-ru! Work hard-er. Work hard-er.'*

The men wash up from breakfast and Vanessa packs the breakfast food and tea back into Dad's old ammunition box. We scramble up into the back of the Land Rover and sit in a circle, perched around the impala. The men begin to sing, picking up songs and tunes from each other. They are songs of work and love and war. They are the songs of men who live too long at a stretch without women.

When we reach the permanent camp on the banks of the Turgwe River, Dad skins the impala and hangs it from the bush pole that holds up the tarpaulin under which we keep food, dishes, and the drums of water for washing. Dad points to the drums. 'Don't ever drink this water,' he tells Vanessa and me. It comes from the shrinking, slime-frothed pools of water, warm and green with stagnant life, that are all that remains of the Turgwe River's last flood.

During the day, Dad and the men drive to the fence lines and continue to set stakes in the ground, stretching wire into which they will one day herd the wild Brahmans. Some days, Dad drives all day with maps to find the old, decaying dips and kraals. He leaves a span of men at these old cattle camps to fix the holes in the concrete walls and reinforce the old races. He leaves them with food, cigarettes, matches. 'I'll be back in two days,' he tells them. 'You fix this place by then?'

'Yes, boss.'

'Then *faga moto!*'

Dad wants to dip the wild cattle before the rains come in October–November.

Vanessa and I stay in camp and read, or climb the boulder that overlooks the Turgwe River and sing into microphone–baobab pods, 'If you think Ah'm sexy and you want my body, come on baby let it show.'

'Those aren't the words.'

'Okay, then.' I stick out thin hips and rock back and forth: 'There's a brown girl in the rain, tra-la-la-la-la! There's a brown girl in the rain, tra-la-la-la-la-la. Brown girl in the rain. Tra-la-la-la-la. She looks like sugar in your bum. Tra-la-la!'

'I'm telling Dad.'

'What?'

'You said 'bum'.'

I climb higher on the boulder until I am balanced precariously on the thin-shouldered top. 'Bum!' I shout into the stunned midday heat. 'Bum! Bum!'

Vanessa says, 'You're so *immature*.' She goes back into camp and I am left with my bad word echoing around in the dusty quiet bush. *Bum*.

That is a day Dad has gone with old maps to find a kraal and he is late coming back into camp. We have been in camp for two weeks and the drinking water is running low. We must use the drinking water carefully, only for brushing teeth and drinking. When the plastic containers of drinking water have run out we will have to turn to the tanks of river water pulled from the Turgwe. We are already making tea from boiled river water – boiled for ten minutes and strained to get rid of the lumps of dirt, hippo shit, the worst of the silt.

Vanessa is reading under the tree. She has set Shea up as a pillow and is lying on Shea's belly.

I say, 'I'll make a cake.'

Vanessa doesn't answer.

'Do you want to make a cake with me?'

'No.'

I make a cake out of dirt, leaves, bark and water. I decorate it with stones and sticks, sprinkle it with shiny white sand. I put it on a rock to bake in the dying light of the sun. Then I am bored. I lie on my stomach in the flat dirt, poking pieces of grass into ant lion traps. I catch ants and drop them into the tiny tunnel-shaped traps and watch the ant lions scurry up, minute claws waving, to catch the scrambling ants. I lie on my back and squint up at the sky, watching blue through the fronds of the ivory palm tree.

I roll back onto my knees, 'Should we have tea?' I ask Vanessa.

Vanessa has fallen asleep over her book. Shea is sleeping, too. I watch their stomachs rise and fall in soft, warm slumber.

The fire has gone out. I soak a teabag in the tepid water from the drum which sits under a fresh impala carcass. Powdered milk dropped into my cup floats on top of the water in lumpy obstinance. I take a few sips before the taste of it swells in my throat and I grimace. 'Yuck.'

By the time Dad comes into camp, Vanessa is holding me up over a fallen log, rear end hanging over one side of it, head hanging over the other. I am naked; all my clothes are in a bag in the tent, soiled with frothy yellow shit. Vanessa has a grip on my shoulders; there is shit streaming from my bum, vomit dribbling into a pool between Vanessa's feet.

'She drank the wrong water,' says Vanessa when Dad comes. 'She made tea without boiling the water first.'

Then there is nothing left inside me. I gag dryly, my bowels clutch and spasm but all that comes out of me is thin yellow liquid. Vanessa wipes my mouth and bum with a fistful of leaves and grass. She bathes me, running water over my burning skin from a bucket, and then wraps me in a towel. She carries me to the tent, which is rank with the smell of my soiled clothes. Dad throws them into a pit fire at the back of the camp where we burn garbage – old baked-bean tins, cigarette packets, empty cereal boxes, and used teabags. Vanessa props me up and tries to feed me some hot tea. I am so thirsty my throat seems stuck together, my tongue feels swollen and cracked. As soon as the liquid hits my belly, I vomit again.

My bum and mouth are raw and both begin to bleed.

Dad says, 'We should have packed some Cokes.'

'And loo paper,' says Vanessa. She licks her finger and wipes the edges of my mouth with her moist fingertip. I loll back against her arm. She says, 'Hold on, Chookies.' She strokes sweat-wet hair off my forehead and rocks me. 'Hold on,' she tells me.

We have a radio in the Land Rover. Dad drives up to the top of a small rise overlooking the river and calls headquarters. The radio hisses and cackles.

'Devuli HQ, Devuli HQ, this is Devuli mobile. Do you read? Over.'

The radio squeaks, swoops, *'Wee-arrr-ooo.'*

Dad calls again, but there is no answer.

Dad comes back to camp. 'We'll have to try again at seven, when they're waiting for us.' We have been checking in every evening at seven to see if Mum has had the baby.

He says, 'I'll mix up some rehydration salts.' He stirs two level teaspoons of sugar and half a teaspoon of salt into a litre of boiled water. Vanessa holds up my head, and Dad feeds teaspoons of the liquid into my mouth. I start to retch; bile dribbles, bitter and stinging, down my chin.

At seven, Dad drives the Land Rover back up to the rise and radios again. 'Bobo's sick; vomiting and diarrhoea. She's too sick to move. If we try and move her . . . she won't make it back. Any advice? Over.'

The ranch manager's wife comes onto the radio. 'Have her sip some salt, sugar, and water. You know the amounts? Over.'

'Affirmative. We've tried that. No go. Over.'

The manager's wife is quiet. At last she replies, 'Don't know what to say, Tim.'

Dad slumps over the radio.

*

The next day Dad stays in camp with me instead of going out to herd wild cattle. I am feeling light-headed, losing the feeling of my body. When Dad pinches the skin on my arm, it stays puckered up in a tiny tent of skin. My feet are starting to swell.

He tells Vanessa to keep on trying to feed me the rehydration salts. I keep vomiting. By late the next afternoon, I am too tired to keep my eyes open. Vanessa goes into the old ammunition box and finds a wrinkled orange, the last saved piece of fresh food in our store. She slices it open and comes back into the tent. 'Here,' – she presses a quarter of orange between my teeth – 'suck on this.'

Dad says, 'I don't think she should eat fruit.'

Vanessa looks at him.

Dad hunches miserably. He lights a cigarette. 'You're right,' he says. 'Might as well, hey. Try it.'

The orange juice trickles down my throat and falls into my empty, air-blown belly. It stays.

That night Dad feeds me a bowl of soft, watery sadza. He says, 'Eat this. If this doesn't plug you up, I don't know what will.'

The mealie porridge sticks against my teeth and slides into my belly.

'One more bite.'

I swallow and take one more bite, then I say enough and lie back on my cot and shut my eyes.

I can hear the men around the camp fire singing softly, taking it in turns to pick up a tune, the rhythm as strong as blood in a body. The firelight flickers off the blue and orange tent in pale, dancing shapes and there is the sweet smell of the African bush, wood smoke, dust, sweat. My bones are so sharp and thin against the sleeping bag that they hurt me and I must cover my hip bones with my hands.

I make a vow never to leave Africa.

Ranch Work

Meat

We're running out of water again: the second tank of brackish, throat-clinging water from the river has nearly run out. Our tea has started to taste like the bottom of the water tank, metallic and singeing. It's so hot, the bush feels narrow, slender, barely-hanging-on. Everything is still. We drive past impala and they barely flinch, shoulders hunched under the thin, fluttering shadows of thorn scrub. The only things moving are their little, alarm-flashing tails. Even the wild cattle are subdued by the heat. Dad has them in the kraal. They bleat weakly; their sound is dry and wispy, evaporating into the dust. There is a wood fire in which there are four branding irons, getting hot. And a kettle in which Dad is boiling water for tea.

Dad tells the men to push the cattle through the chases. They make a run at the cows. The cows stir; dust rises and is a blinding, blonde mist. They begin to cry like foghorns. Dad says, 'Bloody idiots.' And then 'Stop!' These are lowveldt men, who have never herded cattle before. They are bush men. They can make fire by rubbing two sticks together and they can kill impala with a spear. They can snare rabbits and live off stagnant river wells. They can tell their way from one end of the ranch to the other in the dark by reading stars, but they cannot herd cattle.

They are herding cattle the way they would herd impala into a baobab-rope net. Waving arms, coming at a run, 'Woooooop!'

'Stop!'

The men stop. The dust settles. The cows are jittery now, ready to startle.

Dad says, '*Pole, pole*, eh?'

'Boss?'

'Slowly, slowly, catch a monkey.'

The men look confused.

'Come on, Vanessa. Bobo. Let's show them how to herd cows.'

We come at the cows slowly. 'Dip-dip-dip-dip-dip,' we sing. The cows start to move forward. The herd leader – an old, scarred bull with a mean slant to his horns – is anxious. He looks over his shoulder and makes a sweeping, half-threatening gesture at Dad that could also be a halfhearted attempt to shoo a fly. Dad has him cornered. 'Dip-dip-dip-dip.' Dad lowers his eyes, sticks a shoulder out and down: 'Dip-dip-dip-dip.' The old bull begins to make his way into the races.

Dad won't allow sticks, shouting. He won't allow the cows to run. 'Stress them, and they'll drop their babies too early. They'll lose weight. They'll sicken and die.' Dad comes from the side, showing the cow his shoulders. He whistles gently. The cows stop looking panicked and they begin to move calmly towards the race. They have dumb cow faces on now, they will go anywhere. 'Treat your cows nicely and they'll treat you nicely,' says Dad.

Charlie Chilvers

Leopard skin: Devuli

Dad knocks on the door. 'Tea's ready!' It's still dark, not quite four o'clock. Dad has lit a candle in the bathroom and there is a paraffin lamp hissing bluely on the dining-room table where Thompson has laid out tea. He has already put a basket in the car with our breakfast: boiled eggs; small twists of newspaper containing pinches of salt; slices of buttered bread; bananas; and a thermos flask of black coffee. The milk is in a small, separate plastic bottle.

Before five, we pile into the Land Rover and head for Mutare. Dad likes to get to town by nine in the morning, when the shops are just starting to open. Dad shops like a man who hates the exercise, spinning in and striding the aisles, paying with scribbled cheques, and hurrying out, buckling and overladen with baked beans, candles, soap, oil, yeast, flour, engine oil, toilet paper enough to last a month or two. The young grocery clerks, who run from the stores in their aprons, anxious to help with the bags and boxes and earn a tip, are growled away. Vanessa and I are not allowed in the stores with Dad; we have to guard the car.

We eat lunch in the car, waiting for Dad while he flies around in Duly Motors or the Farmers' Co-op yelling his orders, shouting his hellos and goodbyes, waving over the back of his head as he leaves, and then we drive home so that we are back at seven or eight, in time for a warm beer and hot supper.

Today, the mourning dove is just starting to call as Dad starts the Land Rover. '*Wuwu-woo. Wuwu-woo.*' His lament is drowned out by the rattle of the Land Rover on the pocketed, spiny road. We drive out of HQ (the sleepwalking watchman opens the gate for us and salutes blearily to a cloud of swallowing dust) and turn left into the faint glimmer of a sunrise, crawling over the bridge spanning the Devure River. Vanessa and I bump sleepily next to Dad. The Land Rover makes such a roar it is impossible to talk. My mind is empty of everything but the road ahead; the flashing baobabs; the droppings on the road which I silently acknowledge as having been left by impala, kudu, hyena (bright white, like bones on the road). At ten o'clock Dad shouts above the noise the engine is making, 'Anyone hungry?' We nod together.

Dad pulls up under a baobab tree and switches off the engine. The sounds of the bush suddenly flood in on us. Hot, crackling, dry-bush sounds: crickets, doves, grasshoppers. Vanessa unpacks the picnic basket while I run around trying to find intact baobab pods so that we can crack open their hairy shells and suck the sour white powder off the seeds. The baboons have beaten me to it.

We each find a rock to sit on and a patch of shade to sit under. The cover of the baobab's leafless branches is sparse. We eat quietly, dipping our peeled boiled eggs into the twists of salt and biting off hunks of buttered bread. Dad pours the coffee and hands us each a tin cup. The coffee is sweet and strong. We eat and drink without talking and then silently pack up the debris of our picnic before the mopane bees and wasps and ants are attracted. Dad lights a cigarette and Vanessa and I breathe deeply to catch the first, fresh, breath of newly fired tobacco. He sits back down on his rock. Vanessa and I sit next to him. Vanessa is mindlessly drawing designs in the sand, tracing patterns. I lean my chin on my knees and watch ants bump against my bare toes, scuttle across the top of my feet. I stroke a small stick in their path to watch them jolt out of their busy line, the line leading toward the few spare crumbs dropped on our picnic. I sigh happily.

The world looks better when your belly is full, brighter and more hopeful.

*

After Dad has done all the shopping and we are sweaty, sticking to the seat where flesh meets vinyl, he says, 'Let's see how Mum's doing, hm?' Which is what Vanessa and I have been hoping for.

Mum is in bed, looking pale, almost grey and too old to be having a baby. There is a woman in the bed next to her who has had a baby girl the day before and the little girl is covered from head to toe in thick black hair like a baboon.

Afterwards, in the car, Vanessa says, '*Ohmygod*, all that hair!'

'It's called lumbago. It's normal,' I say.

'No, it isn't.'

'Yes, it is. I read it in a medical book.'

Dad says, 'Lumbago is what old men get.'

'See?'

'Or something like that. Anyway, it'll fall out.'

'How do you know?'

'I read it.'

'Maybe the mother'll shave it.'

'I promise you, it'll fall out.'

Vanessa says, 'I hope our baby isn't a hairy baboon.'

Mum holds us close to her, a woman thirsty for her children, and breathes deeply, almost drinking us. And then she wrinkles her nose and says, 'Whew! When was the last time you two washed your hair?'

Vanessa and I look at each other. Dad hates hospitals and he's self-conscious about the woman with the new baby in the bed next to Mum's. He's terrified she might start breastfeeding.

He says, 'Grub all right in here, Tub?'

Mum says, 'When was the last time the girls washed their hair?'

'I don't know. They're old enough to wash their own hair, aren't they?'

'You have to supervise them.'

'In the bath?'

'Yes, Tim. In the bath. Or get Judith to stay late.' Mum sighs and presses herself back on her pillows.

Vanessa says, 'It's okay, Mum, really. We'll wash our hair. Dad doesn't need to watch.'

*

Vanessa has boobs now. She stands in front of the only mirror in our house, which is in the bathroom, and jumps up to catch fleeting, bopping glimpses of them. Once she stood on the washing basket, to get a glimpse of her boobs in the mirror without having to flop up and down, but the lid fell through before she could get a good look.

'They're nice,' I assure her. 'Quite big.'

She says scornfully, 'What do you know.' She adds, 'You have holes in your knickers.'

Which is true.

'And you don't sit with your legs together, so everyone can see you have holes in your knickers. And they're grauby.'

'What are grauby?'

'Your knickers. They're all grey and holey.'

'Well . . .' I am close to tears. 'They're handed down from you,' I say, 'that's why. You get new knickers and I have to get your old knickers when you've *peed* in them for three years.'

'I don't pee in my knickers.'

'*Ja, ja.*'

Vanessa shuts her eyes at me in exquisite pain and sighs deeply.

*

And then Mum notices our fingernails and says, 'For heaven's sake, Tim, no wonder Bobo got diarrhoea.'

I say, 'Mum, can I feel the baby?' I stretch out my hand, ready to put it on her belly.

'No,' says Mum irritably. She sighs again, like she's on the edge of screaming or crying. 'Have you been riding?'

'Every day when we haven't been camping.'

'Good girl. Wear your riding hat.'

'I will.'

And then to Vanessa, 'Are you drawing?'

Vanessa nods.

Mum closes her eyes. We kiss her cheek. 'Have the baby soon,' I say.

Vanessa says, 'I'll get the baby's room ready.'

Dad says, 'Pecker up, Tub.'

*

We leave Mutare and now we're on the strip road leading home. All of us miserable, lonely without Mum. We don't want to wash our hair alone and have no one to tell us to cut our fingernails. We want Mum to come home. Our want floods the inside of the Land Rover and spills out behind us with the diesel fumes.

It's past the place where Dad needs to pay attention to the

road – there hasn't been any other traffic for miles and miles – when we see the white woman hitchhiking.

'A hijacker!' says Vanessa.

'It's a lady.'

'We can't leave her there,' says Dad, stomping out his cigarette in the spilling ashtray above the gear stick. He pulls up. The woman, who has been bent over an ambitiously swollen backpack, looks up at us, pushes a fringe of clean blonde hair out of her eyes, and smiles. 'Hi,' she says, her voice flat with Australia (dust, boomerangs, kangaroos, convicts, eucalyptus, sheep), 'I'm Charlie Chilvers.'

Dad says, 'Budge up, kids.'

Vanessa and I squash together.

'Where are you going?'

Charlie Chilvers says, 'Wherever you're going, mister,' and she smiles again and her smile is such a smile. Just so. A smile with nothing behind it. And her face is without worry and anxiety and anger and loss. Her face is hopeful and open and hungry for experience.

Dad says, 'Hell, you don't want to go where we're going.'

'Where's that?'

'To the dogs,' says Dad, 'to the bloody dogs.'

Charlie laughs and climbs in. 'Hi, kids,' she says.

Dad says, 'Mind if I smoke?' I've never heard him ask anyone's permission before and it makes me stare at Charlie harder. She's crisp and sharp-sweet, like the white under the green skin of a Granny Smith apple.

Charlie says, 'Hell, no,' and I am already in love with her.

That night Charlie helps Vanessa and me wash our hair. She has strong, smooth, brown, muscled arms. By breakfast the next morning, it feels as if Charlie has been with us for years.

She says, 'Who wants to go riding today?'

'I do, I do.'

Even Vanessa says, 'Maybe.'

Dad says, 'I'll see you girls later. Charlie, you all right here?'

'This is great,' says Charlie, 'it's a luxury to be sitting still for a while.'

*

Every night we go to the manager's house to get the phone call from Mutare General Hospital and Vanessa and I have to sit on the manager's wife's dining-room chairs while Dad shouts down the line at the nurse. And the news is always the same. Mum's fine, no baby.

Then one night Dad says, 'What? Say again?' and we sit up.

'What? Dad! What?'

'Hold on!' shouts Dad. He puts his hand over the receiver and shushes us. 'I can hardly hear. The line . . .'

So we hold our breath.

'A boy.'

'Weee-oooop!'

Dad puts his hand over the receiver again and tells us, 'Hey, keep it down, you two! I can't hear a thing.'

Vanessa says, 'Let's call him Richard.'

'Steven,' I say.

'How about Richard Steven?'

'Richard Steven Fuller,' I agree.

But Dad looks worried, almost cross. 'Shhh.' He frowns at the manager's wife.

She takes us out of the room. She looks worried and cross, too. It isn't the look most people have when a new baby has just been born. She says, 'Would you girls like some Milo?'

'No, thanks.'

But she makes us wait in the long, dark corridor (in which there are photos of her and her son and her husband standing next to various shiny, fat cows and woolly sheep).

'You wait here.'

Her dogs – a German shepherd and a Chihuahua – follow her into the kitchen. Vanessa and I don't look at each other, we look at the photos of the ranch managers and all their prize animals. The door to the dining room is shut. I can't hear Dad's voice. I try putting my ear to the door.

Vanessa says, 'Don't.'

'I want to hear.'

'Look at these photos.' She points to a photo of the wife standing next to a ram.

'They don't take very good care of their sheep now,' I say. The ranch sheep live in a pen near our house and they're always dying of starvation and malnutrition. Dad won't let me rescue them. He says, 'It's not your problem.'

'Look at those balls,' says Vanessa, pointing to the swinging hammock of the ram's testicles.

Which makes me snort.

'Shhh.'

The wife brings us two cups of cold milk in which floats a crunchy layer of undissolved chocolate granules. She shows us the sitting room and points to the sofa. 'You sit there.' She has enormous bosoms, which seem to have a life independent of her own. They are like two great, pointy globes sailing across the room at us, armoured in a tight 1950s cotton farm dress. She sits opposite us in an armchair, watching us, her strong rancher's-wife hands on her knees. The ranch manager is sipping a brandy and Coke. He doesn't say anything, either. I hate both these people. I think, 'Leopard killers.'

When Dad comes out of the dining room he looks tired, as if he's been up all night, and his face is red. If I thought my dad ever cried I would have said he had been crying.

The manager says, 'Brandy?' But the drink is offered medicinally, not in the form of celebration.

The Milo is making me feel sick.

Dad says, 'Okay. Thanks.'

The manager goes to the drinks trolley and pours Dad a brandy.

'If you need help with the girls . . .' says the wife. 'I mean, while you . . .'

Dad shakes his head. 'We've got a hitchhiker staying. An Australian girl.'

'Oh I wondered who that was . . .'

'She can keep an eye on the girls.'

'Oh, that'll be nice. Won't that be nice?' asks the wife, turning her bosom and beaming it onto Vanessa and me. We nod miserably.

'Well, it's better than nothing,' says the manager's wife, her voice laced with irritation. 'We must all make do and be brave, mustn't we?'

I scowled at her and thought, 'What do *you* have to be brave about?'

Richard

Dad

We walk home in the dark behind Dad, without a torch, following the silvery gleam of the sandy road in the moonlight.
I follow the red cherry of Dad's cigarette. I want to hold his
hand, but he's too bunched and quiet and angry.

The next morning, when we wake up, Dad has left. Charlie
Chilvers says he has gone to Mutare General Hospital to see
Mum.

'And bring the baby home?'

'Right,' says Charlie.

'Do you have a brother?' I ask her.

'Yes.'

'Any sisters?'

'One.'

'Like us. Hey, you're like us?'

Charlie says, 'Eat up your porridge.'

'But I'm not hungry.'

'You're always hungry.'

'Is everything okay with the baby?' says Vanessa.

'Hm,' says Charlie vaguely.

'There's something wrong, isn't there?'

'Why don't you eat up?' says Charlie.

Vanessa sighs and pushes her plate away. 'It's too hot to eat,' she says.

Vanessa and I spend two days making up a baby's room out of the storeroom at the end of the corridor. We assemble the crib and mattress, and when we shake out the blankets they smell of Olivia. Baby smells. We take the tins of vegetables and floor polish and bottles of oil and shampoo and rolls of spare toilet paper off the shelves and find all the stuffed toys we own to put in their place. Two bears and a knitted green snake, one blue poodle, and a brown knitted dachshund which Olivia won at the Umtali fair for being so beautiful in a beautiful-baby contest. The place still looks bland and white. We Sellotape cut-out calendar pictures to the wall. The calenders have been sent to us by Granny in England and show west-coast-of-Scotland scenes or breeds of horses standing politely in green fields.

On the morning of the fourth day Charlie says, 'Your mum and dad have gone on a little holiday.'

'With the baby?'

'Without us?'

'Yes.'

'Where?'

Charlie clears her throat. She says, 'Just to Inyanga.'

'They're going fishing?'

'Without us?'

'With the baby?'

Vanessa takes me by the hand in such a violent grip I protest, 'Owie man, let go.'

She says in a dangerous voice, hissing like we're going to be in trouble, 'Let's empty the baby's room.'

'What?'

'Let's take everything out.'

'Why?'

'Shut your trap, Bobo. Can't you shut your stupid trap?'

I shut my stupid trap and try to stop the tears squeezing out from under my eyelids.

We spend the next two mornings emptying the baby's room.

'But where will he sleep?'

'He's not coming home.'

'Then where's he going?'

'How can you be such a doofus?' says Vanessa.

'I'm not a doofus.' I start crying.

'Bring the tins back from the kitchen.'

Vanessa replaces the tinned vegetables, the oil, the toilet paper. She puts the stuffed toys away in a trunk, which she pushes under her bed. She folds up the crib. She tears the pictures off the wall and crumples them into the dustbin.

*

When Mum and Dad come home, Charlie says, 'I'll just go for a walk.'

Mum and Dad look pale when they climb out of the car. I run up to Mum.

Dad says, 'Careful.'

Mum is walking hunched over, as if she has suddenly grown very old. She puts up her hands to stop me, like I'm one of the dogs, liable to jump up. 'Gently,' she says. She leans over and I can kiss her cheek. She has dyed her hair, dark over the grey.

'Where's the baby?'

Vanessa says, 'Oh *jeez*.'

'Come inside,' says Mum. She takes me by the hand to her

bedroom and makes me sit down on the edge of the bed. It's only then I notice that her eyes are shiny and half-mast, but not in a drunken way. This is a more profound half-mast; deep enough to slow the way she moves and talks, but not so deep as to make her slur and sing. She hands me a new brown canvas satchel. 'Look what we bought you.'

I look inside the satchel and start crying. 'But where's Richard?'

'Who?'

'The baby.'

'He's not here. He . . . went away.'

'Where?'

Mum shrugs helplessly. She says, 'That's what happens when you have a baby in a free African country. A government hospital . . .' Her voice is tight and cold, brittle like thin slides of glass.

I say, 'What happens?'

Vanessa is standing at the door. She says, 'He's dead, Bobo.'

The sob that comes out of me is racking, like vomiting. I feel my face and hands and the skin on my arms go cold.

Mum looks away as if I disgust her.

'How did it happen?' I am screaming.

Vanessa says, 'Shhh.'

I turn on Mum. 'How do you think I feel?' I ask her.

She looks at me astonished. 'Well, how do you think I feel?' she asks. She sinks down onto her bed; I can see from the way she goes down like that, suddenly, that she has lost the strength in her legs.

Vanessa says, 'Come, Bobo. Let's leave Mum alone.'

Mum is lying down now. She says, 'I'm very tired.'

I am still crying noisily, but Mum has closed her eyes and she is either asleep or she is pretending.

Vanessa pulls me away.

'Then why didn't we have a funeral? If he's dead we would have had a funeral.'

'Dad just buried him.'

I shake my head. We had a funeral for Olivia. We have funerals for all the dogs and horses that die. We would definitely have a funeral for a baby. 'Maybe they gave him away.'

'No, they didn't.'

'Then where's his grave?'

'It's unmarked. He's buried with all the rubbish from the hospital.'

'You're lying.'

'Think what you like.'

*

The next day Charlie hugs Vanessa and me and says, 'Time for me to hit the trail.'

Dad drives her to Masvingo and leaves her in the middle of town. When he comes home, he has the horses brought to the house and he takes me out riding until after dark, and he doesn't talk except to say 'Race you down the airstrip' and 'Race you up the river' so that we don't walk for long enough to talk and the horses come back in a shiny sweat and I am scratched from dodging camel-thorn branches.

*

Mum's okay in the mornings when she's just on the pills; she's very sleepy and calm and slow and deliberate, like someone who isn't sure where her body ends and the world starts. At night she has a few drinks and some more pills and then a few more drinks, and that's when things start to not be so okay. She gets drunk enough by six o'clock that Dad runs her a bath and says, 'Go on Tub, why don't you have a bath?' And she is obedient, stunned, taking a brandy with her into the bath, and I can hear her in there crying softly to herself. Then she comes into the sitting room, wringing wet, wrapped only in a towel, so Dad goes into the kitchen and tells Thompson it's okay, he can knock off now. Mum puts on the old Roger Whittaker record and stands in front of the window where she can see her reflection and she dances to herself and sings softly, 'I'm gonna leave old London town, I'm gonna leave old London town . . .' And the towel gapes open in the rear and exposes her naked bum. I point and giggle and Vanessa hisses at me sternly, 'It's not funny.'

I snort. 'Yes it is,' I insist.

'No, it's not. Mum's having a nervous breakdown.'

'Oh.'

Vanessa lays the table for supper, since Thompson can't come out of the kitchen with Mum half-naked in the living room. We eat impala steak, potatoes, tinned peas with a cup of milk, and Milo. Dad says, 'Come and eat, Tub.'

But Mum is swaying and singing. She has put the record back on from the beginning. It's the background music to her nervous breakdown. Dad serves up the food. He says, 'Sit up straight. Mouth closed when you chew.'

Night after night for the rest of the holidays it's the same.

*

When Mum and Dad drive us back to boarding school at the beginning of term, some of the other mothers ask Mum where the baby is. And they peer over Vanessa and me, as if we might have the baby hidden behind our backs. Mum has to say, 'We lost him.'

'*Ohmygod*, I'm so sorry.'

'Yes.' Mum's eyes are shiny glazed. She's holding on to my hand so tightly that her rings bite into my flesh. I hold on to her back. When she kisses me goodbye, she wraps me briefly in the safe, old smell of Vicks VapoRub, tea, and perfume and it's only when I look into her eyes that I remember she is in the middle of a nervous breakdown. She says, 'Be a brave girl, okay?'

'You, too.'

She smiles at me.

Dad says, 'Come on, Tub.' He says to me, 'Pecker up.'

'Ja. Pecker up to you, too.'

Nervous Breakdown

Long road

Things get worse. When Mum is drugged and sad and singing tunes from the Roger Whittaker album every night, that is one thing. It is a contained, soggy madness, which does little more than humidify the dry, unspoken grief we all feel. But then the outside world starts to join in and has a nervous breakdown all its own, so that it starts to get hard for me to know where Mum's madness ends and the world's madness begins. It's like being on a roundabout, spinning too fast. If I look inward, at my feet, or at my hands clutching the red-painted bar, I can see clearly, if narrowly, where I am in spite of a sick feeling in my stomach and a fear of looking up. But when I pluck up the courage to look up, the world is a terrifying, unhinged blur and I cannot determine whether it is me, or the world, that has come off its axis.

*

Thompson is beaten up in the compound. One day he comes to work and his eye is purple-black, the skin split open on the brow. He says it's because he's from a certain tribe in the east and these people are from a different tribe from the south and they fear and hate him.

'Fear and hate you for what?' I ask.

Thompson shrugs. 'I am not one of them.'

'But if they fear you, then why did they beat you?'

'Because they hate me more than they fear me.' And, 'Fear makes anger.'

Dad says, 'Thompson was probably after their wives.'

But I shake my head.

*

When we first moved to the ranch, before Richard died, in the brief, blissful period when Mum was well enough to be at home – with her health, and with her swelling belly, and with the end of the war, it seemed as if we might at last be allowed some peace and undisturbed happiness. There was then a pause in my life of uncomplicated childhood, a period of delicious hubris. In those days, I explored the ranch as if I were capable of owning its secrets, as if its heat and isolation and hostility were embraceable friends. I covered the hot, sharp, thorny ground of the ranch on horseback, foot and bicycle, ignorant of her secrets and fearless of her taboos, as if these ancient, native constraints did not apply to me.

Most mornings, I rode Burma Boy across the river in search of kudu and impala, the dogs panting through the bush on either side of me. In the afternoons, I walked, or rode my bike, down towards the compound past the old airstrip (a hangover from the ranch's more prosperous days) and searched the ground for wildlife finds. Once, I discovered the skulls of two impala rams, their horns locked into an irreversible figure-of-eight; the two animals had been trapped in combat, latched to each other during the battle of the rut. The harder they had pulled to escape from each other, the more intractably stuck they were, until they had fallen exhausted, to their knees, in an embrace of hatred that had killed them both. When I picked up the skulls to add to my growing collection of what Vanessa called 'Bobo's smelly pile', the hooked horns fell away from each other and the story of the impalas' death struggle was undone.

On one of my rides, I had found a game track to the surprising *kopjes*, which bulged with dark, shiny boldness out of the flat blonde savannah, alluring in their strangeness, small islands of secret life. I circled an outcrop, looking for an obvious way up, into the dark creases of rock, but the routes were too intimidating for me. Besides, I was afraid of the leopards I knew might be panting silently in the kopje's caves, or the snakes that lay like fat coils of rope, sunbathing, on the heat-absorbing rocks.

Then one day Vanessa suggested we take a picnic and explore the kopjes.

'What about leopards?'

'It'll be okay.'

'What about snakes?'

Vanessa said, 'Don't be a scaredy cat.'

'I'm not a scaredy cat,' I whined, 'it's just . . .'

'It's just you're a scaredy cat.'

'Better take someone with you,' said Mum, 'just in case.'

'See,' I said, 'even Mum thinks it might not be safe.'

'I didn't say that,' said Mum. 'And make sure you take your hats, it's hot out there on the rocks.'

It was Cephas's day off, so we were sent with Thompson, still gleaming in his white kitchen uniform, as an escort. Thompson carried a string bag with oranges, boiled eggs, an old wine bottle, corked, with water, and a fragrant clutch of warm buns fresh from the oven that morning. When we reached the kopjes, we chose the one closest to the road to climb. Thompson let Vanessa and me go ahead, helping us up over the steep sections of rock until at last we were panting, itching with sweat, on top of the world, able to see as far as the river over the top of the grey-hot haze and the mopane trees. Thompson sat on his haunches and peeled an orange, the creases of his hands turning chalky white with the juice. He handed sections of the fruit out to Vanessa and me, and we ate quietly. Happy with our accomplishment.

It was later, after we had eaten our oranges and climbed around on top of the kopje singing, 'Needles and pins-a', that Vanessa and I found the old grave sites, cool dark places of ritual and burial where half-broken pottery, cracked, blackened jewelry, dull arrowheads, and crumbling water gourds lay heaped on top of pyramids of rocks. We scrambled excitedly through our find.

'What do you think it is?'

'I don't know, maybe people lived here.'

'Maybe they died here.'

Suddenly Thompson was upon us. 'What is it?' He was frowning into the gloom of our narrow cave.

'Look!' I showed him two pieces of pottery, which put together made up part of a zigzag pattern. 'It's an old pot.'

'Leave that stuff!' said Thompson. He had almost shouted, raised one prohibiting hand.

I looked at him with astonishment. I had never been spoken to – ordered around – by an African before. My nannies had never dared speak to me so sharply. But Thompson was stumbling back, out of the cave, as if he had seen a snake's hole.

'I want to take it home to show Mum.'

'You must not touch the things of the dead!'

I had my head to one side and my mouth drawn up, to show I was sceptical, but still, I came out of the cave, as slow-casual as I could, holding the piece of pottery, and I said, 'How do you know they are dead people's things?'

'Anyone can see these are graves,' said Thompson. 'Don't touch! You mustn't touch.'

I laughed. 'It's a bit late for that, Thompson.'

'Please picannin madam.' Thompson looked as if he were about to fling himself backwards off the bald head of the kopje.

'Well, if the people are dead, they won't mind.'

'No, they will mind. They will think of you most terrible things.'

'Thompson, don't be so superstitious.' In an effort to rid myself of the tainted pottery and to still maintain my superiority, I tossed the pottery carelessly back into the cave and dusted my hands on my shorts, 'There. Happy?' And then casually, 'I didn't really want it, anyway.'

Thompson looked as if I had struck him, as if I'd thrown the pottery in his face. He said, 'Oh you should not have done that, picannin madam. You shouldn't have *thrown* it like that.'

Vanessa was ducking out of the cave behind me. Her face had changed, the way a shadow comes when a thin cloud scuds across the sun. She said, 'Come on, Bobo, let's go home.'

'But we haven't even eaten our picnic yet.'

Thompson, his shoulders poking and bony out of the back of his thin cotton uniform, was already scuffling down the face of the boulder that made up the top of the kopje. He had the string bag of uneaten food over his shoulder.

'Come on, you guys, I'm hungry. Let's eat first.'

Thompson didn't even turn around, much less slow down.

'Why are you frightened?' I had to quickly scuffle down on the seat of my shorts to keep up with Thompson and Vanessa.

'You touched the things of the dead,' said Thompson. And I saw then that he was beyond scared, he was angry too.

*

I remember the soft, silty, gritty feel of the grave pottery when I see Thompson, his eye split open like that. And then I think of Richard dead, and Mum gone crazy. And I think that if I hadn't touched the things of the dead we wouldn't be having all this bad, bad luck.

*

And then Oscar, our Rhodesian ridgeback, is found lying on the road outside our house and he has been sliced up and down with a panga. Mum is screaming at the front door, holding his body in her arms. He is so weak from lack of blood he doesn't even struggle. 'Those bastards! Those bloody, bloody bastards.' I open the door and Mum staggers in, barely able to hold herself up with the dog pressed against her chest.

'Is he still breathing?'

Mum lies him down and covers him with blankets. 'We need to get fluids into him.' She feeds him whole milk, with the cream, dry-season thin and pale, floating on the top. Oscar gags and the milk dribbles back out of his mouth. 'He can't even swallow,' says Mum, her hands slippery with the milk. She finds a vein in his back leg and punctures it with a needle, letting a bag of intravenous fluid seep into his body. She stays like that, crouched over the dog with the plastic bag of saline solution held up over her head, until Oscar begins to struggle. Then she pulls the needle out of his leg and sits back on her haunches, wiping sweat off her forehead.

'Who did this?' I ask.

Mum says in a hoarse whisper, 'They did,' and lifts her eyes toward the ranch manager's house.

'Oh. The ranch managers did this?'

Mum nods.

I let this sink in for a moment. 'Why?'

Mum rolls her eyes and says in a soft voice, like she's telling me a secret, 'They want to kill me, too.'

'They want to kill you?'

'Yes.'

'Why? Why would they want to do that?'

'Because I know about them.'

'You know about them.'

'They're crooks and they're poaching leopards.'

'We all know they're poaching leopards.'

'Watch yourself,' says Mum. 'Watch yourself.'

*

A week later, Burma Boy contracts horse sickness, and he is barely recovered from that when he comes down with tetanus.

Mum says, 'We need to get fluids into him.'

She fills a bucket with water and empties a bag of brown sugar into it. Burma Boy sucks at the water weakly to get to the sweet silt at the bottom of the bucket, and then he collapses. Mum puts blankets over him and lies with him in the garden for four nights. The dogs curl up next to her. Even Oscar, who has been allowed to sleep inside, on the sofa, during his convalescence, relinquishes his comfortable position and crawls onto the blanket under which the horse lies quivering with rigid spasms every time there is a loud noise.

*

Thompson gives notice and goes back to the eastern highlands. He says, 'This place is poisonous.'

Dad says, 'It's time we moved on, too.'

That night it is so hot that we sit outside in the dark with the windows to the living room open so that we can hear our records. We have managed to hide the Roger Whittaker album in a Chopin sleeve. Dad is playing Tchaikovsky's *1812 Overture*.

'Loud enough to scare the bloody elephants.'

'There aren't any elephants.'

'That's because we scared them with the *1812*.'

'Ha.'

We eat a supper of impala steak, balancing plates on our laps. When we look up the sky is deep, lonely black. We can hear the jackals starting to trot the perimeter of the security fence, yip-yipping. They have come for the weak, undernourished, diseased sheep and for the wobbly-legged lambs. A nightjar sings.

Mum is not eating, again. I haven't seen her swallow a decent mouthful of food since the baby came, and went.

Suddenly Dad says, 'I'll go fishing for three days.'

'Can I come?'

'If the fishing is good, we'll stay here and make a go of it. If the fishing is bad, we'll leave.'

'Why?'

'We can't live where the fishing's lousy.'

'Leave to where?'

'Better fishing.'

'Can I come?'

'No.'

'Why not?'

'Because then what if the fishing is good for you and bad for me? We can't confuse the issue.'

'Oh.'

'I'll leave sparrow's fart tomorrow.'

*

The next morning, very early, Dad leaves with his coarse-fishing rod, spinners, thick line and weights. He has packed brandy, tins of baked beans, salt, boiled eggs, tea, powdered milk and bread into his old ammunition box.

'You're not going trout fishing?'

'No.'

Dad goes fishing for bass and bream and tiger. He's never been much of a coarse fisherman.

I say to Mum, 'We might as well start packing. Dad never catches anything if he isn't using a fly.'

Mum is lying in bed staring at the ceiling, as if she doesn't care.

'Should I bring you some tea?'

'That would be nice.'

Mum spends most of the day in bed. When she gets up, after tea, she is groggy, unsteady on her feet. She makes it as far as the sitting room and sinks into an armchair with a sigh. Her face is longer and older; there are sad lines by the sides of her mouth and under her eyes that didn't use to be there. Her hair has grown out, the wings on her temples are grey.

She made the house cheerful and homely when we first came here. She made bright new curtains and cushions, she hung pictures and put ornaments on the mantelpiece. Judith/Loveness had polished the floors until they shone like marble, and Thompson hammered drooping gauze tightly on the windows and whitewashed the walls inside and out. Mum wrote a list of chores to be done every day and pinned it to the kitchen door: dusting, sweeping, brushing, polishing, shining. Now Mum looks as if she doesn't care. The list of chores has turned yellow and is splattered with fly shit and has begun to curl up at the edges, and the house is starting to look dishevelled without Thompson. There is a population explosion of cockroaches in the kitchen, and the cats are finding rats everywhere; we see them crouched and crunching over their rodent carcasses and we trip over half-eaten remains.

I watch Mum carefully. She hardly bothers to blink. It's as if she's a fish in the dry season, in the dried-up bottom of a cracking riverbed, waiting for rain to come and bring her to life.

Vanessa says, 'Leave her alone, she's depressed.'

Vanessa seems a bit depressed herself.

I say, 'Anyone hungry?'

Mum pours herself another brandy.

'Aside from me?'

Since Thompson left, Judith/Loveness has been the only help in the house, but she can't clean very well and she really can't cook. I tell her to open a tin of baked beans and cook some bread on the wood fire to make toast for supper.

'With some boiled eggs,' I add.

When supper arrives I lay the table and shout, 'Grub's up!'

but Mum doesn't want to eat, and Vanessa pushes a few beans around on her plate before going back to her room. I am left to eat toast, an entire tin of baked beans, and three boiled eggs on my own.

Mum goes into the bathroom, where she wallows around in a humid steam for some time before emerging stupefied and reeling, wrapped in a towel. I have been entertaining myself, feeding the dogs the leftover supper one baked bean at a time.

Mum stands in front of the window in the living room, without music, swaying to nothing. I put the supper dishes on the floor for the dogs to lick and fish the Roger Whittaker record out of the Chopin sleeve. It seems better if Mum is swaying to music, even if the music is Roger Whittaker, than if she is swaying into the deep, animal-scampering, cricket-calling, moth-bashing silence.

'Ahm gonna leave ole London town, Ahm gonna leave ole London town . . .'

I stand in front of her, in an effort to distract her. Her eyes slide glassily past me.

'Mum!'

She says in a low whisper, 'You know they tried to kill Oscar.'

I say, 'I know. You told me already.'

Mum looks over her shoulder and leans forward, almost overbalancing. 'They think I'm unstable.'

'Do they?'

Mum smiles, but it isn't an alive, happy smile, it's a slipping and damp thing she's doing with her lips which looks as much as if she's lost control of her mouth as anything else. 'They think I'm crazy.'

'Really?'

'But I'm not, I'm not at all.'

'No.'

'It was a *warning*.'

'What was a *warning*?'

'First Thompson, then Oscar, then Burma Boy . . .'

'But Burma Boy got horse sickness and tetanus. The managers had nothing to do with that.'

Mum's eyes quiver. Her towel is slipping. 'I'm next, you know.'

'For what?'

'But it doesn't scare me.'

'No.'

The towel falls off completely. I retrieve it, and Mum clutches it over her breasts. 'I know what they're up to.'

'Oh, good.'

'No, it's not good.'

'No.'

'A leopard a week. I see them. They think I'm crazy, but I see them. It's illegal, you know.'

'I know.'

'Leopard are Royal Game. You have to have a permit.'

'I know.'

'They could go to jail.'

'I know.'

Vanessa comes out of her room; she turns off the record player and takes Mum by the elbow. 'Why don't you go to bed, Mum? I'll bring you some hot milk.'

'Yuck.'

'Cold milk.'

'Yuck.'

'How about some tea?'

Mum allows herself to be led to the bedroom. Vanessa dresses her and puts her into bed. 'Stay there, okay, Mum?' As she leaves the room she hisses at me, 'Don't let Mum get out of bed.'

'Right.' I sit on the edge of the bed pinning down the bedclothes and watch Mum, who is staring at the ceiling. 'They invited me to a party,' she says in a dreamy voice.

'Who?'

'The managers. They had houseguests from town.'

'When?'

'You were away at school.'

'Was it fun?'

'They tried to poison me.'

'Oh.'

'Then when I was in the bathroom trying to throw up the poison, one of their guests tried to . . . to assault me.'

Mum suddenly sits up and I am scared of her, the way I would be scared of a ghost. I draw back, suppressing an urge to run away. She is behaving supernaturally. She is pale and drawn and there is sweat on her forehead and a thin moustache of sweat clings to her top lip. Her eyes are shining like marbles, cold and hard and glittering. She says, 'You watch out for yourself.'

'I will.'

Vanessa comes in with the tea. 'Go and bath, Bobo.' I flee, relieved.

*

Afterward Vanessa comes into my room and says, 'You mustn't pay too much attention to Mum. She's just having a *nervous-breakdown*.'

I have an arrow, confiscated from a poacher, hanging on my otherwise bare walls.

Vanessa frowns at it. 'It's about time you had some pictures in your room.'

'Why?'

'You'll get morbid, looking at that thing all the time.'

'I like it.'

'*Ja*, but it's not normal.'

'Nothing's normal anymore, hey. Everything's wrong.'

'It'll be okay.'

'Why are the managers trying to kill Mum?'

'They aren't.'

'That's what she told me.'

'They aren't, okay?'

'They tried to kill Oscar.'

'Maybe that was the Africans.'

'And they beat up Thompson.'

'That *was* the Africans.'

'Mum said they tried to poison her.'

'Ignore her. I told you already, she's just having a *nervous-breakdown*.'

'Then why are there so many bad-luck things at once?'

'Bad-luck things happen. That's just the way it is. They happen all the time. It doesn't mean anything, Bobo. It doesn't mean that the bad-luck things have anything to do with each other. If you start thinking that bad luck comes all together on purpose or that it has to do with the managers or with you or with anything else, you'll go bonkers.'

'Mum's already bonkers.'

'Which is why she thinks all the bad-luck things are to do with the managers.'

I wipe my nose on my arm.

'You've really got to stop doing that,' says Vanessa.

*

Dad comes back from fishing. He has had one bite in three days, and has caught nothing.

'We'll move to a place where we can catch a fish just by yawning in the right direction,' he tells us.

I look at Mum and wonder how we're ever going to move her anywhere.

'What do you think, Tub?'

Mum gives Dad her glazed smile and says, 'Sounds fine.' Her voice is blurred.

'Mum hates fishing,' I point out.

'Yeah,' says Mum, laughing in a wobbly unhappy way, 'I hate fishing.'

'See?'

'Well, we can't stay here,' says Dad.

'Come back for my body in the dry season,' says Mum.

'What?'

'Nothing.'

*

I say to Dad, 'I don't think Mum's well enough to go anywhere.'

'The change'll do her good. She'll be fine once we're in a new place.'

'How do you know?'

'Because we've done it before. It's no good wallowing around in the same place too long. Too much . . . too many . . . It makes you morbid.'

'Vanessa says I'm morbid.'

'See?'

I stroke the dogs with my foot. 'What about Oscar and Shea? And the cats?'

'We'll bring everyone with us.'

'And the horses?'

'We'll see.'

Moving On

Dad

Mum is living with the ghosts of her dead children. She begins to look ghostly herself. She is moving slowly, grief so heavy around her that it settles, like smoke, into her hair and clothes and stings her eyes. Her green eyes go so pale they look yellow. The colour of a lioness's eyes through grass in the dry season.

Her sentences and thoughts are interrupted by the cries of her dead babies.

*

Only Olivia has had a proper funeral. Richard and Adrian are in unmarked graves. They float and hover, un-pressed-down. For them, there is no weight of dignity such as is afforded the dead by a proper funeral. There is no dampness of tears on earth, shed during the ceremony of grieving. There is no myth of closure.

All people know that in one way or the other the dead must be laid to rest properly: burnt, scattered, prayed over, laid out, sung upon. Earth must be thrown upon the coffins of the dead by the living hands of those who knew or loved them. Or ashes of the dead must be scattered into the wind.

'We have offended against thy holy laws, we have left undone those things which we ought to have done, and we have done those things which we ought not to have done; and there is no health in us.'

It doesn't take an African to tell you that to leave a child in an unmarked grave is asking for trouble. The child will come back to haunt you and wrap itself around you until your own breathing stops under the damp weight of its tiny, ghostly persistence.

*

Mum's world becomes increasingly the world she sees in the reflection of the window at night when the lights are humming, high and low in tune to the throb of the generator, and Roger Whittaker is playing on the record player. Mum's towel slips lower over her full-of-milk breasts. I hear her crying in the bathroom when she's squeezing them empty. Milk for no one, down the plug. Her towel hangs open at her bottom, where her thighs are blood-smeared from the tail end of childbirth. She seems to be grieving for the loss of this new baby in every way a body can grieve; with her mind (which is unhinged) and her body (which is alarming and leaking).

While Mum sways damply in the insect, hot-singing night, crooning with Roger, 'Ahm gonna leave ole London town,' Dad sits in the corner, under the lightbulb, ducking the moths and rose beetles that come in search of the light. He reads to himself, eyebrows raised in distant absorption, and smokes quietly.

He is stretching a brandy and Coke into the night, sipping at it as if it were a delicate treat, although it has long since gone warm and flat. The dogs lie flattened on the concrete floor, their ears pressed to their heads, eyebrows anxiously raised.

That night I go into Vanessa's room after the generator has been switched off.

'Van.'

'*Ja?*'

'Are you awake?'

She doesn't answer.

'What do you think?'

She still doesn't answer.

'Why won't you talk to me?'

'You're asking stupid questions.'

I grope my way to the end of her bed and lower myself next to the rising, bony hump of her feet.

'What do you think about Mum?'

'Well . . .' What about Mum?'

Silence.

'Don't you think?'

Vanessa sighs and turns over. She's fourteen now. I can feel the suddenly heavier, womanly shift of her. The bed sags under her newfound weight. She smells different, too – not dusty and metallic and sharp like puppy pee, but soft and secret and of tea and her new deodorant which comes in a white bottle with a blue label and which I covet. It's called Shield. She says, 'If Mum and Dad catch you out of bed you'll be in the dwang.'

'They won't catch me.'

Vanessa knows I'm right. She says, 'I'm trying to sleep. You're bugging me.'

Suddenly, surprisingly, I'm crying; mewing my sadness. Vanessa sits up and puts her arms awkwardly over me. 'It's okay, hey.'

'What's going on, man?'

Vanessa rocks me. 'Shhhh.'

'Why is everyone so crazy?'

'It's not everyone.'

'It feels like it.'

Vanessa says, 'If you promise to go to sleep, I'll make a plan, okay?'

I sniff and wipe my nose on the back of my arm.

'*Sis*, man. I've told you about that.'

'I don't have any bog roll.'

'Well get some. Blow your nose. Then go to bed.'

*

The next morning, when I wake up, later than usual, with the sun already eight o'clock high and hot in the dust-flung pale sky, Vanessa is already dressed. She has been arranging for the family's healing; she has collected our fishing rods and hats and has packed a cardboard box with reels, fishing line, boiled eggs, beer, brandy, a cheap bottle of red wine, a loaf of bread, biltong, thin-skinned and bitter wild bananas, oranges.

'I've made a plan to go to the dam,' she announces at breakfast. 'Let's go fishing for catfish.'

Dad looks up from his porridge, surprised.

'I really think we should go fishing.'

'Mum hates fishing,' I say. 'She isn't even up yet.' Mum is having tea in her room.

Vanessa glares at me and then stares at Dad intently. 'We need to go for a picnic.'

Dad says, 'I have work . . .'

'And we'll take our fishing rods so you don't get bored.'

Dad looks as though he's about to protest further. He opens his mouth to speak but Vanessa gets up, pushes her hair out of her eyes, and says, 'I've packed the lunch. I'll go and get Mum.' She cocks her head. 'Why don't we ask that visitor chappy to come along?'

There is a young law student from South Africa staying on the ranch. His grandfather had been one of the original homesteaders of Devuli Ranch. Vanessa and I have been watching him hungrily through the binoculars since he arrived a few days earlier. He has a mass, like a wig, of curly blond hair. He's been staying with the ranch managers, with whom we have been unofficially at war since Mum's nervous breakdown (in case her mad accusations might have some grounding in reality). Vanessa and I met the visitor (we had stalked him) at the workshop and I grilled him unabashedly – who was he, what was he doing here, how long was he staying – until Vanessa dragged me off by the wrist and hissed at me, 'You're so embarrassing.'

'Why?'

'*Why?*'

'What did I do now?'

'Oh, God. Where do I start?'

*

Our captured guest (whom I have gloated over victoriously since his arrest, which took place in the ranch manager's compound: 'Come fishing with us. Please,' and then, not wanting to scare him off with my eagerness, 'If you'd like') has the unsettling, potentially unhealing name of Richard. But he's young and cheerful and appears innocent of our recent and past traumas and Mum has responded to him, to his freshness, with the first true, unwobbly smile since she came back empty-armed from the hospital.

Vanessa and I make room in the back of the Land Rover for Richard, who swings up onto the little metal bench over the wheel with long-legged ease. I stare at him intently and smile fiercely. Vanessa nudges me hard in the ribs. She is looking nonchalantly out of her side of the Land Rover, aloof, composed. She has stopped wearing her hair in braids. Now it falls across her face in a blonde sheet, so that she has scraped it around the back of her neck and is holding it against the slap of wind. She closes her eyes and lifts her face to the sun. I resume my hopeful, maniacal grinning, fixed on Richard.

It's pointless trying to start a conversation with our captive, although I am tempted to warn him (to be fair) that Mum is crazy. The Land Rover rocks and swings and plunges, its engine roaring with the effort of off-off road. We have long since left the rib-shattering relative speed of the main dirt road (where the short wheelbase smacks the corrugations in the road at just the right interval to wind us) and we are beyond the barely made tracks which are really nothing more than an indication – some telltale wear – that someone else has come this way in the past. (In the thin, brittle soil, barely held together by the soft, burnt-up weight of grass, tracks from a single vehicle, covering the ground a single time, can show for years.) Now we are plunging between buffalo thorn and skirting anthills and we, in the back, are forced to swing forward (our hands tucked under us to prevent them from being raked by thorns) and duck.

We pass, without comment or surprise, small, rain-ready herds of impala. The ewes are swollen with impending babies, but the babies will come only with the first rain. Dad stops to let a pair of warthog charge fatly in front of us, round-bottomed and heads held high. A kudu bull stares us down – the perfect white 'V' on his nose a hunter's target. He is sniffing the air and then, with a magnificent leap, his horns laid across his back like medieval weapons, he is gone, plunging greyly into the cross-hatched bush.

It is late morning by the time we get to the dam, and the sun has settled into the shallow, blanched mid-sky. The dam is shrinking, muddy, warm; its waters have receded, leaving a damp swath of cracking mud and strong smells of frog sperm and rotting algae. Egrets are poking along the edge of the dam. They rise when the dogs come flopping towards them, and settle, just beyond reach. Busy weavers chatter and fly, darting back and forth from their watertight, snake-savvy nests with pieces of grass trailing from their mouths.

It is the wrong time of year to be here. The sun has scorched the shade off all the trees, whose limbs now stretch, thin and hungry, into the arid, smoky sky. The ground is glitteringly hot. Vanessa pulls out some cushions and a deckchair and sets the chair up for Mum under the lacy protection of a buffalo thorn. Mum pours herself some tea from the thermos and, with the remote distraction she has maintained since Richard died, begins to read.

She smiles at Richard – 'This is nice, isn't it?' – and I want to sing wildly and shout for joy because it is such a normal thing to say, even though it is a lie. I want everyone to notice what a normal thing to say this is. I want to ask Richard, 'Don't you think she sounds normal?'

Dad and I find logs near the edge of the dam and begin to fish for barbel, whiskered fish that bury themselves into the mud in the drought years and re-emerge only after the first rains. They are like vampire fish, coming back to life with a creepy insistence, year after year – even after years that have left a trail of skeletons in their wake. These fish are very hard to kill. We bash them brutally, headfirst, on rocks; still they thrash and squeal. They don't seem fragile or fishlike at all. Dad and I take turns to jump on them, but they slither out from underfoot. Then we wrestle them to the ground (they are black and muscular, and slip easily from our grip) and one of us holds them down while the other smashes rocks on their heads. We leave their battered bodies in a net, suspended in the water so that they won't rot in the heat.

'We'll take them home for the *muntus*,' says Dad.

'What do they taste of?'

'Mud. They taste like the smell of this,' says Dad, digging his toe into the visceral dirt.

'Yuck.'

'*Ja*, but a *muntu* will eat anything.'

Vanessa has walked to the other side of the dam, where she can see Mum and where she can be seen by Richard, who has stationed himself, precariously, on a log that overreaches into the dam. He is straddling the log, head bowed exposing white neck to hostile sun, and is threading a worm onto his hook. His back is to Dad and me; his neck is already turning stung pink. The dogs nose around, always keeping one anxious, faithful eye on Mum, who looks unmovable, unmoving, unreading. In spite of her stillness, she is the one who seems most restless, her energy is snaking out of her like heat waves, dancing across the water to us, hot and insistent. Or perhaps it is my anxious energy dancing towards Mum; I'm like one of the dogs, trying to read her mood, her happiness, her next move.

Suddenly, Mum gets out of her chair and walks across the damp patch of smelly sticky mud towards the water, kicking mud off her toes as she walks, girlish in the gesture. Vanessa lifts her head – as if sniffing the air – and puts down her fishing rod. She has been watching Mum out of the corner of her eye all this time, but now that Mum has moved, Vanessa is rivetted with indecision. Dad and I have propped our rods against rocks and have been crouched, haunches hanging, waiting for another bite. Dad shifts when Mum gets up, almost rising himself. The dogs come bounding back from where they have been exploring, mixing and stirring at Mum's feet, suddenly playful. Only Richard is unaware of the un-drama unfolding at the water's edge.

Like a woman hoping to drown, Mum is walking into the dam, fully clothed. She walks softly, shimmering behind the veil of heat.

'What the hell's she doing?' Dad gets to his feet.

'Mum!' Vanessa starts to run toward her.

Mum continues to wade. Her shirt has floated up and is spread out on top of the water, blue and dry, briefly, until the muddy weight of the dam sucks it down. Mum can swim – poorly – but we all know that she has the willpower, the leaden weight of heartsickness, not to swim if she chose to let the murky water swallow over her head.

Vanessa is lumping awkwardly, slow-motion-panic, through the mud. 'Mum!' Her voice is made sluggish with the dense heat.

The water is up to Mum's chest now. She raises her arm, and it is only then that I notice she is holding a beer. 'Cheers!' she shouts. Then, 'It's not very deep.'

For a moment we're all too stunned to react. Then, 'Is it nice?' I shout.

'Nicer than outside.'

Vanessa pokes one toe into the water and then, with sudden resolution, wades out to Mum.

'Why don't you bring a beer in, Tim?'

By the time Richard dives off his log and swims towards us, we are all up to our chins in the water, sipping beer.

'Get yourself a drink, Richard.'

'The beers are a bit warm, I'm afraid.'

Mum says, 'There's nothing worse than warm beer' – she pauses – 'except no beer.'

And we laugh and laugh. I am deliciously, carelessly drunk. I throw my empty bottle to the shore and declare my intention to swim to the log. I soon discover that the dam is shallow enough for me to wade chest-deep the whole way. The dogs swim circles around me.

We eat lunch in the dam. Then Dad opens the wine, and we pass the bottle around. 'We need a table,' he says.

'And a roof,' I say.

'A lodge on stilts,' says Vanessa.

'A butler,' says Mum.

Richard is smiling, 'This is very civilized,' he says.

'It seemed the only sane thing to do,' says Mum.

*

That night when we get home, our skins shining with sun, our eyes stinging with sun's reflection on the water, Richard comes in for supper and Mum gets drunk but she doesn't dance alone in front of the window, sad and mourning. She dances with Richard. We roll up the rug, push the sofa aside and put the 'Ipi Tombi' record on the player. We all dance wildly – hips sideways, wiggle-wiggle, shuffling feet, shaking breasts and breastbones – the way we imagine Zulu warriors to dance, up and down the sitting room. 'Ay ya! Ay ya! Ay-ya, oh in-tombi-um. Ipi in-tombi-um. In-tombi-um!'

Mum is glowing, twisting, beautiful again. Her face is pink with sun and wine.

Dad is laughing, 'Let's have a par-ty!' in his signature, sing-song way.

Vanessa is trying to avoid permanent humiliation, but she dances anyway, edging her way around Mum and Richard, 'Uh, uh, uh!'

I am dancing with the dog, her feet caught up in my hands, crouched low; she teeters around for a few steps before her feet slip on the floor. 'Look at Shea dance! Look!'

We dance until the generator dies. And then we sit outside in deckchairs, under the silver moon, and drink Irish coffees. Dad tells stories about the time he went hunting for a zebra and got lost, the time he was chased by a rhino and had to jump fourteen feet into a dry riverbed, the time he saw a man get downwind of buffalo bean.

Beyond the gate I can hear the jackals laughing, their quick, high voices travelling sharply through the dense night.

It's almost midnight by the time Richard leaves and we all climb into bed.

Malawi

Dad with President Banda

North of Zimbabwe (but not bordering it), there is a skinny slice of a country, over one fifth of which is a lake boasting the largest population of freshwater tropical fish in the world. Its highlands are speckled with rivers and lakes that were stocked with Scottish trout before the Second World War and whose waters are still rich with the trout's descendants. The air almost anywhere you go in Malawi is salty and rich with the scent of smoked fish.

To reach Malawi we can go the short, dangerous way, or we can go the long, less dangerous way. We can choose to drive this way: first, west out of Zimbabwe at Chirundu, then north through Zambia, following the spiny Great East Road to Chipata and finally into Malawi – a journey of four or five days on increasingly deteriorating roads, but without war and with few bandits. Or we can choose to drive east through the Tete corridor in Mozambique and be in Malawi in a matter of hours, a full day perhaps.

In any normal situation, the journey through Tete would be the more sensible choice. But this is Africa, so hardly anything is normal. If we go through Mozambique, we will have to elude land mines, Renamo rebels, bandits, and roads so decayed they are worse than the tracks that army lorries and trucks have worn beside them.

For once, my parents are prudent. Dad flies up to Malawi from Zimbabwe, his plane (taking the shortest route) breathlessly flying over the Tete corridor while the passengers anxiously drink Carslberg lager and peer out of the windows. Mozambique slides into, and then out of, view, the years of savage warfare and burnt villages and raped women and child soldiers and no schools and no hospitals and battle-bred malnutrition felt as only a temporary dip of unrelated turbulence. The plane lands in Blantyre – a strangely Scottish-feeling, African-smelling city – and Dad is met at the airport by an unusually tall, unusually dark African who, it turns out, is not Malawian, but from Zambia. Malawians tend to have a reddish complexion and tidy features. Dad's driver stands out, tall and rangy and black, like a palm tree in a mopane forest.

Mum drives the long way around to Malawi, through Zambia, in the Land Rover, with the dogs, the cats, and all our worldly goods. Oscar falls out of the Land Rover somewhere near the Kafue River and is never seen again even though Mum spends two days walking along the river calling for him. At last she gives a schoolteacher in a nearby village some money and says, 'If you find my dog, will you look after him for me?'

'He probably bought beer with the money,' says Dad afterwards.

'You never know.'

'You *should* know by now.'

Malawi was formerly the Nyasaland Protectorate. When we arrive in the country in 1982, it is being run by a lilliputian dictator, Dr Hastings Kamuzu Banda. He is shrunken and very old, although no one is supposed to know exactly how old. His birthday is an official state secret but it is generally agreed that he may have been born as early as 1898 or as late as 1906. Some careless people joke, behind their hands, in quick nervous whispers, that Kamuzu Banda is actually dead. That his body is battery-run by remote control. After all, they point out, he does little in the way of official state business anymore, except wave a zebra-tail fly whisk from the steps leading up to his private jet or personal helicopter.

But most people are careful to keep their mouths shut. Mum says, 'Never say anything derogatory about the government or the President.'

'What if we're alone?'

Mum sighs, as if the dense population of Malawi is pressing air out of her lungs. 'We're never alone here.'

People who disagree with His Excellency, the President for Life and 'Chief of Chiefs', are frequently found to be the victims of car crashes (their bodies mysteriously riddled with bullets); or dead in their beds of heart attacks (their bodies mysteriously riddled with bullets); or the recipients of some not-quite-fresh seafood (their bodies mysteriously riddled with bullets).

*

Revolts by H.B.M. Chipembere and Yatuta Chisiza are crushed in 1965 and 1967. Chipembere dies in exile in the United States.

Dick Matenje (Banda's likely successor) dies under mysterious circumstances in 1983.

Orton and Vera Chirwa are imprisoned for life for protesting against some of Banda's policies. Orton is released, but later kidnapped in Zambia.

Dr Attati Mpakati, leader of the Socialist League of Malawi, is killed by a letter bomb in 1983 in Zimbabwe.

*

Dr Hastings Kamuzu Banda is not only Life President. He is also the Minister of External Affairs, the Minister of Work and Supplies, the Minister of Justice, and the Minister of Agriculture. The airport, most major roads and public buildings, and many schools and hospitals are named after the President. Lining almost all the main roads there are scores of billboards containing a photograph of the President for Life. Many women wear bright cloth chitenges around their waists – as skirts – which contain a photograph of Banda, a younger Banda, whose face shines over round bottoms and swelling bellies. Babies hang from chitenge slings decorated with the President's face, their little faces peeping over the placid, mild gaze of the image of their Great Chief.

When we move to Malawi, the people of this sliver of a country have among the lowest per capita income of anyone in the world. Their numbers are swelling as refugees flood over the borders from Mozambique to escape that country's seemingly endless civil war.

We move to a tobacco farm on the edge of Lake Chilwa, not far, on roads that toss the pickup from one side to the other as if it were a small boat, from Lake Malawi and the Shire River nor from Mozambique. The farm, Mgodi (meaning the Hole), is one of many owned by His Excellency the Life President. It is supposed to be a shining example of what can happen when the President sets his mind to help his people. When we arrive, the estate is a shambles; overrun with weeds, corruption, thieves, threatening Big Men, trembling Little Men, collapsing workshops, and disintegrating roads. The entire place is shuddering under a crumbling infrastructure. It is a smaller, contained version of the Malawian government as a whole.

There are one thousand 'peasant farmers', each of whom

rents an acre of land on which to grow burley tobacco, which they will sell back to the estate. They are also required to grow a patch of maize and a patch of vegetables on a separate acre of land to feed themselves and their families.

By the standards of this tiny, tightly controlled, densely populated country, our farm is remote. It's at least an hour's drive to Zomba, the nearest town. Zomba is built on the edge of a startling plateau on which the Life President has built himself a small palace (one of many scattered throughout the country) and which offers a sudden change of climate. The plateau, whose summit we reach by winding up an 'up'-only road (avoiding the lawless drivers hurtling illegally down) is planted with fresh, sweet-smelling pine and fir trees. Its ground is soft and mossy; the air is thick and cool, and fresh with an almost permanent lick of mist. The dams and streams are stocked with trout; the roads on top of the plateau are hard, red, slick clay, which become so slippery during the rains that our heavy truck slides drunkenly off their spines and into the ditch. Coming down the 'down' road from the plateau, the air thickens by degrees until, by the time we reach the town, we have almost forgotten the tonic of the plateau's summit, its cool, comforting, mossy silence.

There is little to recommend the town of Zomba, or to set it apart from many other African cities of its nature, except the mental hospital on the main street. To the casual observer, the town of Zomba is primarily populated by mentally ill Malawians, escapees from the hospital, who tear around the modest city in sawn-off pink-, blue-, and white-striped pyjamas.

*

By now, Vanessa is sixteen and attending a private coeducational school in Blantyre where the focus is on a cheerful learning atmosphere and where the students are encouraged to express themselves artistically. I am thirteen, at Arundel High School in Harare, Zimbabwe, where the students are expected not to express themselves at all. The focus is on a rigorous academic programme and we will be expected to pass difficult examinations sent out from Cambridge in England.

At our school, we cannot make or receive phone calls except at ten o'clock on Saturday morning, when our conversations are monitored by a matron and we may speak for only five minutes. Our letters out of the school are frequently censored. Our letters into the school are subject to censorship at any time. We may receive only visitors who are approved by the authorities and who appear on a master list, and these only between the hours of three and five on Sunday afternoons. We must attend chapel twice a day. Grace before meals is expressed in Latin.

We must wear our uniforms no longer than an inch below the knee, no shorter than an inch above the knee as measured from a kneeling position; we are required to wear a uniform of some description (there is a school uniform, a Sunday uniform, and an activities uniform) for all but a few hours a day when, between bath time and lights out, we are (in any case) shut up in a classroom attending to homework. We must tie up our hair when it touches our collars. We must wear high-waisted, low-legged thick brown nylon underwear. We may not speak after lights out, or before the wake-up bell, which rings at six. We must wait at the door for our seniors, teachers, visitors.

We are issued packing lists. We must bring (but may bring no more than) everything on the list. Three sets of school uniform, three sets of civilian clothes, five pairs of underwear, a Sunday dress, two pairs of lace-up Clarks shoes bought at vast expense from the aging lady (who seems prewar to me, by which I mean pre-Chimurenga) with flaking pink-powdered cheeks and a bright blonde beehive at the shoe department on the third floor of Meikles in Harare. After we have bought the shoes, Mum will take me out for tea and scones as a treat but I will hardly be able to swallow with the sickening anticipation of school ahead of me. And Mum's mouth has dried up, too, at the thought of all the money we do not have that she has just spent.

In our dormitories, we may only have three posters on our walls and five items on our dressing tables. We may wash our hair only on Saturday mornings. We cannot watch television or listen to a radio except for a few hours on the weekends. If we are caught smoking or drinking, or if we are disruptive, we will be expelled.

One evening, before lights out, a rumour spread through the boardinghouses (hopping the lawns from one hostel to the next) that two teenage boys had scaled the security fence and were at large on Arundel High School property. All the boarding hostels were immediately locked, with us inside of them, roll call was taken, and we were instructed to turn out the lights and undress in the dark (lest the rumoured boys see us as we changed into our pyjamas). Hysteria swept from cubicle to cubicle, from dorm to dorm. Several girls threw their underwear and bras out of the window. One girl burst into tears and it was said that another actually fainted with excitement.

*

At the end of the school term, I fly out of Zimbabwe and arrive at Kamuzu International Airport.

There is a barrage of signs to greet me.

I may not take photographs of official buildings; doing so will result in my arrest.

If I am a man, I may not wear my hair below my collar. My hair will be cut if it is too long.

If I am a woman, I may not wear shorts, trousers, or skirts that show the knee. Doing so will result in my arrest.

I may not bring pornography into the country. Doing so will result in my arrest.

(Pornography laws are so stringent that even the boxes of salty crackers imported from South Africa are censored. The bikini-clad woman on the box of crackers has her shapely legs blackened to the knee by the marker of a pornography official.)

I may not bring drugs into the country. Doing so will result in my death.

There is a small army of customs and immigration officials to greet me as I climb off the plane. I peer over their shoulders, trying to see into the terminal building, but there seems to be no end to the arrival procedures. There are rows and rows of officials and behind them there are poster-sized photographs of the little dictator whose skin, I notice, is shiny, like redwood mahogany. His photograph has been airbrushed into an eternal, tight-smiling youth. Armed guards stand at an imposing wooden entryway, blocking the view beyond the posters.

My school trunk is laid on a table. I am ordered to open it.

Three customs officials descend on my modest pile of possessions.

'Do you have any pornography?' asks one official. He waves his gun casually at the place where my heart is.

'No.'

My textbooks are discovered, opened, examined. Pages of biology, mathematics, chemistry, Latin, and French are carefully turned over until, with an expression of disgust, the official bears down on me and asks, 'Do you have drugs?'

'No.'

The officials find my box of tampons, open the box, unwrap a few tampons and peer down the tubes as if they were kaleidoscopes.

I look around, hoping no one is looking at me. I can feel my face burning. But everyone else is having their possessions fingered in just the same way. I can tell the Old Hands from the New Hands. While the New Hands blush, sweat, and occasionally protest their treatment, the Old Hands have relaxed. They are chatting to each other, smoking cigarettes, ignoring the officials, waving to each other: 'Where did you go?' 'How was your trip?' 'Join us for a beer later?'

'Do you have foreign currency?' My brookies and training

bras, awkwardly neither childish nor yet grown-up, are brought out and shaken, as if money might fall from their folds.

'No.'

The officials frown, suspicious. 'Then how will you pay your way while you stay in our country?'

'My mum and dad,' I say, my voice growing hoarse with near tears.

I burst breathlessly out into the steaming, humid air of the main airport where Mum, Dad, and Vanessa have grown bored, waiting for me to emerge. Mum is reading; Vanessa has wandered outside and is doing handstands on a patch of grass near a bed of bright canna lilies; Dad is smoking and staring at the ceiling.

*

Our letters are censored, clumsily torn open and read by the greasy-fingered immigration officials at the post office, so that by the time we get them, they are smudged and fingerprinted and rumpled and smell of fried fish, Coke 'n' buns, and fried potato chips: the office food of Africa. We may make phone calls only when the operator at Liwonde is on duty so that our calls can be monitored. If the operator is taking the rest of the day off, or is at home with malaria, or if the operator is attending a funeral, we cannot make a phone call.

I do not remember anyone making or receiving a phone call in that house. The Liwonde operator and his family appeared to suffer the most unfortunate ill health.

Touching the Ground

Butchery

Mgodi Estate is set up on gently sloping, sandy soil, seeping into the horizon, where a yellowing haze hanging over Lake Chilwa (less a lake than a large, mosquito-breeding swamp) marks the end of the farm and the beginning of the fishermen and their dugout canoes and their low, smoking fires over which they have stretched the gutted bodies of fish (spread thin, like large irregular dinner plates). From the spot where our garden ends (which Mum immediately encloses within a grass fence), the bodies start, and stretch as far as you can see on any side. Wherever we drive in Malawi there are people, and people in the act of creating food, whether scratching into the red soil with hoes and seed or raking the lakes for fish. It doesn't seem possible that there can be enough air for all the upturned mouths. The land bleeds red and eroding when it rains, staggering and sliding under the weight of all the prying, cultivating fingers.

Our house is big, airy, well-designed, and cool, with a mock Spanish grandeur that holds up only under fleeting scrutiny. Arches and a gauzed veranda surround the house: a large sitting room, a dining room, a passage down which there are three bedrooms and (unheard-of luxury!) two bathrooms. The kitchen, dominated by a massive woodstove and a deep sink, is set in a little cement hut behind the house where its heat and smoke can be contained. Our cook is a gentle, self-contained, avuncular Muslim called Doud whose careful rhythm of prayer and cooking and cleaning washes like a balm from his small inferno behind the dining room and soothes in waves across our house. The floors are covered with shiny, peeling-in-places linoleum and the made-on-the-farm doors and cupboards have swollen in the humidity and must be forced into their holes. Termites and lizards have set up house on the walls.

The large garden is thick with mango trees and is a sanctuary for birds, snakes, and the massive black and yellow four-to-six-foot-long monitor lizards. There are a swimming pool and a fish pond behind the house, but these bodies of water are a stubborn, frothing, seething mess of algae in which monitor lizards float, their small faces hiding their large, hanging bodies, and in which there are scorpions and frogs in staggering numbers. There is still the occasional goldfish, from previous managers, hanging in the murky fish pond, but between the monitor lizards and the fishing birds, their numbers dwindle monthly.

Dad strides down the passage in the morning, when the sun is just beginning to finger the skyline, banging first on my door – 'Rise and shine!' – and then on Vanessa's on his way to the veranda where Doud has set tea and fresh biscuits on a tray. Vanessa and I each have two beds in our rooms. Vanessa has taken the mattress off her spare bed and has laid it up against her door to dampen Dad's early-morning wake-up calls and to ensure that when she doesn't appear for tea he can't come crashing into her room shouting in blustery, sergeant-major tones, 'C'mon, rise and shine. What's wrong with you? Beautiful day!'

Mum and I both work on the farm. Mum walks down to the grading shed (a massive hangarlike structure into which all the tobacco from the farm has been brought) during the reaping season, or is driven down to the nursery where tobacco seedlings strive under the heat during the planting season.

Mum had been issued a motorbike, but after her first lesson ended (with a humiliating burst of feathers from a surprised guinea fowl) in a flower bed, she turned the motorbike over to me and either relied on me to drive her down to the tobacco seedlings, or walked, with the dogs fanning out in a destructive, chicken-killing wake behind her. There were constant requests from Malawians, toting bloodied fowl, for 'compensation for chicken death'. We began to suspect that even Mum's badly behaved dogs could not possibly have the energy (in the thick, swampy heat that hung almost permanently over the farm) to kill such a number of chickens and ducks over such a wide, diverse range (and all, apparently, within an hour or two). But we always paid up.

There was a constant, unspoken tension in the air, expressing the Malawian's superiority over all other races in the country. Even Europeans who had been in Malawi for generations, and who held Malawian passports, were on permanent notice. A complaint from a disgruntled worker could have a foreigner (regardless of citizenship) thrown out of the country for ever.

At the end of the farm, where the road bordered the beginning of the fishing villages, and all through the country, there were the blank faces of elaborately fronted, abandoned Indian stores whose owners had been unceremoniously expelled from the country as unpopular, money-grubbing foreigners. The stores had been handed over to Malawians, who soon lost interest in

Pulling dugout canoe

the long hours and careful scrutiny that are required to make a living from selling small bolts of cloth, single sticks of cigarettes, and individual sweets to an impoverished population. Now the windowless stores baked in the sun, their previously brightly painted walls bleaching, their floors littered with the droppings of fowl and birds, their rafters hung with bats and caked with the crusty red tunnels of termites.

I often ride the motorbike down to these abandoned stores, which are so hung about with ghosts and old dreams and a lost time. Sometimes, I see chickens scratching on the cracking concrete floors where once a tailor toiled strips of bright cloth through his fingers to the treadle of a Singer sewing machine. This is as close as I get to the swamp. From here, I sometimes see men, stripped to the waist, their backs silver-shiny with sweat, as they pull dugout canoes (made farther and farther from the lake as forests disappear into stumped scrubland in the wake of many busy axes) to the lake. The men sing as they pull the craft; their song is rhythmic and hypnotic, like a mantra.

But mostly I don't have time to drive all the way down to

the start of the swamp. I have to work. Dad says, 'You can't have a vehicle unless you use it for farm business.'

I leave the house after tea in the morning; I come home for lunch and then leave again until supper. My arms and legs grow muscled and brown as I manhandle the Honda through thick sand (which quickly turns to impassable mud in the sudden, violent rainstorms that sweep across the farm). I ride the avenues between the one thousand plots that make up Mgodi Estate. I am supposed to make sure that the tobacco has been planted with appropriate spaces, that the crop is weeded, that the plants are topped and reaped correctly.

*

It's a long time past lunch and I have been stuck at the north end of the Estate since mid-morning trying to persuade the Honda out of an abandoned well into which I fell while following the flight of a fish eagle. Now I am hurrying down the avenues, keeping half an eye on the tobacco crop, half an eye on the road, where chickens and children and dogs have settled in the shade cast by straw barns and mud huts. Suddenly, a child runs laugh-crying from a hut, arms outstretched, looking over his shoulder at his mother, who emerges just in time to see the child hit the motorbike side on. I am sent sprawling, the vehicle's spinning wheels kicking up stinging sand into my eyes and face until it stalls. In the sudden, ringing silence, I scramble to my feet, spitting dirt from my mouth and wiping my eyes. I am dizzy with fright, but the child is still standing and unhurt. He is looking at me with astonishment, his arms still outstretched. His face trembles, his lip shakes, and then he starts to cry. His mother swoops upon us and scoops her son into her arms. She shifts a smaller sling of baby, a quiet bulge in a bright hammock of cloth, under her arm to make room for the bigger child. The baby bleats once and then is quiet again.

I stand up and pull the motorbike up. 'Are you okay?'

She shrugs and smiles. The boy nestles into the soft crease of her neck and calms himself with soft, diminishing sobs.

'*Pepani, pepani.* I'm so sorry,' I say. 'I didn't see him. Is he okay?'

The woman shrugs and smiles again and I realize that she does not speak English. I have only learned a few phrases of Chnyanja none of which ('Thank you', 'How are you?', 'I am fine', 'What is the name of your father?') seem appropriate for my current predicament.

I put my right hand to my heart and bob a curtsy, right knee tucked behind left knee, in the traditional way, to reinforce my apology. The woman looks uneasy; she pats her young son's head almost as a reflex and glances, as if for help, into the shadows under the drying crop of tobacco hanging in a long, low shed next to her hut.

'It's no problem, madam,' a man's soft voice says from the shadows. I shade my eyes against the harsh, blanching sun. There, under the cool, damp leaves, on a reed mat, is a man lying almost naked, with a young boy of twelve or thirteen, also hardly clothed, by his side. For a moment I am too surprised to reply. The man, obviously the father of the toddler into whom I just crashed, props himself up on one elbow and rubs his bare, pale-shining collar bone with the thick fingers of one hand. The boy at his side stirs, rolls over, and hangs an arm over the older man's neck, his face stretched up in a grimace which is half-smile, half-yawn. The boy's shorts have worn through at the crotch and his member is exposed, flaccid and long against his thigh.

The man begins to softly caress the boy's arm, almost absent-mindedly, as if the arm draped around his neck were a pet snake. I am suddenly aware of how softly quiet the hot afternoon is: a slight buzzing of insects, a crackle of heat from the drying thatch that covers the barn and house, the distant cry of a cockerel clearing his throat to warn of the coming of mid-afternoon when work will resume. My stomach growls, empty-acid. I feel the sun burning the back of my neck, my eyes stinging, my muscles aching. I pull the motorbike up and have begun to climb back onto it when the man suddenly pulls himself off the mat, the child still hanging from his neck.

The man is smiling. I see now that he is much older than I had first thought. I also see that the boy around his neck is disabled; he is a combination of helplessness (his arms and legs are as thin as bones and devoid of muscles) and of uncontrollable, rigid spasms, which send him backwards against the softly restraining cradle of his father's arms. His head rolls, his mouth sags open sideways, and saliva hangs to his chin. He makes soft, puppy noises. I have never seen this, an African child in this condition. It comes to me, in one sweep, that most children like this boy are probably allowed to die, or are unable to survive in the conditions into which they are born.

The man says, 'Are you fine?'

I nod. 'Thank you.'

He frowns and points at the sun with the flat of his hand, which also supports his son's head, 'You are out now? In this hot sun? You can see from the sun that it is time to rest.'

I nod again. 'I was stuck.' I point to the motorbike. 'I fell in a well.'

'Ah.' The man laughs. 'Yes, that is difficult.'

'I'm sorry,' I say – I indicate the toddler, and then am embarrassed in case the man thinks I am apologizing for his older, disabled child. I quickly add, 'I didn't see your baby.'

'Baby?'

'Your small boy.'

'Ah, yes. I see. We also have a baby, you see.'

'Yes. Big family,' I tell him.

'*Lowani*,' says the man suddenly.

I grin and blink. 'What? I don't speak Chnyanja,' I tell him.

'Come inside,' says the man in English. He speaks quickly to his wife in Chnyanja and she disappears into the hut. 'Please, we have some food. You must take your lunch here.'

I hesitate, torn between lies ('I've already eaten', 'They'll be waiting for me at home') and an impulse to please this man, to make up for the disruption and the accident. I nod and smile. 'Thank you. I am hungry.'

*

And this is how I am almost fourteen years old before I am formally invited into the home of a black African to share food. This is not the same as coming *uninvited* into Africans' homes, which I have done many times. As a much younger child, I would often eat with my exasperated nannies at the compound (permanently hungry and always demanding), and I had sometimes gone into the labourers' huts with my mother if she was attending someone too sick to come to the house for treatment. I had ridden horses and bikes and motorbikes through the compounds of the places we had lived, snatching at the flashes of life that were revealed to me before doors were quickly closed, children hidden behind skirts, intimacy swallowed by cloth.

I am aware suddenly of watching my manners, of my filthy, oil-stained, and dust-covered skirt, of my dirty hands. I turn my dirty fingernails into the palms of my hands and duck out of the heat into the soft, dark, old-smoke-smelling hut. I blink for a few moments in the sudden dim light until shapes swim out of the greyness and form into four small stools crouched around a black pot on a ring of stones. The floor is fine dust, infinitely swept into pale powder. The father is pointing to a stool. '*Khalani pansi,*' he says. 'Please, sit here.'

I sit on the small smoothly worn stool, my knees drawn up above my hips.

The father crouches at the far end of the hut and shouts an order, throwing his voice beyond me and into the hot afternoon; he is half-balancing, half-supporting the retarded boy on his knee, an elbow crooked to catch the youth's head if it should suddenly lurch back. The boy appears to be grasping at the hanging silver particles of dust that jostle in the fine swords of sunlight slicing through the thinning grey thatch of the hut. The mother leans over the fire. She bends at the waist, gracious and limber. Her baby is suckling at an exposed breast. The woman pounds at the pot on the stones where hot nshima is bubbling and steaming, letting out burps of hot breath as it cooks. A smaller pot is emitting fiery gasps of greasy fish.

A girl child comes into the hut, tottering under the sloshing weight of the basin of water that she balances, clearly straining, on her head. She stops when she sees me and looks likely to drop her burden and run.

The father laughs and points to me.

The girl hesitates. The father encourages.

The girl lowers the basin from her head and holds it in front of me. I see that I am to wash my hands. I rinse my hands in the water, shake the drops at my feet and smile at the little girl, but still she stands there, the muscles in her thin, knobbly arms jumping under the pressure. Water and sweat have mixed on her face. Large drops quake on her eyebrow and threaten to spill at any moment.

'Thank you.' I smile again.

The whole family is watching me. '*Zikomo kwambiri*,' I try, smiling in general at everyone, for lack of knowing what else to do. The smell of the food and the heat it is giving off while cooking makes me sweat. I point at the little girl. 'Your daughter, too?'

The father beams and nods.

'How old?'

He tells me.

The mother hands me a plate (enamelled but rusted on the edges). She spoons food.

'Thanks,' I say when the plate is just covered, making a gesture of sufficiency, half ducking the plate out of reach.

Her large spoon hovers between her pot and my plate.

'No, really,' I say, 'I had a late breakfast.'

The mother glances at her husband. He nods, barely, and

Schoolboy

she lets her spoon drop back into the pot. Carefully she covers the leftover food.

'Isn't anyone else going to eat?'

The father shakes his head. 'No, please . . . Thank you.'

The *nshima* is surrounded by a grey sea of barbel and oil. 'This smells very good.'

The children are watching me hungrily. The disabled youth has stopped patting dust fairies and is staring at me. A trembling, nervous cord of saliva runs from the corner of his mouth to his chin. The toddler has started to cry, weakly, plaintively, like a small goat. The mother absently pats the boy, nurses the baby, rocks and rocks, staring at me. The father swallows. 'Eat,' he says. He sounds desperate. I sense that it is only through the greatest exertion of will that my spectators don't fall on the food on my plate in a frenzy of hunger.

'It looks delicious.'

I make a ball of *nshima* with the fingers of my right hand, the way I had been taught to do as a small child by my nannies.

I insert my thumb into the ball, deep enough to make a dent in the dense hot yellow porridge. Onto the dent, as if onto a spoon, I scoop up a mouthful of the fish stew.

Almost before my mouth can close around the food, the young girl (who has not left my side and whose arms still strain at the ends of the bowl) offers me the water and I see that I must wash my hands again. I am conscious of the little girl's breath-catching effort to hold the basin, and of the groaning, sometimes audible hunger pangs that ripple through the hut. The food, which is sharp and oily in my mouth, has been eagerly anticipated by everyone except for me. I know that I am eating part of a meal intended for (I glance up) five bellies.

There are bones in the fish, which I try to manoeuvre around to the front of my mouth. I spit the bones into my hand and carefully wipe them on the side of the plate. I stare at the food. A fish eye stares balefully back at me from the oily pool of gravy. I have a long meal ahead of me.

*

It is mid-afternoon by the time I wash my hands for a final time and swim backwards out of the hut, back into the mellowing heat of a yellowing afternoon, where light from the sun is sucked up and diffused by so many smoking fires over which fish are drying near the edge of Lake Chilwa. I pat my heart and bend one knee behind the other, lowering my eyes. 'Thank you very much,' I say, '*Zikomo kwambiri. Zikomo, zikomo.*'

The family watch as I kick the motorbike into life. I wave, and slowly drive away up the avenue of tenants' houses which no longer feels like an anonymous, homogenous row of grass-fronted, mud-stiff huts.

That evening I return to the hut with a good proportion of my already meagre closet. I have plastic grocery bags hanging from the handlebars of my motorbike in which I have put shorts, T-shirts, skirts, a dress, one pair of shoes (worn through at the toe) and some outgrown toys and books. Mum has stopped me from taking towels and blankets. 'We barely have enough for ourselves,' she told me. But our faux-Spanish house, with its stucco walls and its long, cool stretches of linoleum and its vast veranda and its spacious garden seems, suddenly, exhaustingly, too much.

Mum shakes her head. She says, 'I know, Bobo.'

'But it's so awful.'

'It won't go away.' She is watching me stuff plastic bags with clothes. 'You can't make it go away.'

I sniff.

'It was there before you noticed it.'

'I know, but . . .'

She gets up with a sigh, dusts her knees. She says, 'And it will be there after you leave.'

'I know, but . . .'

Mum pauses at the door. 'And bring back my plastic bags, we're always short of those,' she says.

At the hut, I feel suddenly self-conscious, aware of all the curious, maybe suspicious, eyes on me from all the other huts up and down the road. Children abandon their games and cluster around me. All are in worn-through clothes, most are swollen-bellied. I hand over the plastic bags to the mother of the child I knocked into earlier and I say, 'Here.' She looks at the bags, uncomprehending.

'For you,' I insist.

She looks embarrassed. 'Thank you.' She holds the bags against the round lump of sleeping baby in the hammock at her breast. '*Zikomo, zikomo.*'

I back away into the crowd of children who are now bouncing and dancing around the motorbike. 'Miss Bob, Miss Bob, what have you brought for me?'

When I drive away the children run after me as long as they can keep up, shouting after me, 'Miss Bob! Bob! What have you brought for *me*?'

The Goat Shed

Bobo: Cape Maclear

The T-shirts we buy at the small white hotel overlooking the beach on Lake Malawi or at the small kiosk at the airport declare, MALAWI – THE WARM HEART OF AFRICA.

We call it the Warm Fart of Africa, hee, hee.

Dad's face erupts in boils. Mum begins to grow thick wings of grey at her temples. I become white-gilled and lethargic until Mum diagnoses anaemia and feeds me liver and chopped rape. For the first time, we are all regularly malarial. Vanessa has to be hospitalized, she becomes so ill, yellow, thin, weak, fevered. In the two years we live in Malawi, all three of our dogs die. The new Rhodesian ridgeback contracts a deadly venereal disease; the spaniel contracts fatal tick fever, which turns her gums and eyeballs yellow and then kills her; ancient, faithful Shea spouts foul-smelling lumps, her ears bleed yellow pus, she scratches and whines until we shave her coat in sympathy. And then she dies in her sleep.

We feel more dangerously, teeteringly close to disease and death (in a slow, rotting, swamp-induced fashion) than we did during the war in Rhodesia where there was a zinging, adrenaline-filled, anything-goes freedom and where we were surrounded by violent, quick mutilation and a sudden, definitive end. Which now seems preferable to death by swamp rot. Death by spies. Death by lack of social contact.

In Malawi we frequently see children bent backwards, as easily and rigidly as twisted paper clips, with cerebral malaria, from which, if they emerge alive, they will rarely recover completely. And here we see the effects of malnutrition and the effects of overcrowded, unsanitary shantytowns and overfilled garbage dumps and we see thin, ribby, curly-tailed dogs digging in heaps of decomposing rubbish on which children play and pick and shit.

Our nearest white neighbours are a German couple who have come out to Africa as aid workers. They are our first experience of foreigners in Africa who are here for that purpose; until now, in Rhodesia, we had seen foreigners only as missionaries or mercenaries.

Dad says, 'At least death by mercenary is quicker.'

'Than what?'

'Death by aid.'

But we are desperate enough for company to visit the Germans.

'Perhaps they drink beer,' says Mum hopefully.

Dad lights a cigarette. 'Maybe they cure sausages.'

I have only ever heard of Germans in the context of the Second World War.

I say, 'I hope they don't have a gas oven. Hee hee.'

Mum says, 'Bobo!'

'Okay, okay.'

'Don't mention the war,' says Dad.

'Ve have vays and means of making you talk.'

We start to giggle, hiccupping our hilarity.

But we find, to our surprise, that we are very fond of the Hartmans. Barbara does not wear makeup, she does not shave and she smells naturally (in a pleasant way) of her own clean body: a salty, onion, cooking-bread smell that reminds me of the homely, breast-milk scent of my old nannies. Gerald is keen on saving the environment, which, until then, I had not noticed needed saving. I had been more concerned with staying alive myself.

Gerald lends me books. He is patient, gentle, intelligent, passionate, methodical. I fall in love with his hard accent, the way his words cut so efficiently through the sickly, sticky heat. I listen to the stories he weaves of the living planet around us. 'We are minute,' he tells me. 'We are grains of sand on the beach of time. We are not important. There was a time when the planet was without people and, especially with the way we are going, there will sooner or later be a time when again we are gone from this earth.'

I declare my adolescent difference from my family as a passionate environmentalist, and if I had a choice I'd wear baggy, tie-dyed clothes like Barbara's. Except I don't have a choice. I have to wear what clothes we can find at the secondhand market and castoffs from Vanessa (which I supplement with scarves and wooden beads). I consider taking up vegetarianism, briefly.

*

But mostly we are white and alone, an isolated island in a pressing, restless, relentless sea of Malawians whose lives continue on the periphery of ours in a seeming miracle of survival. At night, by the throb of the generator that gives us a few hours of electric light, we scramble for the tape recorder, on which we now play a recently extended collection of music (Bizet,

Puccini, Chopin, Brahms, Rachmaninoff, Debussy, to supplement our old standards Roger Whittaker and the 1812. Mum is trying to expose us to all the usual suspects in a glut of 'Best of' tapes purchased from the budget bins at classical music stores in England. And we drink Carlsberg lager into the mosquito-humming night which is so dense with humidity we feel as if we might absorb water through our skins, as sheep are said to do.

We play fierce games of poker, Dad, Vanessa, and I. We have no money, so we use Dad's matches as chips. We play for 'If you lose you have to get the next round of beer,' which means asking Mum to hand a beer round to all of us. We play for 'If you lose you have to light the next round of mosquito coils,' which burn fragrantly, like incense, at our ankles and are supposed to ward off mosquitoes although every morning our legs are polka-dotted with bites. We play for 'If you lose you have to bring me a tray of tea whenever I ask for it for the next week,' which is an idle threat because we have a houseboy (who arrived one morning announcing he was here to help Doud in the kitchen) to fetch us tea.

*

The new houseboy scuffles idly at the door of the back kitchen, where Doud is making up the massive pot of nshima that will feed the dogs, cats, chickens. A pungent, oily soup of bones, fish heads, green cuttings and leftovers bubbles on the woodstove.

Mum says, 'Yes?' and glares.

'I have orders,' he announces.

'Orders for what?'

'I have orders to work here.'

'No, you don't.' Mum turns her back on the man and shows Doud a recipe in her well-fingered, brown-spattered *Good Housekeeping Cookbook*.

'But I have orders.'

Mum heaves a deep, irritated sigh and turns back to the man on the doorstep. 'From whom?'

The new houseboy looks sullen. He shrugs his shoulders impatiently under the new crisp cut of his khaki uniform (not issued by Mum).

'It is required that I am hired.'

'Well, I unrequire you,' declares Mum.

But the next day the new houseboy arrives again (late, after we have eaten breakfast) for work and skulks around the house until Mum screams at him.

'You can't fire me,' he says.

'I didn't hire you to begin with.'

The new servant lets this settle for a moment before declaring, 'This is not Rhodesia.'

'I know it's not bloody Rhodesia.'

But he stays. And at the end of the month he is paid along with Doud, the gardener, the watchman, and the driver who make up the household staff. And Mum says, 'I suppose it's just as well. We need someone for Fridays,' which is Doud's day at the mosque.

The new houseboy is caught reading our mail, looking through our drawers, rifling in the suitcases under our beds, but whenever we threaten to fire him, he only bares his teeth and tells us, 'You can't.' And it gradually dawns on us that this little man with the hostile breath and furtive tackies (squeaking sneakily from room to room) is an official employee of the government, sent to spy on us. Thus employed, he is an indifferent houseboy.

When we ask him to fetch us a tray of tea it arrives lukewarm, tea leaves floating damply in the top of the pot, with unmatched cups, and we only glance at each other and obediently drink the inferior brew. He irons wrinkles and scorched, burnt-brown stains into the clothes (he overfills the charcoal iron so that hot coals spill from its lid). He overcooks the supper (meat appears dried and flaking next to shrivelled vegetables and parched rice).

Even the dogs hunch their backs at him and slink wearily from his feet.

All day we must leave unspoken any thoughts that might be taken as negative with regard to the country: the country's government, the country's leader, the country's roads, the country's climate, the country's population. But at night, with the hum of the generator throbbing light into the compound (where the Spy lives with a sad-looking young wife and a fat child always embalmed in pink wool) Mum sits yoga-cross-legged on the chair next to the beer (as if guarding it), and shouts of the conspiracy against us. She hates the Spy. She hates the breath-sucking crush of bodies around us. She hates the censorship that interrupts our mail, our phone calls, our reading, our boxes of South African crackers.

Dad smokes quietly. He looks at me over the top of his cards. He says, 'You're feeling brave.'

I've put down four matches on the strength of my hand. I struggle, unsuccessfully, for a poker face.

Mum's waving a finger in the air. 'Corrupt! Every last one of them. What a bloody country.'

'Don't cheat,' says Vanessa.

'I'm not.'

'You're trying to look at Dad's cards.'

'Am not.'

'They can send their little spies . . .' says Mum.

'You are, I saw you,' says Vanessa, kicking me under the table.

'I am not. *Owie* man. Hey, Vanessa kicked me.'

'It was an accident.'

'Liar.'

Dad squashes out a cigarette. 'Hey, cut it out you two. No fighting.'

'But they can't change the way I think,' says Mum.

Dad smiles. 'Now I have you girls by the short and curlies. A pair of kings, a pair of queens, and three eights.'

'*Jeez,* Dad.'

'You know the little creep is lying to them about you.'

'I'll have another beer, please Mum.'

'What little creep?'

'That little spy of a houseboy. He's reporting everything we do to the government.'

'Can I have a beer, too, please Mum?'

'You need to watch their every move, Tim, I'm telling you.'

Dad lights a cigarette and grunts.

'My God, if we don't get off this bloody farm, we're going to rot.'

Mum scratches her ankles absently. They have begun to bleed from bites on bites on bites.

*

Near the southern tip of Lake Malawi is a bay called Cape Maclear tucked into hills and accessible only by a long, thin, terrible road. The bay is protected on each side by wings of rising rocks and in front by a thin string of uninhabited islands, which are wild and secret and guarded by monitor lizards who lie sunbathing on black rocks. The bay is habitually unruffled and its waters miraculously free of those traditional drawbacks to African swimming – bilharzia and crocodiles – although the occasional hippo has been known to stray up onto the beach.

The beach is two miles long. Black, powdery sand near the water leads to sugar-coarse dunes. Sitting on the beach, we can smell the bitter-sweet pungency of the rising camp settlements behind us. Periodic rain flushes debris and litter down from the shanties onto the beach and into the water.

It is here that the expatriates congregate on the weekends to drink.

'Expats like us,' says Mum. By which she means, Not missionaries or aid workers, 'with whom one doesn't want to drink anyway.'

We find a small patch of land among the other parcels on

Van: Cape Maclear

the edge of the lake where the expats-like-us camp in shacks or tents during the school holidays and on weekends. This is where generators throb all night to keep beer cold and milk fresh and where the beer drinking begins at breakfast, when there is a fatty, salty hum of bacon and eggs coming from each blue-smoked fire and where the crackle of radios or the *bah-bum-bah-bum* of kids' pop music (turn-that-bloody-racket-down) wakes us from our hot, beer-heavy sleep.

Eventually, the morning sun beats us out from under our mosquito nets in search of tea and we join the other pink-shouldered soldiers blearily trudging to the refreshing lap-lap of the sweet blue bay. We swim out to the rocks and back, and then run back to our camp (over already foot-searing hot sand) for goggles and snorkels, cigarettes, towels, books. The day becomes seamless and sunlit, its passage marked only by the diminishing supply of beer in various generator-run fridges and by the peripheral activities of the local fishermen (who leave at dawn in their dugout canoes and return at dusk).

We lie on the beach reading, we swim and drink and try out our new-fledged flirting skills on our friends' brothers, who are either kind and ignore us, or are cruel and take us to heart. All day, there is a sting of petrol in the air from the speedboats that periodically cut drunkenly out across the ripple-free lake, towing the swinging stick figure of a water-skier behind them or bumping the ecstatic bodies of children on its bows. And there is the soft, rotten smell of humid heat and there is the periodic piercing burn of a freshly lit cigarette ('Can I have one?') and the underlying, constant persistence of smoked fish.

When the dug-out canoes come in from the lake, the fishermen bowed silver-backed in the lowering sun as they paddle for shore, we stretch sun-and-sweat-salted bodies, crush out our cigarettes in the sand, and saunter down to greet them. We haggle for their fresh catch, carefully scratching the scales of the fish and sniffing to check for freshness (we want just-caught fish, not fish from the morning that have been recently splashed to make them appear just-caught). We take our fish back up to the various ribbons of blue smoke over which cooks are bending and into which cooks are blowing, sending roaring orange flames into crackling wood. We eat fish and rice and drink local gin, slapping mosquitoes off our ankles and sweating into our tin plates.

After supper, we build bonfires on the beach and sit with toes dug into blood-warm sand, watching the moon's reflection on the lake as it rises over the hills behind us. We smoke and talk, tired from all-day beer-and-sun. Gradually bodies roll back to camp and shack and caravan. The singeing smoke of mosquito coils curls in the air. Some nights, we drag mattresses down to the beach and shake out mosquito nets under trees, hunching sunburnt shoulders to each other, and we sleep next to the silver-edged, moon-and-star-speckled lake, from which there comes an occasional, mysterious splash.

*

It is the beginning of the rains and the Spy takes leave in order to return to his village, where he will plant a new year's crop on his small patch of farm and plant a new year's baby into his mournful young wife's belly. Doud is too old for babies, he tells us. His sons have taken over his small farm now. He tells us he will stay for Christmas. He makes daily attempts at hot mince pies, which are stomach-heavy in the steaming heat but which we swallow dutifully, along with equally unrefreshing mulled wine. There are no fir trees or Christmas decorations, so we decorate a dusty, droughted pine with the cut-out golden stars and globes of old Benson & Hedges cigarette boxes.

The rains are rhythmic, coming religiously in the afternoons (after lunch has been eaten but before tea, so that the nights are washed clean-black with bright pinpoints of silver starlight hanging over a restless, grateful earth). The rains are grey solid sheets of water, slamming into the mock-Spanish house with sudden sideways ferocity and soaking everything, slashing through the window louvres and damping beds and curtains until everything seems heavy and turning-green with moisture. Laundry, which until now has hung behind the cookhouse (and is returned to us fragrant with wood smoke) is never quite dry. It hangs, steaming over Doud's head, from a wire running over the woodstove and now (when it is returned to us) our clothes and sheets and towels smell of the dogs' boiling fish-head stew.

The pet guinea fowl crouch damp and miserable under the dripping trees' inadequate shelter and the chickens stop laying all but the most deformed eggs (from which hatch sickly, one-legged or wingless chicks). Snakes slide onto our veranda, slithering resentfully from flooded holes. Frogs breed energetically in the pool and in the fish pond, where the toads grow so fat and large we suspect them of having eaten the last of the goldfish (which were plagued with unsightly growths anyway); leguaans are washed from their swamps and one of these six-foot lizards even wanders into the sitting room where I am legs-tucked-up-in-a-chair reading a book.

When we peer (lifting tired eyes from books and games of cards) into the grey rain and over the grass fence, we can see the tenants' children run knees high through puddles, mahogany-coloured arms shaking into the air, heads thrown back, pink mouths open. The very little children are shining-naked. They look polished and ecstatic and I am jealous of them.

The daily rains mean that we can no longer camp at the lake and so now our weeks lump ahead of us in a dreary patternless marathon of tobacco planting, trays of tea, card games, beer drinking, rain gazing. Weeks pass. The rains have set in and their generosity is assured. It will be a wet year, and now we all long for one or two days' reprieve. The rains are no longer a cause of daily celebration and relief, as they were a month ago. Even the tenants' children have stopped playing when the heavens burst upon us. Now comes the playless, earnest task of ensuring that all the crops are in before the fields become too wet. And now the flush of weeds, which have sprung up like tufts of unruly hair, must be snatched from the earth before they sap precious food from tobacco and maize. Through the grey, hanging afternoons, tenants and their children are bent over freshly turned fields pressing raw, startled tobacco seedlings into ridges and dropping maize pips into tiny raised mounds of hot, damp, welcoming earth.

Vanessa rescues a rain-sick, one-legged chick from the coop. She keeps it in a shoe box near her bed and spends most of her day trying to tempt lumps of Pronutro porridge down its sickly beak until the porridge oozes out of its nostrils and the creature suffocates. Vanessa wears a black scarf to the sodden funeral in the garden and after that she won't be coaxed from her room except for beer and cards in the evening. Nor will she allow Doud to clean away the deceased chick's shit-smelling shoe box. The house takes on the smell of Vanessa's dead project.

It is too wet for me to get the motorbike through the vlei which cuts through the middle of the farm. I walk the farm for days but the wet is persistent and soul rotting. I give up and read my way through Mum's library.

Mum presses herself into gumboots and spends her mornings

Mum: hair job

hovering over the tobacco seedbeds watching the limp-necked plantlings as they are loaded onto the trailers and taken to the tenants' fields. But when the seedlings have all been transported and planted, there is nothing left for her to do except wait and hope that most of them survive the ordeal. She comes home and we lie on her bed and read books.

I dye Mum's hair a streaky, porcupine blonde and shave my legs just to see if I need to.

Vanessa experiments with eye shadow and looks as if she has been punched.

I try and make meringues and the resulting glue is eaten with clench-jawed dutifulness by my family. Mum encourages me not to waste precious eggs on any more cooking projects.

I learn what I hope are the words to Bizet's *Carmen* and sing the entire opera to the dogs.

Vanessa paints a picture of a girl with long blonde hair. The picture depicts the girl drowning and screaming, her hair spread out around her. She calls it *The Scream–Mgodi*.

Mum rinses her hair in purple wash and her porcupine blonde streaks turn silver.

Dad teaches me to drive the old truck. I have to balance on the edge of the seat to reach the pedals, and the steering is so loose that it bucks my thin arms into the air when we jolt over a bump.

I smoke in front of the mirror and try to look like a hardened sex goddess.

Vanessa declares, hopelessly, that she is thinking of running away from home. I stare out at the nothingness into which she would run and say, 'I'll come with you.'

Mum says, 'Me too.'

*

So Dad takes a gang of men from the farm and in one weekend they erect an open-air hut out of mud, poles, and thatch on our plot at the lake. Its walls reach to my knees, and its primitive thatch hangs down like too-long hair, stopping just above our heads so that any breeze off the lake is free to press through the hut, through the stifling, humid-thick air, to the back of the hut where Dad has fashioned crude slat beds from rough wood. Each bed has a thin foam mattress and a pair of locally made sheets (rough, raw-to-the-toes cotton) and is misted with a mosquito net. He splashes whitewash on the mud hut and covers the mud floor with raked beach sand.

He comes home and declares (in the presence of the Spy, who has lately returned from his village) that we can now escape the farm at weekends. 'Room for everyone,' he declares. 'We built a bloody palace.'

On Friday, we load the pickup. Mum brings last year's unsellable tobacco scraps and sweepings from Mgodi's grading shed to dig into the clay-tight, black soil. She has ripped up runners from the garden to plant a lawn of thick-leaved buffalo grass (which will spread green, quick, grateful fingers over bare soil) and bags of cuttings from the poinsettias, bougainvillea, and snowball bushes. She has jars of fledgling mango and avocado (coaxed to life on the windowsill in the kitchen) pressed up against the burlap sacks of grass. Dad and I struggle under the weight of a real flush toilet (bought from the hardware store at Zomba) on which Vanessa triumphantly balances herself for the drive (and from which she waves victoriously to shrieking children all the way to the lake). We pile up dry firewood (the lake area has been picked clean of kindling) and sacks of mealie meal for the watchman who has been stationed to keep an eye on our new palace. We whistle up the dogs and climb into the truck. I am holding onto a cage, made of bush sticks and bark, from which a cockerel is glaring. He is Marcus, and Mum insists that he is necessary to eat the ants that crawl out of the floor and cover the bush poles with their red, crusty tunnels.

All the expats-like-us bring a servant down to the lake to cook, clean, and run to 'Stephen's Bar' for the daily supply of beer. But we are loaded to the gunwales and are forced to leave the Spy behind. 'Worthless bugger that he is,' Dad says. 'Anyway, the watchman can make a fire for us and clean up.'

'And I'll help cook,' I say, exuberant with escape.

Vanessa retches theatrically.

Mum says, 'It's just this once, Vanessa. We can survive.'

We edge out of the yard, teetering dangerously on top of our heavy load of supplies, and wave to the Spy.

*

And then the Spy outdid himself.

Because of Christmas and New Year, more than two weeks pass before we can return to our palace at the lake. This time we bring the Spy. We arrive to find an excited gaggle of expats-like-us·who report that a Presidential Inquiry was sent to the lake the previous weekend. The Inquiry had apparently come to investigate reports that 'Tim Fuller has built himself a palace at the lake with His Excellency's money.'

The entourage, bad-tempered after an uncomfortable, steamy

journey from Lilongwe (which not even a ride in an air-conditioned Mercedes-Benz could cushion) had arrived at Cape Maclear and demanded to know where Tim Fuller's palace was.

The expats-like-us show them the raw, mud hut.

'This!' The chief government investigator was scandalized; his mouth moved in silent protest until indignation could find words. 'This is not a palace! This is nothing but a goat shed.'

*

The Spy creeps to the back of the hut and makes a fire. He looks furtively at the expats-like-us and then, with obvious dismay, at the hut.

Dad finds a piece of driftwood flattened by water and rock, and Vanessa uses a hot rod of metal, fresh from the fire, to burn THE GOAT SHED into it. We hang the sign from one of the hut's poles.

Federal Fullers

Dugout canoes: Lake Malawi

Vanessa and I are sunbathing on the cluster of rocks at the far south of the beach, where fishermen from the local villages sometimes suddenly appear, as if organically rising from the deep, clear water, their ancient, finger-smoothed canoes smoke-smelling and fish heavy. They try to sell us marijuana (which they will also exchange for cigarettes or fishing line), fish, or sometimes baskets and beads.

I say, 'I'll pay you two *kwacha* for a ride in your canoe.'

'Three *kwacha*.'

I hesitate.

'Okay, okay, two *kwacha*.'

Vanessa sits up and shades her eyes from the sun. 'Don't go too far, hey.'

I scud down the rock, gripping on a narrow ledge, toes stretching towards the canoe.

'Hands first,' says the paddler, holding the canoe steady against the rock.

'How can I put my hands first?'

'Ah, but you must.'

'It'll be all right. You just keep the thing still.' I make a clumsy lurch for the canoe, there is a brief vision of the paddler's dismayed face, and then we are all over, upside down, the water around me suddenly lively with paddles, dead fish, grasping nets, despondent soggy cigarettes.

Vanessa peers over the edge of her perch. 'You're going to have to pay him for everything you've sunk.'

'I will. I will.' I cling to the upturned canoe. 'Sorry,' I pant to the fisherman. But he is too busy recovering his goods to respond. I clear myself from the debris, from the leg-heavy fishing nets which threaten to pull me down, and thrash back to the beach, where I lie on my belly staring at the glassy sand and coughing. The fisherman is still hanging on to his upturned canoe, saving cigarettes, which he is placing in a row on the canoe's sky-facing bottom.

He kicks the canoe to shore. He has lost his day's catch. He does not look at me as he lays out his life on the beach. He has lost not only his catch, but also his knife, a basket, a plastic bag in which he had an old wine bottle filled with cooking oil, and a tin bowl containing a fistful of dry cornmeal for *nshima*. I watch the muscles hop on his angry back and dig my toes into the sand. 'I'm sorry.'

He does not answer.

'I'll pay you. How many *kwacha*?' But even those usually magic words fail to elicit a response.

He turns his canoe upright and pushes out into the lake, balancing briefly, as lightly as a cat, on the gunwale before lowering himself into the canoe, bent like a dancer, from where he digs into the water with his paddle and slides out into the glare of the bright afternoon sun.

I pick my way back up to the top of the rock, where Vanessa's pink shoulders are beginning to hum a more urgent shade of red.

'You're burning,' I tell her.

'That's so typical,' she says.

'Put your shirt on.'

'You're so annoying.'

I sit, contrite, next to Vanessa. 'He wouldn't let me pay him.'

'No wonder no one will snog you.'

I light a cigarette.

Vanessa scratches under her chin, her jaw thrust out. She is looking far out into the water, as if reading it for further insights into my shortcomings. 'Everything you do is a disaster.'

The cigarette is bitter on my tongue. Tears sting behind my eyelids and make a hard painful lump in the back of my throat.

'You're fourteen years old and you haven't even been kissed.'

I shrug. 'Who says I want to be?'

She pushes out her lips at me. 'Can't you be just a little less . . .? Can't you? I mean, can't you just be *normal*?'

'I am normal.'

Vanessa closes her eyes. We have been taking it in turns spraying a bottle of Sun-In into our hair. It has streaked Vanessa silver-blonde and has turned my hair orange, in unsightly blocks. She runs her fingers through her hair and turns her face to the sun.

I have had my hair cut, in an unflattering pudding bowl, by an African hairdresser in Blantyre. My fringe is very short and crooked. I look like a grasshopper wearing a wig. I hang my head on my knees and sigh. Tears roll down my cheeks and splash onto my legs.

'Geoffrey might snog you,' says Vanessa at last.

He looks like a small, greasy weasel. 'Thanks.'

'It's better than nothing.'

*

Which is how I come to be snogged, at the next New Year's party, by the rodent-faced Geoffrey, whose tongue takes me by such surprise that my teeth clamp down on it in a startled reflex.

'Well, what were you expecting?' says Vanessa.

I shrug. 'Not his tongue.'

'What did you think snogging *was*?'

'Not tongues.'

Vanessa rolls her eyes. 'You can't say I didn't try,' she says.

'I know, I know. I didn't.'

Vanessa considers. 'Geoffrey was your best bet,' she says at last.

There are few expats-like-us, which translates to very few snoggable sons. I say, 'I'll be okay.'

'It's not healthy.'

'What isn't?'

Vanessa looks at me, at a loss for words, and waves at me. 'You,' she says at last. 'Your whole . . . everything.'

I press my lips together to prevent tears from coming.

'I hope Geoffrey didn't tell *everyone* that you bit him.'

But he had.

Which is why it is a relief when Dad announces that he will not be renewing his two-year contract with the President for Life as manager of Mgodi Estates.

'We're moving,' he announces.

Our choices are Papua New Guinea, Mozambique or Zambia. It is 1983.

*

Papua New Guinea is floating anonymously off the tip of Australia. I read that it is mostly covered with forest. It is famous for its mineral reserves and cannibals.

Mozambique is seven years into a civil war, which follows on from its ten-year war of independence against the Portuguese. It is widely acknowledged to be the most miserable nation on earth. It is famous for its land mines and child soldiers.

Zambia is recovering from belly-rocking, land-sucking drought. It is famous for its mineral reserves and political corruption.

I am keen to move to Papua New Guinea, which is as far from Geoffrey's injured tongue as we can get without actually falling off the planet.

Dad thinks Mozambique might have a future.

'In what?' Vanessa wants to know.

'A future,' Dad insists. 'Everything has a future.'

'Not if you're dead,' I mutter.

Vanessa looks away. 'Are there any other . . . people there?' she asks.

Dad says, 'That's the best part. There's *no one* there.'

No snoggable sons.

The Germans for whom we would farm in Zambia have clothing factories there. They make a tremendous profit manufacturing uniforms for the various and numerous armies of Africa (no shipment of uniforms without payment). Their seven-thousand-acre farm is a tax ruse but they still want the place to run at a profit. They have found their last three farm managers to be incompetent, dishonest, and drunk (usually in combination).

The Germans have offered to buy Mum horses if Dad will agree to work on their farm. They will pay for Vanessa and me to attend our private schools (in Zimbabwe, where Vanessa is now at secretarial college) and they will buy us tickets to and from Zambia so that we can fly back home during the holidays.

So Mum and Dad go to Zambia and take a look at the farm. There are virgin forests and three dams, two rivers and passable roads. There is a large main house and a guest cottage, and a total of three flush loos at our disposal (if you count the loo in the guest cottage). There is more or less full-time electricity (when the Zambian Electricity Supply Commission can compete with summer storms). There is a schoolhouse and a building for a clinic for the farm staff (neither have operated for some years). There are whitewashed stables and a dairy, an old, dry orchard ('But it might revive with some water and fertilizer') and there is a swimming pool ('A bit green and slimy, but that's all right').

There is a farming community of twenty or thirty families in Mkushi district (where the farm sits), not far from the border with Zaire. If Zambia were a butterfly, our farm is situated right where Zambia's wings would meet.

If we move to Mkushi, we will neighbour Yugoslavs, Afrikaners, Englishmen, Zambians, Indians, Greeks, Czechs.

'Too many people,' complains Dad.

'You don't have to *socialize* with them.'

'It's the bloody League of Nations.'

'So?'

Dad mutters something.

Mum says, 'If we move to Zambia, then we will have lived in every country in the former Federation.'

And the symmetry of this fact seems to be enough to seal the decision. We will move to Zambia in January, too late to catch even the tail end of the planting season.

Mkushi

Mum with horses

Depending on the state of the roads, our farm is three to six hours from Lusaka and two to four hours from the Copperbelt.

Either way you arrive at it, the farm does not come as a surprise.

Drive out of Lusaka, its shantytowns spreading like a tea stain away from the city centre and its hum of commerce. Drive away from the clamour of market women in their shack-shanty stalls where they trade vegetables, oil, cloth, clothes. Drive past the Planned Parenthood building and under the great, stark, concrete archway proclaiming Zambia's freedom, ONE ZAMBIA, ONE NATION. Leave the city concentration of poverty behind – leave behind its stench and the place where social diseases come together to shout the misery of the truly almost-dead-from-it poor. And the one-in-three with AIDS and the one-in-six with TB. Leave behind the Gymkhana Club, where red-faced expats-like-us drink and shout their repeated stories to one another, cigarettes waving. Leave behind the expat, extra-marital, almost-incestuous affairs bred from heat and boredom and drink. Leave behind the once-grand, guard-dogged, watchman-paced, glass-top-walled compounds of the rich and nervous.

Msasa forests are thicker here.

And the trees are swollen against each other, giving the impression that they can outlast the humanity which presses up against them. Charcoal burners trudge toward the grey-haze of the big city, pushing piles of charcoal in burlap bags strapped high on to bicycles, but their axes don't seem to have dented the forest yet. The road is a narrow strip of potholed black on which few vehicles swing and rock, avoiding the deeper holes and slamming into some of the shallow, surprising dents.

We hurry through the rotten-egg stench of Kabwe, which belches smoke from copper and cobalt mines. There are, here, some reminders of our European predecessors, who long ago returned to the ordinariness of England where they now remember (with a fondness born of distance and the tangy reminder of a gin-and-tonic evening) the imagined glory of sunburnt gymkhanas and white-clothed servants. These long-gone Europeans had tried to turn Kabwe into something more powerful than its smell (which is strong enough to taste; bitter, burning, back-throat-coating, like the reminder of vomit). There are some surviving trees from the dream of the Kabwe Gardening Club – dusty, droughted, diseased, root-worn. These expat trees (brittle frangipani, purple-flowered jacaranda, and pod-exploding flamboyant) line the streets like soldiers who continue to stand, even as their comrades fall.

The mine houses, which are now sand-covered and chicken-littered, contain some reminders of the mazungu madams who once designed a water-sucking lawn and rose gardens around a gauzed veranda. There is the Elephant Head Hotel (peeling paint, stained green plaster, urine-smelling), a Church of England, and a hospital (where lines of fevered patients curl out of the door). A magnificent green and white onion-domed mosque rises out of the centre of Kabwe; neither colonial decomposing, nor yet postcolonial socialist (which is to say grey cement-block) but of some other resilient culture, defying time and place.

At Kapiri Mposhi (comprising a railway stop, whore-riddled bars and an Indian store where everything from bicycles, to nylon scarves, to made-in-China sunglasses, pencils, and alarm clocks is sold) we will turn right. But first there is the third of the four roadblocks we must negotiate from the city to our farm. Back-to-front spikes tooth the road, sandbags burst heavily and spill white onto the tarmac, and the military lounge on their rifles. We must produce passports, reflective triangles, the car's registration; but all this can be avoided if we would only produce a fistful of notes and some cigarettes, soap, oil.

Dad loses his temper. It's hot and we have been up since long before dawn in order to make it to and from town before dark, when bandits, the poor roads, and unlit, sometimes drunkenly driven vehicles make travel hazardous. Dad lights a cigarette and stares out of the windscreen; he is seething, very quiet, but he seems to be in his own thought world, completely ignoring the antagonism of the militia man. Finally Dad turns to the man with the gun and says, 'For God's sake, either let us go, or shoot us.' The man with the gun is clearly drunk, but he is startled into a brief state of alertness.

In the backseat Vanessa and I sink into ourselves. I want to say, 'He was just kidding. Only a joke. Don't shoot, really.'

But the soldier starts laughing. 'Ah, Fuller,' he says, 'you are too clever. Too clever.'

Dad doesn't wait for him to wave us through, but drives

ahead; the wheels of the car spit gravel up against the drums that guide us away from the spike-toothed barrier.

People have died like this. They have driven through roadblocks when it has not been clear that they have been waved through and a drunken sergeant has pumped several rounds of ammunition into the backs of their heads. Cause of death: accident.

We say, 'Acci-didn't. Acci-didn't stop. Ha ha.'

There is a madman who lives on the road to Mkushi. Every full moon he comes out onto the tarmac and digs a deep trench across the road. Dad would like to find the madman and bring him back to the farm. 'Think what a strong bugger he is, eh?'

'Yes, but you could only get him to work when there was a full moon.'

'Which is twice as hard as any other Zambian.'

We cross the second bridge (one more roadblock) and reach the gum trees, their ghostly white limbs stretching into the sky, and now we are almost home. The road is dirt, washed, potholed and ribbed from here, spitting up a fine red, throat-coating dust, but the peace of the farm is already spreading her fingers towards us.

The farm does not come as a surprise, because it's where I would put a farm. It's where any sensible person would put a farm. We have driven hundreds of kilometres and each kilometre brings land more beautiful and fertile and comforting and with each passing kilometre the air clears and the sky appears wider and deeper. And then, when it feels as if the land could not have settled itself more comfortably for human habitation, there it is – Serioes Farm – lying open like a sandy-covered, tree-dotted blanket. Softly, voluptuously fertile and sweet-smelling of khaki weed, and old cow manure and thin dust and msasa leaves. It seems the logical place for this family to stop. And mend.

*

Zambia has been independent since October 1964.

The president, Kenneth Kaunda – affectionately known as KK – is a deeply religious teetotaller, the son of a missionary. He is prone to tears and long speeches and calls himself a social humanist. He speaks of love and tolerance and reconciliation.

'One Zambia, one nation.'

'UNIP is the people's party.'

UNIP stands for United National Independence Party. It is the sole legal party in Zambia.

KK orders his critics and those who oppose his government to be tortured, killed, imprisoned. He is the only presidential candidate at election time, winning a landslide victory against no one year after year.

Election times come and go and nothing changes; the point-less elections are not memorable.

The occasional, quickly squashed coup attempts are what I remember.

Anyone can stage a coup. I have the impression that even I could arm myself with enough gin and anger to walk into the radio station in Lusaka and break off the nightly broadcast of African rumba to declare myself the new leader of the country.

'Stay calm,' I would say into the microphone, 'it is me, Bobo Fuller, in charge. I hereby declare the third Republic of Zambia.' And by the time my words reach the rural areas (days, maybe weeks later) I will have been locked up and will be on my way to death.

The leaders of the coups, the political detainees, the student rioters, are quickly forgotten in jail. Their heroic dissent melts in the tropical heat and washes away with the next rainy season.

*

Vanessa is away at secretarial college in Zimbabwe when we arrive on the farm, that first night. The workshop manager – a rough-looking ex-Rhodesian named Gordon ('Call me Gordy') – has been instructed to stock the kitchen with enough food to get us started. Accordingly, there are half a dozen beers and a few slabs of meat in the leaky gas fridge, a loaf of stale crumbling bread, an old jam jar containing oil, and a small bowl of salt. Gordy says, 'We haven't had electricity for six weeks. These bloody guys, hey? The first rains and all the lines go down and then you're fucked-excuse-my-French.' We smile politely, excusing his French. 'So you'll have to build a fire for your supper, hey?'

'That's okay,' says Mum.

'I brought a *muntu* for you. He used to be the cook here.' An African in a grubby khaki uniform grins broadly behind Gordon's shoulder.

'Hello,' Mum says to the African.

I say, 'How are you?'

'*Bwino, bwino, bwino.*'

'What's your name?' Gordy asks him.

'Adamson,' says the African.

Gordy shrugs. 'I can't keep track,' he says, 'they like to change their names like it's going out of style, hey.' He waves in the direction of Adamson, as at a mosquito or a fly.

Gordy has preceded us on the farm by a couple of months. He is supposed to be fixing the stable of tractors, combine harvesters, motorbikes, generators, water pumps, and trailers with which Dad will rework – regenerate – this exhausted, lovely farm. Gordy lights a cigarette and tells us, 'Aside from your truck, there's only one working vehicle on the whole bloody farm.' He takes a drag off his cigarette and adds, 'Which is my motorbike.'

The kitchen sighs and creaks to itself, settling around us.

Gordy kicks himself into action. 'So you have everything you need?'

We nod.

'I'll see you tomorrow then, hey?'

We troop back out of the kitchen, into the long concrete drain that lines the front of the house, and watch Gordy spin up the driveway on the only working piece of machinery, aside from our truck, on the farm.

Dad lights a cigarette.

Mum says, 'His wife's quite pretty. Pregnant, too.'

I wrinkle my nose. 'She must have got that way through wind pollination, then.'

'Bobo!'

*

For supper, we eat fried meat on top of fried bread, with boiled black-jack greens on the side. Mum found the black-jacks growing in what had once been the vegetable garden and is now overgrown with weeds and encroaching bush.

'You eat?' Adamson points incredulously at the weeds.

'Black-jacks are jolly good for you,' Mum tells him, 'taste like spinach.'

'For African, yes, madam. But for *wazungu*?'

'Beggars can't be choosers.'

We drink the barely cool locally brewed Mosi from the leaky mildew-smelling fridge, keeping an eye out for UFOs, unidentified floating objects, in the bottles. We had been warned by Gordy, 'I know a bloke who found a muntu's finger in his beer, hey. *Struze* fact.' The beer is yeasty and mild and flat, but it tastes better than the red-brown water that splutters out of the taps.

I take a few swallows of the meat and bread and then push my plate away. There is a taste in African meat sometimes that is strong, like the smell of a sun-blown carcass. It is a taste of fright-and-flight and then of the sweat that has come off the hands and brows of the butchers who have cut the beast into pieces. It makes the meat tough and chewy and it jags in my throat when I swallow.

'Not hungry, Chooks?'

'I'm okay.' I sip my beer and stare up at the ceiling, which is flecked with thick crusts of fly shit, most concentrated directly above the dining-room table.

Adamson appears to clear the dishes (the kitchen door is coming apart; it is two pieces of plywood held together by a handle and it chatters to itself whenever it is opened and closed). Adamson says, 'I can cook Yorkshire pudding.'

'You can?' says Dad.

'I work for Englishman, many years.'

'I see,' says Dad.

'I work for the last *mazungu* bwana here.'

'Ah.'

'And now I am to cook for you.'

'Good.' Dad puts both hands down on the table in front of him, looks up at the cook, and says, 'Then no silly buggers with Mr Fuller, eh?'

'No, Bwana. No.'

Adamson has a large, sorrowful head, so heavy and bone-dense it looks as if it is straining to stay upright on his neck. His lips are massive and sagging, very red, revealing a few stumps of teeth. He nods sadly and says, almost to himself, 'Buggers can't be choosers.'

The farm has been without proper management for years. Even before the Germans acquired it, a series of alcoholic, occasionally insane *mazungus* (mostly burnt-out Rhodesians, fleeing the war) have run the place into the ground. The house and garden have been allowed to fall into tropical collapse. The carpet tiles in the hall are floating up, peeling and green-grey, from where they have been soaked during the rainy season. There are pots and pans all over the house, set out to catch rainwater from the leaking roof. Mosquitoes breed happily in the stagnation.

That night, the first night on our new farm, while I am sitting on the edge of my bed contemplating my new bedroom, a rat the size of a small cat runs over my foot.

Balm in the Wounds

Mum

We whitewash the walls, clean the carpets, curtains, furniture. Mum hangs pictures, puts out her books and ornaments, and cuts wild plants which she dries on the veranda and then sets about the house in vases and jars where they quickly become places for spiders' webs. Adamson is issued new uniforms and a pair of shoes. Mum instructs him not to smoke marijuana in the house. The vegetable garden is dug up and replanted with tomatoes, rape, pumpkins, green peppers, carrots, potatoes, green beans, strawberries, and onions. The flower garden is watered, and spread over with tobacco scraps, and the roses are pruned into spikes. The bougainvillea creeper, which had become massive and unruly and threatened to drop out of its tree and onto the house (bringing the tree with it), is trimmed and thinned. The honeysuckle on the garage wall is coaxed back into life where its sweet, orange flowers hang like clusters of tiny trumpets over the entrance.

The dairy, which had been surrounded by a deep moat of cow shit, is cleaned up and the skinny, overmilked cows fed and pampered until their coats are glossy and their milk thick, sweet, and prolific. We adopt and buy enough dogs to clutter the space at our heels, we are given a white kitten whom we name Percy, and the Germans (as promised) purchase for us two mares, one of whom is in foal.

The farm succumbs to the gentle discipline of careful farming. Exhausted pastures are fertilized and then allowed to lie fallow. The cattle are dipped, dehorned, counted, branded and inoculated, and the barren cows culled from the herd. The tobacco barns are patched and made watertight, airtight and windproof. The roads are graded and, in places, crushed bricks fill in holes and sandy patches, so that tractors and trailers are not stranded on far reaches of the farm. The silt is dug out of the dams and their shores are lined with sandbags. Gordon finds work elsewhere and the farm's vehicles run again.

*

We've been riding all morning, out across the vlei, where Dad has organized the planting of rows of young, thin-necked, grey-blue-skinned gums. It's been a hot, high morning, the sun pale and intense, sucking the colour out of the sky. Mum has found that the trailer, which is holding the rows of wilting gum seed-lings, has broken down. When we get back from our ride, she drives up to the workshop to organize a mechanic. I am sitting on the veranda in my jodhpurs, horse sweat stinging my hands, my eyes burning with the heat. Adamson shuffles through from the kitchen with a tray of tea for me. A thick joint hangs from his lower lip and drips ash and fragrant flakes of weed onto the tea. I light a cigarette. 'Thanks, Adamson.'

I watch the horses saunter out into the paddock. They find sandy patches and throw up clouds of dust, rolling the morning of hot riding off their backs, legs paddling the air. There is a singing chorus of insects and birds; yellow-feathered weavers crash out from the bougainvillea where their nests hang like tiny, intricate baskets. The dogs lie belly flat on the veranda, pooling saliva under dripping tongues. I push Percy off my lap. 'Too hot, Perks,' I tell him.

I finish my tea and contemplate a trip down to the yard, where Dad is in his office and where I can usually find work to justify my luxurious life and my daily ration of cigarettes and beer. As I get up, I see Mum in the pickup, barrelling back up the driveway from the workshop. There is a thin, sandy, two-mile-long road between the house and the workshop, and the funnel of dust has kicked up as far as I can see. Even from here, shading my eyes against the sun, I can see the pickup juddering over the ribby wash of the road. The horses startle and bolt at her approach. The dogs leap off the veranda and run tail-high to meet her.

Mum skids to a halt in front of the garage. I run out to see what has happened. She emerges awkwardly, kicking at the dogs, who are leaping up to investigate her lively parcel. She is holding at a cautious distance something wrapped in a sack, 'Quick, Bobo, get me a box,' she says.

We call him Jeeves. He's a spotted eagle owl. The Zambians here are deeply superstitious about owls. They believe that if an owl lands on a roof and hoots, an inhabitant of the house on which the owl lands will die. Mum found Jeeves at the workshop, legs bound together with coarse rope; he was being spun, helicopterlike, over the head of a young man while a circle of the man's friends stood and cheered each time the owl crashed to the ground, his wings spread out and limp.

By the time Mum ran, screaming with rage and horror, into the cluster of jeering spectators, the owl was dust-covered, bleeding, with one leg and one wing broken.

The gardener is ordered to build an enormous cage in the garden, under the shade of the tree. Jeeves is installed in his new home; it boasts the thick branches of dead trees for a perch, a soft green carpet of lawn, and a small brick kennel with a roof for rainy days.

Jeeves is furious. He glares at us from his perch, his massive yellow eyes sliding over us eerily. When anyone approaches his enclosure he hisses and clacks his beak at us. Once in a while he calls, 'Voo-wu-hoo', and the Zambians shudder and hunch their shoulders, as if against a stinging dust storm.

Mum tries to feed Jeeves chunks of meat. 'Come on,' she tells him, 'it's my best bloody steak.' But Jeeves hisses and glowers and the meat sits untouched on his perch, turning from red to brown to grey until it is removed. The staff observe Mum, slant-eyed and peripheral, and sulk at the waste of food. Some children who have come with their mothers for the daily clinic at the back door cover their mouths with their shirts and jerk quick, furtive looks at the bad-luck bird. Their mothers pull them closer and smack them.

It has been three days, and still the owl won't eat. Mum rakes through her books and sees that, in the wild, an owl of Jeeves's order would eat insects, reptiles, mammals, and other birds. She shapes the steaks into small-mammal and lizard sizes and tries to make them act alive, piercing the meat on the end of a stick and having the morsel jerk and scamper around the enclosure before coming to a shaky rest near Jeeves's feet. He blinks and turns his head completely away from Mum and her offering.

So we drive off the farm, across the railway line and out towards the main road, to Barry Shenton, who was one of the earliest game wardens in the country: a legendary guide and tracker turned soy and maize farmer. We wait while Marianne, his Swedish wife, pours tea (she offers lemon *or* milk and for a moment we are stunned, overwhelmed by the idea that anyone would drink anything but strong black tea topped with strong thick milk). Marianne has a walled garden, like something I imagine out of England. She is slender and vegetarian and drinks hot water and lemon instead of tea. She has travelled to India recently. We listen politely, riveted, as she tells us of her adventures there.

This is the African manner. We must follow the ritual. There is no direct way to come to a point of business. Whether we have come for a spare tractor tyre or some advice on feeding an injured owl, we skirt the point at issue. There are no reliable telephones in Mkushi, so all business is done in this way, over tea or sometimes over whisky and beer. Social contact is limited, precious. We milk it, luxuriate in it. We bathe in the company, the strangeness of another home's smells and habits. We admire the flowers Marianne has grown against her redbrick wall; we accept a second helping of the dry lemon-carrot cake. Mum talks about the difficulty of finding decent flour. We agree to swap butter for flour. Meat for rice.

At last we tell the story of Jeeves and the now urgent problem of getting the owl to eat. Barry smokes thoughtfully and says, smiling gently, 'No, he won't eat meat like that. It must be covered with hair.' He tells us that the owl needs the hair on its prey to help it digest the meat.

When we get home, Mum (who has wavy, thick, shoulder-length bottle-auburn hair) sits in front of the mirror in her bedroom and crops her hair short, right up to the neck. The staff are scandalized into silence when Mum emerges from her room with hacked-off locks in hand and wraps them around chunks of meat. 'Does that look like a mouse to you?' she asks.

I shake my head. 'Not really.'

'Do you think Jeeves will know the difference?'

I say, 'Probably.'

Mum grits her teeth. 'You're not being very helpful, Bobo.'

'I can't believe you chopped off your hair.'

'What else could I do?'

'Catch a rat,' I tell her.

'How?'

'Steal them from Percy.'

Mum rolls her eyes.

'There are a couple in my room that shouldn't be too hard to corner.'

'Why don't *you* try catching them.'

'It's your owl,' I tell her.

We let ourselves into the enclosure. Jeeves puffs himself up, clacks his beak, and hisses. His broken wing hangs like a heavy over-the-shoulder cloak, draping past his feet. Mum had tried to bandage the wing to Jeeves's body but Jeeves had attacked the bandage until Mum, fearing Jeeves would harm himself, had removed the bandage. Mum impales the auburn-hair-wrapped meat onto her sharpened stick and waves the stick at Jeeves. 'Gourmet,' she tells him, 'come on, boy.' Jeeves shudders. I laugh. Mum scowls at me.

'He shuddered,' I point out.

'He was only shaking down his feathers.'

'Hair-wrapped meat. Yuck.' I tell Jeeves, 'I don't blame you. I wouldn't eat it either.'

*

Mum sends out a message to the labourers' children. She will pay five ngwee for mice, ten ngwee for rats. The rodents spill onto the back porch, where they are counted by Adamson, who pays the grinning children. He puts the limp rat bodies (like old small grey socks) one on top of the other into the fridge, where they startle a visitor from town who wanders into the kitchen searching for a cold beer.

Jeeves eats the rodents. He becomes diurnal. He waits for Adamson now, who is the only member of staff who will agree to feed the bird. In the morning and in the evening Adamson comes hunched out of the kitchen, carrying a tray of mice and rats, like a great, grey owl himself, a long, newspaper-wrapped joint hanging from his bottom lip. He squints through the sweet, pungent smoke of his joint and talks softly to the owl, who eats from the tray. Adamson waits for Jeeves to finish and then he shuffles back into the kitchen.

He is a man who has seen too much pain of his own to ignore the pain of a fellow creature. His third-to-youngest daughter was born with severe disabilities, and lives crawling in the dirt, head-jerking and prone to frequent infection; she is a constant source of worry to her father. And now his eldest daughter has been stabbed by the cattle man (whose name is Doesn't Matter Dagga) and she is dead. She survived two days and two nights with a spear through her middle (we were away in town at a tobacco sale at the time of the stabbing) and she died when someone finally summoned up the courage to pull the spear from her middle. Adamson told Mum that the girl's intestines came out with the spear and that she died screaming.

There is no more bad luck an owl can bring this man.

*

I tell Mum she has to do something about her hair.

'What about my hair?'

'It looks as if you've been run over by a lawnmower,' I say.

So the next time we are in town Mum, uncharacteristically, spends time and money on herself. There are some Zambian hairdressers in Ndola who Marianne tells us can cut *mazungu* hair.

Dad, Vanessa, and I find a piece of shade under which to eat our jam sandwiches and boiled eggs and to swallow our thermos of coffee (bitter with too much boiling and made palatable only by powdered milk and spoons of sugar). We smoke and Dad reads the paper. We keep half an eye on the hairdresser's.

When Mum emerges, we are momentarily startled into silence.

'Well?' she says, blinking into the hot midday sun. She has brought with her the flowery, powerful chemical smells of the hairdresser. The scent of the lotions used to straighten kinky hair, to perm and colour *mazungu* hair, to cleanse and condition any hair, have wafted onto her clothes and skin and she is conspicuous against the hot, salty, dust-smelling African town.

Her hair is cut very short, elfin, up above her ears and spiky short on top. Its colour is deep auburn, the layers of hair that have been hiding from years of sun and wind. Her eyes are pale and startling; they appear bigger and more piercing than I remembered them an hour ago. Her cheekbones are sculptured, down into a full mouth (freshly painted). Mum has always been small-boned, athletic, hard and muscled from years of riding and walking and lean farm living, but the short hair shows off her spare frame.

Dad slowly puts down his paper and clears his throat.

'What do you think?' says Mum.

'Very respectable,' says Dad.

'You look great,' says Vanessa.

I nod. 'Smashing.'

Mum smiles broadly, shyly.

'Who's ready for a beer?' says Dad.

By the time we are ready to leave town for the farm, in order to get back before dark, we are all gently, heat-of-the-afternoon drunk. Mum's hair stands up well under the pressure.

The Last Christmas

Rainstorm at Serioes

The year I turn eighteen, the rains are late.

The first rain had come as usual, in early October, and the world had turned a hopeful, premature green. But now that early green has turned a limp, poisonous, scorched blue-grey. The air is thick with mocking and sucks back the moisture from the plants. The clouds that form from this stolen earth-plant water scud north and south, torn by hot wind, and are left scattered like a thin white scarf across the sky. It makes us thirsty for beer.

The pump spits mud into the water tank from the sinking, stinking dam, and the water chugs from the tap thick and red and muddy. We can only have water for drinking and we share baths. A small frog is spat into the hot bath one night. It is boiled, petrified, eyes wide open, dead and astonished. The boreholes dry-heave, and the thin trickle that issues from the lips of their pipes is as yellow as bile. The riverbed glitters glassily up from between islands of rock. A farmer next door says he saw a crocodile sauntering across his fields, prehistorically out of place, in search of water.

It is the year that Vanessa, who has been working in London for a children's television channel, comes home to travel Africa with her English Friend. The friend is sexy and worldly and she dances at a party at the Mkushi Country Club and the old Greek-coloured who, it is known, hasn't smiled in forty-something years, raises his glass of beer to the ceiling and his eyes grow glassy and his lips grow wet and if he could find the words, he would say, 'Here's to women with legs that go on for ever!' His trembling lips break over his teeth.

I say he smiled.

Dad says it was a prelude to a stroke.

I am in awe. I start trying to emulate the way she smokes, slow and needy and intimate. I get smoke in my eyes and revert to smoking the old way, like an African, with the cigarette between thumb and forefinger.

I have briefly, and not very seriously, found God, and I have stood up in front of the charismatic church (which I attended, briefly, in Harare) and accepted Jesus Christ as my Saviour. The rest of my family finds this development eye-rollingly embarrassing. Once (when drunk) at a neighbour's house I take the conversation-chilling opportunity to profess to the collected company that I love Jesus. Mum declares that I will get over it. Dad offers me another beer and tells me to cheer up. Vanessa hisses, 'Shut up.' And I tell them all that I will pray for them. Which gets a laugh.

To be just like the English Friend, I am – to everyone's collective relief – restored to godlessness.

But still the rains do not come.

*

We hold a rain dance. We invite all the neighbours. There are Greeks, Yugoslavs, Zambians, Czechs, Coloureds, expats-like-us, Afrikaners, a woman who is said to be part Native American, a Canadian, the English Friend, and one Indian.

We make a fire outside (under the brittle, chattering, weaver-bird-full bougainvillea) over which we braai steak and boervors. Adamson, tottering with filched booze, brings out trays of parched grey-boiled greens and boiled potatoes and soggy-hot, peanut-oil-covered salads from the kitchen. The ash from his joint and sweat from his brow drip into the food tray. We drink into the lowering, relentless sun until the groom is called from his Sunday beer-drink to saddle the horses and we go out riding, looking for rain beetles. Mum (who is the best horsewoman among us) slides off her saddle (but does not spill her drink). She is still laughing when she hits the ground, and for quite some time after that. Someone heaves Mum back onto her mount, where she slowly tips forward in a perfect Pony Club exercise: 'Now children, everyone touch your nose to the horse's mane.'

None of us can catch rain beetles (which are the cicadas whose dry, thirsty rasp has been reminding us of our drought day in and day out). We ride home for more beer.

Dad threatens to find a virgin, to sacrifice to the gods. None among our party are considered worthy. Instead, several of the female guests are thrown into the drought-stagnant pool.

And still the rains do not come.

*

Since October, Mum has been using a hypodermic needle to inject the Christmas cake (bought months ago in the UK) with brandy. Needles and syringes are scarce; we boil and reuse those we have. The cake, however, has designated instruments of its own.

'He, he, he,' says Adamson. 'Madam, the cake is sick?'

'That's right,' says Mum, 'I'm helping it get better.'

Adamson chuckles and shakes his massive head. His face seems to be dissolving in sweat. It glows in a shiny film. He shuffles outside, where he sits on his haunches under the great msasa tree and smokes. His head hangs, his arms are stretched over his knees, and, except to adjust the angle of the joint on his lower lip, he is a motionless figure, gently wafting blue marijuana smoke.

The heat in the kitchen is breath-sucking. There are two small windows at either end of the huge tacked-together room, and one stable door, which leads off to the back veranda where the dairy man (surrounded by a halo of flies) labours over the milk churn (milk spits into buckets, cream chugs into a jug; both are in danger of going off before they can reach refrigeration). The fridges, unable to compete with the heat, leak (they bleed, actually: thin watered-down blood from defrosting chunks of cow) and add a fusty-smelling steam to the atmosphere. The aroma here is defrosting flesh, soon-to-be-off milk, sweating butter, and the always present salty-meat-old-vegetable effluvium of the dogs' stew toiling away on the stove.

The end of the kitchen is dedicated to laundry, where a maid (a baby asleep on her back) with a charcoal iron sweats over piles of clothes. She sprinkles water onto the back of her neck and onto the clothes and slams the charcoal iron down onto the table where her ironing lies. Her sweat sprinkles the cloth along with the specks of water, and singes up with the steam. The crescent-shaped air vents in the iron glow fiercely red with fresh coals. The clothes are ironed to paper in the heat and are crisp, starched with sweat.

Every time any of us walks outside, we glance upward automatically and search the sky for likely clouds. Still, it does not rain.

*

This year, we chop down a drought-dry fir tree and set it up in the sitting room. Mum spends hours gluing candles to the tree with wax.

'If that thing doesn't spontaneously combust,' says Dad, 'I'll eat my bloody hat.'

'Are you sure that's safe?' I ask.

Mum (defensive) says, 'It looks *festive.*'

'Looks like a bush fire waiting to happen.'

Vanessa, as designated artist in the family, spends one afternoon supervising the decoration of the tree. In the four years since leaving Malawi, we have accumulated a small box of real decorations (angels, trumpets, halos, doves), which are lost among the balls of cotton wool and the candles. We dare not put anything too close to the candles.

On the veranda, stands a dead protea bush we have dragged from the north, sandy end of the farm. It still boasts the odd, brown, head-hanging bloom, to which we add cutouts from old Christmas cards, sewn with red thread into hanging loops. Two lizards set up house on the tree and add to the decoration.

'Couldn't buy a decoration like that at Harrods,' says Dad.

The lizards lurk, waiting, tongue-quick, for flies (of which there are plenty). They are as thick as the air.

*

Christmas Eve. It still hasn't rained. By now, the tobacco seedlings are thin-necked, yellow-pale, growing into the heat with telltale signs of drought on their leaves already. We have filled the huge trailer water tanks and they stand, like army equipment awaiting battle, at the seedbeds. We have already planted fifteen acres of tobacco, but those plants are lying flat and parched, draped thinly over the top of the soil. When we dig our fingers into the ploughed soil which holds these nursery transplants, the ground is searing hot and parched. Dad says we mustn't plant any more tobacco until it rains. So the water tanks wait. The seedlings wait.

Mum spends half an hour crawling around the Christmas tree lighting all the candles. This is the first Christmas Eve on which we still have electricity. Usually, by now, thunderstorms have brought the lines down and we are without power until the rains subside in March.

Then Mum says, 'I think that's the lot.'

And we switch out the lights and briefly enjoy the spectacle of the flaming tree before Dad loses his nerve and orders the thing extinguished. We switch on the lights again. Beetles and ants and earwigs that have made their home in the dried-up fir tree have sensed forest fire and are scurrying in panic across the sitting room.

'Eggnog, anyone?' says Mum.

It's too hot for eggnog. We drink beer. Mum has cut the top off a watermelon and filled it with gin and ice cubes. We take it in turns sucking from the straws that spike from the watermelon's back, a sickly-prickly porcupine of melting ice and gin in thinned watermelon juice. By bedtime, we are too drunk to sleep.

It is Dad's idea to drive around the neighbourhood and sing Christmas carols. We set off in the pickup, the English Friend driving, with Dad as chief navigator. Vanessa and I are in the back. Mum says she'll stay home with our house guests, a family from Zimbabwe.

We kidnap the husbands, guests, and sons of our neighbours. We acquire two guitar players, one of whom is too stoned to play anything but Eric Clapton's 'Cocaine'. We override his intense, druggy riffs with loud, drunken renditions of 'It Came Upon a Midnight Clear' and snatches of the 'Hallelujah Chorus' (to which we know only the word 'Hallelujah').

We disturb the malarial sleep of a Greek farmer's wife.

We narrowly avoid being shot by Milan the Czech, who sleeps with a loaded handgun by his pillow.

'Jesus!'

'Told you not to sing bloody "Jingle Bells" to a Yugoslav.'

'He's Czech.'

'Same thing.'

'No, it's not.'

'It is to me.'

'Not to him.'

'Hey, Milan! Hold the fire!'

The stoned boy is shocked by the gunfire out of his 'Cocaine' reverie. He thinks deeply for a moment and then starts to sing (accompanying himself badly on the guitar), 'All we are saying, is give peace a chance...' He has to keep repeating the word 'peace' until he finds the right chord. 'All we are saying is give peace... peace... peace... peace...'

We drink hot, mulled wine with Swedish aid workers.

It is dawn and we still have to sing for the Indians and the Yugoslavs.

Dad says, 'Look at that bloody sunset, would you? Never seen a sunset like it.'

'Sunrise, Dad. Sunrise.'

And it is truly a stunning, low-hanging, deep-bellied sunrise. A vividly pink sky under thick grey clouds. Thick, grey, massing, rolling, swollen-bellied clouds. We blink into their pile upon pile of grey and we are briefly, startlingly sober.

'That looks like something.'

Vanessa sniffs the air.

The guitar player says, 'Man. I think this is it.'

Dad has fallen into a quick coma-drunk sleep on the English Friend's shoulder. We wake him up. 'Looks like rain.'

'Great sunset,' mumbles Dad. 'No one shut any doors or windows.'

Finally, rain.

The English Friend drives towards the gathering clouds and

Mum and Dad with tobacco

they come tumbling out of the west to meet us, gathering and rolling until suddenly the sky sags open and the road is instantly as thick and sticky as porridge.

We lie in the back of the pickup with our mouths open. 'It's raining, it's pouring, the old man is snoring!' The pickup churns and slides through thick heavy mud. The English Friend is driving like an East Africa Rally driver.

Dad, awakened by the storm, is still chief navigator, although as far as we can tell he no longer knows which way is up, nor is he consistently conscientious. '*Pamberi*!' he shouts above the whine of the labouring engine. It is the slogan of the ruling party in Zimbabwe: '*Pamberi* to final victory!'

In the back we are clinging to each other, wet to the skin, skin-against-skin, drunk, screaming into the great grey sky. Hair slicks over our foreheads.

By the time we get home, just before lunch, Dad is in drag. We take off the black Afro wig and put him to bed.

Mum has told the farm labourers she will pay a ten-kwacha bonus to anyone who comes out to plant tobacco. She takes a hip flask of brandy and rides out in the rain (horse steaming saltily under her) to the fields. The labourers are already drunk. They crawl, stagger, supporting each other, singing and damply cheerful out to the field. The crop is planted, but the tobacco is not in straight lines that year.

We are supposed to be holding a proper English Christmas lunch at noon for our house guests and various neighbours. The electricity is out. Adamson has been passing out beers to anyone who comes up to the back door. He is crouched over a fire he has made on the back veranda and is roasting the Christmas goose, though he is almost too drunk to crouch without toppling headlong into the flames. The only thing that seems to keep him a reasonable distance from the fire is his anxiety not to catch the end of his enormous, newspaper-rolled joint on fire. He rocks and swings and sings. Everyone within a thirty-mile radius of our farm is drunk.

Except our freshly arrived guests, hair uncomfortably pressed into place, polite in new Christmas dresses and ties, throat-clearing at the sitting-room door.

Mum, mud-splattered and cheerfully sloshed, is determined to inject the Christmas cake with more brandy before its appearance after the goose.

Dad is in a worryingly deep alcoholic coma. His lipstick is smudged. His snores are throaty and deep and roll into the sitting room from the bedroom section.

It is long after noon when the goose is cooked, by which time our Christmas guests are drunk, too. One has fallen asleep on the pile of old flea-ridden carpets and sacks that make up the dogs' bed.

We wear paper hats and share gin from another watermelon porcupine. We eat goose and lamb, potatoes, beans, and squash all rich with the taste of wood smoke. Adamson is asleep against a pillar on the back veranda; the rain blows in occasionally and licks him mildly wet. His soft, enormous lips are curled into a happy smile.

When the Christmas cake appears on the table, there is a

moment of quiet expectation. It is the ultimate gesture of a proper English Christmas. Mum has made brandy butter to accompany the cake.

'I've soaked the cake in a little brandy, too,' says Mum, who is as saturated as the cake by now. She tips a few more glugs onto the cake, 'just to be on the safe side', and refills her own glass.

'Now we light it,' says Vanessa.

Mum struggles to light a match, so the guest from Zimbabwe offers his services. He stands up and strikes a match. We hold our breath. The cake, sagging a little from all the alcohol, is momentarily licked in a blue flame. A chorus of 'Ahs' goes up from the table. The flame, feeding on months of brandy, gathers strength. The cake explodes, splattering ceiling, floor, and walls. The guests clap and cheer. We rescue currants and raisins and seared cake flesh from the pyre and douse our scraps in brandy butter.

Zoron (a Muslim) raises his glass. 'Not even in Oxford,' he pronounces in a thick Yugoslav drawl, 'can they have such a proper, pukka Christmas, eh?'

Charlie

Bo with Charlie

I've been overseas, in Canada and Scotland, at university. The more I am away from the farm in Mkushi, the more I long for it. I fly home from university at least once a year, and when I step off the plane in Lusaka and that sweet, raw-onion, wood-smoke, acrid smell of Africa rushes into my face I want to weep for joy.

The airport officials wave their guns at me, casually hostile, as we climb off the stale-breath, flooding-toilet-smelling plane into Africa's hot breath, and I grin happily. I want to kiss the gun-swinging officials. I want to open my arms into the sweet familiarity of home. The incongruous, lawless, joyful, violent, upside-down, illogical certainty of Africa comes at me like a rolling rainstorm, until I am drenched with relief.

These are the signs I know:

The hot, blonde grass on the edge of the runway, where it is not uncommon to see the occasional scuttling duiker, or long-legged, stalking secretary birds raking the area for grasshoppers.

The hanging grey sky of wood smoke that hovers over the city; the sky is open and wide, great with sun and dust and smoke.

The undisciplined soldiers, slouching and slit-eyed and bribable.

The high-wheeling vultures and the ground-hopping pied crows, the stinging-dry song of grasshoppers.

The immigration officer picks his nose elaborately and then thumbs his way through my passport, leaving greasy prints on the pages. He leans back and talks at length to the woman behind him about the soccer game last night, seemingly oblivious to the growing line of exhausted disembarked passengers in front of him. When, at length, he returns his attention to me, he asks, 'What is the purpose of your visit?'

'Pleasure,' I say.

'The nature of your pleasure?'

'Holiday.'

'With whom will you be staying?'

'My parents.'

'They are here?' He sounds surprised.

'Just outside.' I nod toward the great mouth of the airport, where there are signs warning tourists not to take photographs of official buildings – the airport, bridges, military roadblocks, army barracks, and government offices included. On pain of imprisonment or death (which amount to the same thing, most of the time in Zambia).

The officer frowns at my passport. 'But you are not Zambian?'

'No.'

'Your parents are Zambian?'

'They have a work permit.'

'Ah. Let me see your return ticket. I see, I see.' He flips through my ticket, thumbs my inoculation 'yellow book' (which I have signed myself – as Dr Someone-or-Other – and stamped with a rubber stamp bought at an office supply store to certify that I am inoculated against cholera, yellow fever, hepatitis). He stamps my passport and hands my documents back to me. 'You have three months,' he tells me.

'*Zikomo*,' I say.

And his face breaks into a smile. 'You speak Nyanja.'

'Not really.'

'Yes, yes,' he insists, 'of course, of course. You do. Welcome *back* to Zambia.'

'It's good to be home.'

'You should marry a Zambian national; then you can stay here for ever,' he tells me.

'I'll try,' I say.

*

Vanessa gets married first, in London, to a Zimbabwean.

The little lump under the wedding dress, behind the bouquet of flowers, is my nephew.

Mum, very glamorous in red and black, sweeps through the wedding with a cigar in one hand and a bottle of champagne in the other. She looks ready to fight a bull. She takes a swig of champagne and it trickles down her chin. 'God doesn't mind,' she says. She takes a pull on her cigar; great clouds of smoke envelop her head and she emerges, coughing, after a few minutes to announce, 'Jesus was a wine drinker himself.'

*

In the end, I don't marry a Zambian.

I've been up in Lusaka, between semesters at university, riding

Van and Mum

Dad's polo ponies, when I spot my future husband. I've just turned twenty-two.

I can't see his face. He's wearing a polo helmet with a face guard. He is light in the saddle, easy with the horse, casual in pursuit of the ball.

'Who *is* that?'

An American, it turns out, running a safari company in Zambia, whitewater and canoe safaris on the Zambezi River.

I ask if he needs a cook for one of his camps.

He asks if I'll come down to the bush with him on an exploratory safari.

Everyone warns him, 'Her dad isn't called Shotgun Tim for nothing.'

Dad is not going to have two daughters pregnant out of wedlock if he has anything to do with it. Dad has told me, 'You're not allowed within six feet of a man before the bishop has blessed the union.' He has set a watchman up outside the cottage in which I now sleep. The watchman has a *panga* and a plough disk of fire with which to discourage visitors. Although any visitor would also have to brave the trip down to the farm on the ever-disintegrating roads. Anyway, since Vanessa left home and married, the torrent of men that used to gush to our door from all over the country has dwindled to a drought-stricken trickle.

*

Charlie tells his river manager to make up a romantic meal for the wonderful woman he is bringing to the bush with him. Rob knows me. He snorts, 'That little sprog. She's your idea of a beautiful woman?'

Rob knew me when I was tearing around the farm on a motorbike, worm-bellied and mud-splattered. He saw me the first time I got drunk and had to go behind the Gymkhana Club to throw up in the bougainvillea. He knew me before I was officially allowed to smoke. He used to look the other way while I sneaked cigarettes from his pack on top of the bar.

Charlie and I leave the gorge under hot sun and float in canoes into the open area of the lower Zambezi. At lunch we are charged by an elephant. I run up an anthill. Charlie stands his ground. When we resume the float, several crocodiles fling themselves with unsettling speed and agility into the water, where I imagine them surging under our crafts. We disturb land-grazing hippos, who crash back onto the river, sending violent waves towards us. When we get to the island on which Rob (coming down earlier by speedboat) has left tents and a cold box, Charlie disturbs a snake, which comes chasing out of long grass at me.

We set up the tent, make a fire, and then open the cold box for reveal Rob's idea of a romantic meal for a beautiful woman: one beer and a pork chop on top of a lump of swimming ice.

That night there are lion in camp. They are so close we can smell them, their raw-breath and hot-cat-urine scent. A leopard coughs, a single rasping cough, and then is silent. A leopard on the hunt is silent. Hyenas laugh and *woo-ooop*! They are following the lion pride, waiting for a kill, restless and hungry and running. Neither of us sleeps that night. We lie awake listening to the predators, to each other breathing.

*

The next weekend I take Charlie back to Mkushi with me to introduce him to Mum and Dad.

Dad is standing in front of the fireplace when we arrive. It's a cool winter day and now the fire is lit at teatime. Mum is all smiles, great overcompensating smiles to make up for the scowls coming from Dad.

She says, 'Tea?'

We drink tea. The dogs leap up and curl on any available lap. The dog on Charlie's lap begins to scratch, spraying fleas. Then it licks, legs flopped open. Charlie pushes the dog to the floor, where it lands with astonishment and glares at him.

Dad says, 'I understand you took Bobo camping.'

'That's right,' says Charlie pleasantly. He is tall and lean, with a thick beard and tousled, dark hair. He is too tall to see into the mirror in African bathrooms, he told me. So he has no idea how his hair looks. It looks like the hair of a passionate man. A man of lust.

Dad puts down his teacup and lights a cigarette, eyeing Charlie through the smoke. He says, 'And how many tents, exactly, were there?'

'One,' says Charlie, blindsided by the question.

Dad clears his throat, inhales a deep breath of smoke. 'One tent,' he says.

'That's right.'

'I see.'

There is a pause, during which the dogs get into a scrap over a saucer of milk and the *malonda* comes noisily around the back of the house to stoke the Rhodesian boiler with wood, so that there will be hot water for the baths tonight.

'There's a very good bishop,' Dad says suddenly, 'up in the

Copperbelt. The Right Reverend Clement H. Shaba. Anglican chap.'

It takes Charlie a moment or two for the implications of this statement to sink in. He says, 'Huh.'

'My God, Dad!'

'One tent,' says Dad, and puts down his teacup with crashing finality.

Mum says, 'I think we'd all better have a drink, don't you?'

'Dad!'

'End of story,' says Dad. 'One tent. Hm?'

*

We are married in the horses' paddock eleven months after we first meet. Bishop the Right Reverend Clement H. Shaba presiding. Mum is wearing a vibrant skirt suit of tiny flowers on a black background, with hat to match. Vanessa is billowing and mauve, pregnant with her second son. Trevor, her first son, is in a sailor suit. Dad is dignified in a navy-blue suit, beautifully cut. He could be anywhere. He comes to fetch me in a Mercedes-Benz borrowed from the neighbours, where I have spent the night before the wedding. He says, 'All right, Chooks?'

I've had a dose of hard-to-shake-off malaria for the last two weeks. 'A bit queasy,' I tell him.

It's ten thirty in the morning. Dad says, 'A gin and tonic might buck you up.' He has brought a gin and tonic on ice with a slice of lemon in a thick glass tumbler from the farm. It's in a cardboard box on the passenger side of the car.

'Cheers.' I drink.

'Cheers,' he says, and lights a cigarette, shaking a spare stick to the surface of the packet. 'Want one?'

'I quit. Remember?'

'Oh, sorry.'

''S okay.'

We drive together in silence for a while. It's June, midwinter: a cool, high, clear day.

Bo and Dad

'Pierre's cattle are holding up nicely,' my father says.

'Nice and fat.'

'Wonder what he's feeding?'

'Cottonseed cake, I bet.'

'Hm.'

We slow down to allow a man on a bike, carrying a woman and child over the handlebars, to wobble up and over the railway tracks.

'Daisy, Daisy, Give me your answer, do . . .'

Dad looks at me and laughs. Now we're close to the farm.

'Oh, God,' I say.

'What?'

'Nerves.'

'You'll be all right,' says Dad.

'I know.'

'He's a good one.'

'I know.'

I pull down the mirror on the passenger side and fiddle with the flower arrangement on my head. 'I think this flowery thing looks silly, don't you?'

'Nope.'

'You sure?'

'You're not bad-looking once they scrape the mud off you and put you in a dress.'

I make a face at him.

'All right, Chooks.' He leans over and squeezes my hand. 'Drink up, we're almost there.'

I swallow the rest of my gin and tonic as we rock up the uneven driveway, and there is the sea of faces waiting for me. They turn to see Dad and me climb out of the car. There are farmers from the Burma Valley and Malawi in too-short brown nylon suits. There are the farmers' wives in shoulder-biting sun dresses, already pink-faced from drinking. Children are running in and out of the hay bales that have been set up for the congregation. Old friends from high school wave and laugh at me. Farm labourers stand; they are quiet and respectful.

Bobo's wedding. It is a big day for all the farm. Dad has brought drums and drums of beer to the compound; enough for a huge farm-wide celebration after the wedding. We feed hundreds of people; the entire front lawn is converted into a massive walk-through braai place.

*

The wedding party carries on for three days after Charlie and I leave for our honeymoon safari in South Luangwa National Park. Adamson, who has given me a small carved wooden box for a wedding present, has stopped trying to go home. He sleeps under the ironing table and re-emerges periodically to drink beer, smoke marijuana, and cook for the surviving guests. Mum takes them on rides around the farm, for extended drunken picnics. Several are last seen slipping wearily from the saddle and are found afterwards by the groom asleep on the sandy road or under the gum trees. They sleep in shifts on any available space: bed, sofa, carpet. Dad keeps the champagne and beer and brandy flowing, which is lucky because the water runs out

Charlie and Mum

when the pump is exhausted. The gardener runs up from the dam with buckets of water and guests are instructed to rest the plumbing and use the long-drop, dug especially for the wedding, in the back of the garden. Dad fries eggs and bacon and bananas and tomatoes and serves breakfast for thirty while Adamson snores softly under the table with the dogs.

The party ends when the electricity fails and Dad sets himself alight, as a human torch, for the common good.

*

The flowers for the wedding have been done by a drunken homosexual from the Copperbelt. His flower arrangements, his way of life, his entire philosophy, everything about the man is centred upon the theme of disguise. My wedding bouquet is made from wild African weeds, not flowers. The stagnant green pool is hidden with brightly coloured balloons. White building sand covers the cow and horse shit in the paddock where Charlie and I exchange vows. The trees (bare-limbed in mid-winter) are festooned with crepe-paper-covered hula hoops.

Dad puts all the hula hoops over his body, one on top of

the other. He says, 'You miserable buggers want light. I bring you the Timothy Donald Fuller Electricity Supply Commission.' He lights a match and sets himself on fire.

Mum, singing and arms raised in triumph, shouts, 'Hoo-lay!'

Dad is extinguished with a bottle of champagne by an alert, alarmed American guest.

*

I couldn't be more thoroughly married.

Now

Natasya and her father: Zambia, 2001

Mum has been diagnosed with manic depression.

She says, 'All of us are mad,' and then adds, smiling, 'but I'm the only one with a certificate to prove it.'

She went to what she calls the loony bin in Harare after a particularly manic phase.

Birds started to talk to her. And she listened to their advice.

She couldn't sleep and wouldn't eat and didn't speak except in a mad voice, not her own.

Her eyes went pale yellow, the colour of a lion's eyes.

She began to try and be drunk by breakfast, so that the voices, the noise, the buzz in her head weren't so loud.

She forgot to bathe or change her clothes or walk the dogs.

Then, one night, she was found by a nice middle-class Zambian couple on Leopards Hill Road. She was, she told them, running away from home. Dad was in bed at Oribi Ridge with all the dogs and only realized she was gone when the neighbourhood watch appeared in their pickup and with two-way radios crackling to tell Dad that Mum had been last seen with a nice Zambian couple and what did he want to do about it.

The nice Zambian couple had picked Mum up and driven her to their house, where they tried to get her to tell them who she was and what she was doing. But Mum wouldn't talk. They made her a cup of tea and radioed the neighbourhood watch, and while they were distracted by the radio communication, Mum ran out the back door, climbed their fence, and kept running.

She ran to the small private clinic where she remembered the nurses had been kind when she had gone in a year earlier for an emergency operation on her stomach. She beat on the gate and shouted until the watchman woke up. 'Let me in,' she was crying. 'For God's sake let me in.'

The watchman opened the gate cautiously. He peered suspiciously around the gate.

'Ah, but madam . . .'

But Mum rushed into the yard, past the watchman, and into the clinic, where she surprised the night nurse. 'Please,' she begged, sobbing with the effort of having run twelve miles in the dark in inappropriate shoes, 'please, you have to help me.'

The nurse was astonished.

'I just need to sleep,' said Mum. 'Put me to sleep.'

Mum slept on and off – mostly on – for almost two years. Overtired from life.

Dad took her down to the loony bin in Harare, through the border at Chirundu, where she now looked less like her passport photo than ever.

They gave her so many drugs that she lay flattened on the sheets of her bed like a damp towel. Barely able to speak. Unable, for the first time in her well-read life, to lift a book.

'It wasn't so bad. I wasn't really there,' says Mum. 'I was just sort of floating. Not feeling. It wasn't good, it wasn't bad. It really wasn't anything. Whenever anything like a feeling floated to the surface, they gave me more drugs and the feeling went away and I found I was so heavy and flat . . . I just slept, mostly.'

Then one morning a fellow patient let himself into Mum's room, stood on her bed, pulled out his penis and peed on her. Mum was too weak to react. She tried to scream.

'I would have knocked the bloody fellow out,' says Mum. But her arms and legs and voice wouldn't work.

'That's when I knew that the only thing worse than being crazy was being like this . . . like a lump.'

*

Mum and Dad have a fish farm now, on the Lower Zambezi. For a couple of years after Mum's major nervous breakdown, they lived in a thatched hut. Their dining room was a table under a tree. Their kitchen was a fire under another tree. The bath was a tin tub under the stars, surrounded by a grass fence. I could look up from my tub and stare at the black, deep sky pinpricked with silver stars. The toilet was a ridiculously narrow hole in the ground, a long-drop the size of which, when I was visiting from America, I protested against.

Dad said, 'We don't make long-drops in stretch-limo size out here. We Africans don't need supersized holes.'

They split their time between the cottage at Oribi Ridge and the farm in Chirundu. Once their new house is finished, they will live full time at Chirundu. Their nearest European neighbours are some Italian nuns who run a hospital for local villagers and a family who run a fishing lodge. The villagers have traditionally made their living through poaching wildlife, fishing the perilously crocodile-thick waters and chopping down slow-growing hardwood trees to make charcoal, which they sell in Lusaka. Chirundu is one of the least healthy, most malarial, hot, disagreeable places in Zambia. But it is, as Dad says, 'far from the madding crowd'.

'Because even the madding crowd aren't mad enough to live there,' I point out.

'Yup.' Dad pauses to fiddle with his pipe. 'But we have hippo in the garden.'

As if that can make up for the thick clouds of mosquitoes, the isolation, the insufferable, deadening heat, the lack of rain.

Mum takes little white pills every day now. She says, 'They're just enough to keep my brain quiet, but not so much to knock me out.'

She repeats her stories. They said that would be a side effect. I said, 'You've always repeated stories.'

She has twenty feet of copper wire hanging from the trees, attached to shortwave radio. She is reading, planting a garden, listening to the radio, talking to her dogs, supervising lunch, and trying to write a letter all at the same time. She is gently manic, in a pottering sort of way.

Vanessa left her first husband, and has re-married and now lives a few hours up the road from Mum and Dad in a house facetiously called the rock palace, a beautiful, fanciful settlement frequented by snakes. She has just had her fourth baby.

*

A letter to me in America, from Mum in Zambia, dated 12 December 2000, reads, in part,

When we get water, then I'm going mad on the garden and lawn. I keep putting trees in, which the staff resent because they've got to haul water from a well to water them, and the beastly Madam crawls from plant to plant and bird table to bird bath the minute I get there from Oribi Ridge – the birds down there are wonderful!

Our house is coming along – sitting room plain, high rectangular – needs ceiling when we can afford it, and slates, tiles – something – for the floor which is still cement. Bedroom walls up – such an odd shape – Dad insisted on different shape and drew something out with a stick on the ground – then the builder said 'How do we put the roof on?' and Bwana didn't know – but Madam, of course, came up with a brain wave – but we'll see if it works first.

Thatch house leaks, had low ceiling of black seedbed sheets which sagged and trapped frantic lizards who can only get rescued when Madam went down (from Oribi Ridge). No, this was a sweat box – a torment chamber of note – in that heat I could not stand it – now Banda [Dad's longtime right-hand man] had to crawl around and tuck plastic against the thatch as a neat lining – NOT his plan of sticking plastic over the roof – can you imagine – more like township squalor every day.

Poor Van going mad with depression and pain and waiting (for the baby to come). They've moved into Dunc and Nicollet Hawkesworth's house (closer to the clinic) . . .

That's enough waffling for now!

All our love and thoughts will be with you at Christmas . . .

Lots of love,
    Mum and Dad

Vanessa's baby came the day after Christmas. She named her Natasya Isabelle Jayne.

Jayne in memory of the baby none of us will ever forget, Olivia Jane Fuller.

This is not a full circle. It's Life carrying on. It's the next breath we all take. It's the choice we make to get on with it.